WHATEVER HAPPENED TO DIANA TRASK

A Memoir

WHATEVER HAPPENED TO DIANA TRASK

A Memoir

DIANA TRASK
with Alison Campbell Rate

M
MELBOURNE BOOKS

Published by Melbourne Books
Level 9, 100 Collins Street,
Melbourne, VIC 3000
Australia
www.melbournebooks.com.au
info@melbournebooks.com.au

Title: Whatever happened to Diana Trask: A Memoir
Author: Diana. Trask
ISBN: 9781877096808

NATIONAL
LIBRARY
OF AUSTRALIA

A catalogue record for this
book is available from the
National Library of Australia

www.dianatrask.com

*I dedicate this book to Murphy,
my dearest husband.*

Preface

For the past fifty years, at least once a week, whenever I told someone my surname I would be asked, 'Are you related to Diana Trask?'

A similar fate has befallen all of our family. To set the record straight, I am a first cousin of Diana Trask. My father, Francis Trask, and Diana's father, Llewellyn, were brothers and I have followed Diana's career very closely over the years.

This is the story of a beautiful young girl from Melbourne with an outstanding voice, who is invited to tour Australia as a support act for Frank Sinatra in 1959. At the age of eighteen she flew alone to the USA, where her childhood dreams of stardom came true when she made her debut at the famous Blue Angel Nightclub. Diana succeeded in popular music and then reinvented herself to carve out a new career as a successful country singer, touring the world and performing for fans in the USA, UK, Europe, Canada, Australia and Japan. But, as you will see, it was not all smooth sailing.

I guess Diana was one of the first popular Australian singers to be successful in the USA and many others followed: Helen Reddy, Olivia Newton-John and in recent times Keith Urban. American audiences have fond memories of Diana's appearances on the television series *Sing Along with Mitch* then her hit songs on the Country Billboard charts.

I work in the media presenting nostalgic segments on commercial radio in two Australian states and have always been interested in showbusiness. I am continually amazed at how strongly people remember Diana – and not only here in Australia. I have the great privilege of conducting celebrity radio interviews with film stars and television legends in the USA and the old question often comes back – 'Are you related to Diana Trask?' I am always delighted to say, 'Yes, I am. Diana is a beautiful person and I love her dearly.' Our family and fans worldwide have been proud of her achievements.

When Diana asked if I could assist with her autobiography I did not hesitate to say 'yes'. This book is a fascinating read and we hope that when you get to the last page you will have a deeper appreciation of Diana Trask – not just the singer but Diana the person.

There is great interest in what happened to Diana Trask and this book will answer all your questions. Country fans will love it.

Enjoy.

Kevin Trask

Little Bit

for Thom
1927 – 2009

It's just that little bit,
that little, little, little, little bit
that makes you shine, that means you're mine.
Yes, it's that little bit,
that little, little, little bit
that makes you shine, that means you're mine.

Well, there's some anger in your stride,
a touch of toughness in your hide,
a little hope, a little pride
and lots of love and warmth inside.

It's just that little bit,
that little, little, little, little bit
that makes you shine, that means you're mine.
Yes, it's that little bit,
that little, little, little bit
that makes you shine, that means you're mine.

Well, there's some danger in your smile,
a touch of daring in your style,
I feel a warmth of welcoming,
two lovin' arms to hold me in.

It's just that little bit,
that little, little, little, little bit
that makes you shine, that means you're mine.
Yes, it's that little bit,
that little, little, little bit
that makes you shine, that means you're mine.

Diana Trask Ewen

ONE

Why Was I Born?

Smile For Me, My Diane... It was the song my mother heard nearly every day on the radio when she was carrying me. She was often heard to say, 'If this baby is a girl, by God, her name is to be Diane.'

***

'Curtain in ten!'

Ten minutes. I drew another shaky breath. From my spot in the wings I looked out across the stage. A crew member was tucking electrical leads out of sight. The hand mike was there on the stand, waiting for me. The guys in the orchestra were shuffling music; Al Alvarez, our conductor, was giving last-minute instructions; the horn players were cracking quiet jokes, trying to dispel first-night jitters. *I'll joke with you later, boys. When this is over.* My mouth felt dry.

'Watch it!'

Two crew men whizzed past with a ladder and I stepped back hastily. A spotlight had blown and tension spiked backstage as they raced to fix it. I watched the man climb up into the blackness above the curtain. Hand over hand, grip and pull, face to the top, never look back. I knew what that was about. I'd done my share of climbing to get here. This was the Frontier Hotel. This was the Strip. This was big time Vegas.

'Curtain in five.'

The audience was buzzing behind the thick velvet. I knew the house was packed with show business critics, high rollers, top hotel echelon and agents by the score. They were here to sit in judgment: *Country music on the Strip? Are they serious?* Voices came up from the past:

... 'What are you going to be when you grow up, Diana?'

A famous singer!

... 'What are your ambitions, young lady, now that you've won this competition?

To go to America!

... 'Just say the word, kid, do you want my help?'

No, thanks anyway, Frank. I need to do this on my own ...

And here I was. Opening night at the Frontier on the Strip with *The Roy Clark Show*. Country music was going mainstream and I was part of the breakthrough.

I'd climbed the slippery show business ladder since I was sixteen, a girl from Melbourne, Australia where my parents still lived, always waiting for news and longing to know I was okay. I'd belted out jazz tunes in countless clubs and restaurants, on small town tours and no-name radio stations. I'd skipped several rungs at once in coming to the States, starry-eyed from a successful tour with Frank Sinatra. I'd climbed out of the pit of crushing loneliness as I made my faltering way in New York. I'd landed prime time television exposure on *Sing Along with Mitch* and recording contracts with Columbia, toured alongside Jack Benny, Tony Bennett and many other greats, and then slipped right back to near show business oblivion. *Hand over hand, grip and pull, face to the top, never look back.*

Country music had given me a second shot at my dreams. It had also brought me blessings I hadn't expected and my heart suddenly filled with gratitude for all I had. The journey continues. The climb takes you places you never expected. Thom was at my elbow, as always my rock. He squeezed my hand.

'Just stick your feet in the stage and sing, baby.'

'Ms. Trask, you're on.'

'Here she is, ladies and gentlemen, a Country star in the Vegas sky – Miss Country Soul!'

My intro sounded.

Do or die.

I walked out onto the stage, picked up the hand mike and turned towards the light.

***

'It's a girl!'

I was born on the 23rd of June 1940 in the leafy suburb of Camberwell, Victoria, Australia. While I was busy making my grand entrance, Dad – true to the ways of most fathers in those days – was playing a leisurely round of golf on the links in Warburton, about forty miles away. Mom's doctor was almost as excited as she was at my safe arrival. He knew the pain that my parents, Lew and Thelma, had recently been through with the death of my sister, Patsy Anna.

Patsy Anna had been born prematurely and died at the age of two after contracting a terrible sickness called Pink disease. This disease is caused by exposure to mercury which, at the time, was a common additive in teething powders and other baby products. Children susceptible to mercury poisoning were affected and many, like my poor sister, suffered greatly and eventually died, their parents tragically unaware of the cause of the illness.

Mom and Dad had sweated out the next pregnancy, desperately wanting another girl. It must have been a long, hard nine months for my mother, particularly as my father did not like the look of pregnant women and seemed to be embarrassed to be around them. I came into the world a healthy ten pounds and have complained ever since that I was born heavy and destined to fight the 'battle of the bulge' all my life. I was also born with an unusual double amniotic sac. Mom often laughed about my relatively painless arrival.

'The only time in your life you were not a pain,' she reminded me more than once.

The doctor commented that the double water bag may have indicated a twin that did not make it.

'I've always said she was just plain lucky,' my grandmother was fond of saying.

In due time I was gathered up and taken to the family home in Camberwell where my older brother Peter was waiting to see his new little sister. Dad hired a nurse to help my mother and they all watched carefully for any signs of the disease that Patsy Anna had contracted. All was well and the nurse remained with us until we moved about eighteen months later.

In February 1942 the Japanese began bombing raids in the north of Australia as the war in the Pacific gathered momentum. The city of Darwin was repeatedly bombed and many civilian lives were lost. For the first time Australians felt the insecurity of knowing war was on their very doorstep. Even though Victoria was a long way from the north, Dad decided to move his family into the country for safety.

My parents had spent their honeymoon in the mountains of Warburton about forty miles from Melbourne in the lush Upper Yarra Valley and they loved the area. As young people they were both very sporty, playing endless games of golf and tennis. My father in particular was a great golfer and he loved the scenic golf course at Warburton. It was in this town that Dad decided to build the family's new home.

My mother designed the layout and in time there emerged a graceful white weatherboard house, sitting on a rise and looking out over the river and up into the mountain ranges and beyond. The house had a long front verandah, which was typical of many Australian homes. Verandahs were useful as well as beautiful as they gave shade in the summer and helped to cool the house. Ours also took advantage of the gorgeous view. Mom was really into views, something she instilled in me. Our verandah faced west and was a wonderful place to dream, and we would sit there at night in the summer and stare at the breathtaking vista of bright stars. Mom would tell us stories and plots of the recent books she had read. One I particularly remember was *The Sea Around Us* by Rachel Carson.

Thrusting through the canopy of the surrounding eucalyptus forest were the blackened relics of burnt trees from 'Black Friday' 1939, when 71 people were killed in bushfires that raged right across the state of Victoria. Dad called these dead tree limbs 'sailors' and told me they were very dangerous, as in high winds they could break off and sail through the bush, sometimes dropping to earth and killing the loggers that worked below.

In the summer of 2009, the people of Victoria endured an even worse bushfire event that took the lives of more than 170 people, left thousands homeless, and injured and destroyed whole townships in this beautiful area around my hometown.

Fire can be both friend and foe. We had a wonderful big brick fireplace in the house that put out the best heat of any I have ever known. It was the only source of warmth apart from the old kerosene heater and the cooking stove so it was extremely important in the cold winters. Many a log was thrown on that fire and many a story told around it. I particularly loved to warm up my pajamas there before putting them on for bed.

The trains ran on the line behind our house, going down to Melbourne in the morning and chugging back noisily at night. Mt. Little Joe sat at our back doorstep, peppered with old mine shafts from the gold rush days and the Yarra River flowed at our feet. The air was scented with boronia and eucalyptus and was so clear in winter it actually hurt your lungs to inhale. Massive white gum trees towered all around. I sometimes think that I must have done something really wonderful in a past life to have been lucky enough to be raised in such a beautiful valley. I was always taught to appreciate the beauty around me.

The town of Warburton was quiet and very small, nestled in a valley under Mt. Victoria, Mt. Donna Buang and the Upper Yarra ranges. The main street shopping area sported a straight line of stores fringed with their broad shady verandahs – a typical Australiana look – and a small park where the fire bell stood at the ready for bushfire season. Mrs. Duck ran the main grocery store where you ordered items over the counter. No touching anything until you bought! The river ran parallel to the main street and was criss-crossed by three bridges for cars and foot traffic.

There was a little suburb attached to the town with the strange name of La La, after nearby La La Falls. A feature of La La was the Seventh-day Adventist Sanatorium and Retreat, and their Sanitarium Food factory where Weet-Bix breakfast cereal was made. Mom worked there for a short time after the war and I would watch as she deftly packed up the boxes of breakfast cereals. Not far from town, the asphalt petered out into a dirt road that led on into the great Australian bush which stretched for hundreds and hundreds of miles to the east and north.

In those days there were no supermarkets in the cities, let alone Warburton, but Mr. Inveriaty, the grocer from La La, would deliver our groceries to the house. He would first call in on Mom and over a cup of tea would recite a monotone litany of all the current supplies he could remember. She would order what she wanted and they were delivered to the back door. Rather like modern online shopping but with that personal touch.

Laundry was done in a large copper on Mondays – an all day job. Mom would dip the whites into the bluing mixture to keep them bright and then all the wet clothes were put through a wringer. I loved to work the wringer and watch the flattened shirts and pants and socks squeezing out between the rollers. Then we hung out the clothes on the line outside. The only trouble was in the winter when clothes ended up all over the house and under the verandah as Mom tried to dry them – every mother's bane.

The local iceman delivered large blocks of ice to the ice chest where perishable food was kept. We had a dog at the time called Chad, a very lovable Red Setter. Inexplicably, he loathed the iceman and would wait in the shadows until the poor man had delivered the ice to the house. Then he would spring from hiding and chase him through the backyard to the gate. After the first few ambushes, the iceman would open the back door very carefully, looking both ways. With no Chad in sight he would begin to tiptoe towards the gate, then sprint like a champ when Chad bounded out after him. It was obviously great sport for Chad who would be nipping at his behind the whole way. When Chad took the rear right out of the guy's trousers, that was it – no more ice deliveries to the Trasks' back door.

On top of a hill near us was a large guest house, The Chalet, which was commandeered during the war for the care of American soldiers suffering shell shock or other war related mental illness. Quite a few lived there although we rarely saw them in town. My first time seeing a Yank was as a small child when I was dressed up as a little angel with wings for a fancy dress ball. I won my section and was called onstage to be presented with a trophy. A big tall Yankee soldier bent down to give me a kiss but I did a backbend to get away. I didn't understand that this strange man with the funny accent was just trying to be sweet. Some nights there would be a dance across the street from us at a restaurant called The Cabaret, where these soldiers would come to relax, and although I never saw them, I would fall asleep to the music drifting in through my window.

Dad planted a rose garden and a tulip tree that grew into a spectacular flowering beauty in front of the house. We must have cut that thing back about twenty times for fear it would swamp the house but it still grows huge today. The bush around us was very lush and birds of all kinds came to our garden, flashing their colors and bringing their own music – brilliant rosella parrots with their high-pitched squeaks, the iconic 'laughing' kookaburras, chortling magpies and raucous cockatoos. I still love the bubbling, liquid song of the 'maggies' to this day.

Kookaburras are meat-eaters and we would lure them with tidbits of steak to our front verandah where they would consent to be handfed. Wallabies and kangaroos were rarely seen in town – they are generally shy and stick to the bush. One day, though, a kangaroo appeared in our backyard and Mom took after it with a broom, me howling like a banshee behind her while it jumped the fence to get away.

My father owned a furniture factory in Melbourne and later would own a small timber mill in the town. The bush around us held many valuable trees which the government controlled, carefully selecting those that could be logged. Logging trucks rumbled through the township every day with their cargos of huge tree trunks on their way to Melbourne.

My dad had a crew of loggers that would spend weeks at a time felling trees and hauling them over rough terrain, sometimes by horse power alone. He would travel to Melbourne during the week and come home to 'Warby' for the weekends. My brother Pete, nine years older than I, would travel with Dad to Melbourne where he attended boarding school. That left my mother and I in the country by ourselves during the week and I tended to lead her a merry dance.

My parents loved the outdoors and I inherited my love and appreciation of nature from them. They were both excellent gardeners, as were my grandparents – my mother's parents. Most people grew food in those days and took great pride in their gardens. After the war we were on coupons for food, so gardeners filled the larders and were very necessary.

My grandparents were a big part of my early life. They lived in Tunstall, later named Nunawading, about thirty miles away. Grandma Julia grew the most wonderful grapes and veggies. She was of Scottish descent, born in Tasmania and one of seven daughters. Her light red hair was very long and she wore it braided and wrapped around her head like a cap. She always loved to visit her family in 'Tassie' and would board a ship to cross Bass Strait at least once a year. She slathered ripe red tomatoes on my sunburn (one of my first natural health memories) and was a world of knowledge on common ailments. Her recipes for beetroot and candy have been my all-time favorites.

My grandfather, George, had been born into great wealth but his family lost it all in the Great Depression. He'd inherited his genteel manners, though, and I always thought him very aristocratic, even as he dug ditches and spent his life 'riding the steel' building Melbourne's skyscrapers. His step sister, Amelia Goss, was an operatic singer of note and a student of the great Australian opera star Dame Nellie Melba. Amelia toured and sang for the soldiers of World War One and I still have the crucifix they gave her in recognition of her work.

My grandfather was skilled with cement and laid the paths and driveway at our new house. He was carefully smoothing the wet concrete for a new pathway one day when I decided in my childish way to put my foot in it. He laughingly lifted his trowel and admonished me not to do that. I turned tail and ran screaming into the house.

'Poppa hit me in the head with a shovel!' I yelled to my mother.

That caused a ruckus indeed. My first lesson in the art of exaggeration. And not the first time I 'put my foot in it', so to speak, as future events would prove.

When I was five, my parents sent me to the local state school. I didn't mind the prospect too much. I had a little friend, Barry Mayer, who was also there and I liked being with him. Children can be mean, though, and I had trouble with the fact that Dad was better off than most and I tended to be chubby. Being called 'Fatty' leaves an indelible mark on a child and I would often go home in tears when the taunts were persistent.

But I learned my ABCs happily enough and took comfort from the presence of my special friend – a blue-tongue lizard that I carried inside my shirt. I had befriended my lizard in the backyard one day, feeding and talking to him. He freely let me pick him up and showed me his beautiful midnight-blue tongue. To my mother's horror, he liked to sleep inside my shirt against my skin and soon I was carrying him everywhere. He was wonderful ammunition for kids I didn't like as he would poke his head out dutifully and even snarl if I nudged him. Even with his support, there were many days when I was reluctant to go to school and my mother was often at her wits' end.

One day many years later when I was back home for a visit, I went walking along the river track. From the undergrowth beside the track a large blue-tongue jumped out, startling the life out of me.

'Hey, you better be nice to me, I know your grandmother!' I yelled automatically.

My brother Peter hunted the hills on weekends and worked a string of rabbit traps. Rabbits were an introduced species and with no natural predators in Australia their numbers had gone wild. We ate rabbit many a night thanks to Pete's traps. Then the Australian Government introduced Myxomatosis – a disease – to control the rabbit population and that meant wild rabbit was off the menu. The menfolk also hunted the hills for venison, which my grandma cooked to perfection.

Pete had a series of dogs that would walk the trap line with him. Most memorable was Spike, a hound. He was just a puppy the first time Pete took him out and he came home so exhausted he fell in a heap and did not move until the next day. A routine developed whereby Spike would recuperate through the week until Pete came home from boarding school and then greet him, fit as a fiddle and ready to hunt again. Out they would go in the morning light and Spike would return and collapse, tongue hanging out until the following weekend.

Pete and I both inherited our love of dogs from Dad. He always had hunting dogs around, mostly pointers. Many years later we looked up the Trask Coat of Arms and, lo and behold, pointer dogs appear on the emblem. I loved all our dogs and would have many wonderful dogs of my own in the years ahead.

I had an affinity for cats too and badgered my father for a kitten, but he wasn't at all keen. I was so desperate I wrote him a long letter, pleading my cause. Nothing came of my eloquence and I remember getting so mad at him. All was not lost, however. On a night of teeming rain I found a little kitten, soaked and miserable. *She must be lost! Dad couldn't turn away a lost kitten!*

Home I went, carefully holding the tiny scrap of wet fur, and I begged Dad to let me keep her. I painted a heart-rending tale of that kitten's future if she was cast outside in the cold and wet. There is a limit for all parents and he had clearly reached his. When he finally said 'yes', I hauled her off to my room before he could change his mind. She washed herself all over and slept, curled up and purring like a little motor on my bed.

My room was originally designed for my parents but they did not like its central placement so I inherited it and it had plenty of space for me and any number of kittens. I also shared my room for many years with a resident huntsman spider who crawled over the ceiling every night in search of mosquitoes and other insect snacks. I was never scared of him as he stayed up high.

A big change came to my life when, at the age of seven, my parents decided to send me to the Sisters of Mercy Convent School in Lilydale, twenty five miles from Warburton. My mother thought the bush state schools were too rough for me and wanted me to get a better education. Travel was hard in those days so I would have to be a boarder like my brother Pete, coming home only on weekends – I did not take to this idea at all. I would also have to become a Catholic.

My father was Catholic and my mother Anglican (Episcopalian) but I had been baptized an Anglican. It was decided that I would be baptized again in the Catholic font. I've often wondered about that – did I really need to be cleansed twice? Theological conundrums aside, one Sunday in La La at the Sacred Heart Church I was duly baptized for the second time – Diana Roselyn (after my two great aunts, Rose and Lyn) Margaret (my Catholic saint's name) Trask. I later added 'Veronica', the patron saint of compassion, at confirmation.

It was a pretty impressive name, eclipsed only by that of a dog I had when I was married. More of that later. Now I was a Catholic and acceptable to the convent. Mother purchased the necessary list of uniform items and other essentials and the inescapable day dawned.

The building was cold, gray stone, large and austere. It sat atop a hill with a commanding view of the town of Lilydale and its surrounds. As we drove up, fear welled up inside me and I fingered my new uniform nervously. I had never been dressed up like that in a stiff pinafore and a hat, all in dark colors. We trod up the front steps and entered, my mother almost as overwhelmed as I was.

Her health was not good at the time and, with Dad in Melbourne during the week, I think she felt I was too hard to handle on her own. I was definitely strong-willed, precocious and a bit of a dare devil and that's tiring for any parent. She considered she was doing it for my own good but when the day came she hated handing me over. She gripped my hand tightly as we walked into the lobby and when it came time to say goodbye she held onto me, tears falling fast.

I was aware of a large woman approaching, flowing black clothes, a face wrapped in white, the clicking of beads. I had never seen a nun in full regalia and to me she looked forbidding indeed, even monstrous. Her face wore an expression of stern composure as she detached me from my mother's arms and took me from the room. The heavy door closed behind us, leaving my mother on the other side. That was our goodbye.

The nun led me away. A confusion of images followed – a dark cavernous room that smelled of furniture polish; our shoes clanging loudly on a concrete floor; a sense of extreme cleanness; cold, hushed air. I scurried along quietly in her wake, too frightened to speak, too awed to take anything in. Tremors were running up and down my spine but finally we emerged into a noisy anteroom full of other girls who all seemed to know what to do and how to do it. It is a survival instinct amongst children – fit in as fast as possible – so I quickly latched on to a girl who seemed knowledgeable and did as she did.

After a time I was shown my dormitory where I could put down my belongings. It was a large room with about thirty steel frame beds. The floors were bare and the wind whistled in through a whole wall of open windows which I learned would stay open, summer and winter. My mom had provided me with heavy bedding for which I was very grateful.

In my dormitory the children ranged in age from six to nine but there was another room that housed girls as young as three. It is hard for me to believe now that parents could send their babies away at that age. I was in that dormitory later and my heart bled for one little child who was constantly upbraided for wetting the bed. She was three and a half.

A bell rang and I joined the hustle and scurry downstairs to a barely edible dinner, most of which had to be consumed in silence. Maybe that was a wise move – given the use of my voice I might have said what I really thought! I normally had plenty to say about most things. The imposed silence continued for a while and then another little bell rang.

'You may speak,' we were told.

After a few minutes the bell was rung again. 'No more talking!' and the meal was completed in silence. My mother had sent me here for discipline and it looked as though I would be getting it.

The first lesson I learned was not to cross certain nuns, especially my dormitory nun who I think hated the entire world. Corporal punishment was handed out regularly for very small 'sins' and with very little oversight. My dormitory nun had a special treatment with the edge of a ruler. She would make you extend your hand with the knuckles bent and exposed and then, turning the ruler onto the edge, she would shave your knuckles, leaving them torn and bleeding. This really hurt in cold weather. After the first dose I refused to extend my hand in that fashion so I always got the ruler around the legs.

A big blackboard was mounted at the end of the wash room and we were awarded stars for performing chores well and for earning no black stars. A black star was given for very ordinary misdemeanors – dawdling, running in the corridors, wetting the bed, speaking out of turn – the sort of things all little children do! The older girls rose each morning at six for Mass and were warned not to swallow the water we brushed our teeth with as this would break our fast for Communion and that would be a sin.

One icy morning I was due to take my bath, a bi-weekly event, and I must have fallen back asleep. The routine was that after shaking you awake, the dormitory nun would go to the bathroom and start the bath water running. You were supposed to be up and ready to turn it off when the tub filled. I jerked awake, heart suddenly pounding with fear, and raced up to the bathroom to find the floor completely flooded. Water was pooling inches deep. As I stood there, horrified, the nun came up from behind and slapped my face hard several times over, yelling and screaming all the while. I reeled back, clutching my face, overcome with shock and remorse. I had never been treated this way! My parents had never hit me! The nun ordered me out of the room and I stumbled past her in a daze. No bath for me that day. The injustice of the punishment hurt as much as the blows.

My face was swollen and sore as I miserably joined the file of girls making their way down to breakfast that day. As I took my place I heard some whispering at the seniors' table. Heads were looking upwards and then over at me. I saw some furtive smiles. Our bathrooms were located directly above the seniors' dining tables and my bath water had seeped through the ceiling. The ceiling was bowed and looked ready to fall in at any minute. Droplets of water were descending into the cereal bowls laid out below.

More smug looks passed my way and I felt a smile creep to my aching face. Suddenly, mysteriously, I was part of the 'in' group. A curious camaraderie grows amongst children in these circumstances, something like what I imagine is the case in prisons. During the whole time I was at that school, the ceiling remained in that state, a silent reminder of my crime, punishment and compensation.

The one thing I did love about that school was my second-grade teacher, Sr. Paschal. She was a gentle soul, patient and kind, and I adored her. Quite simply, she made my life worth living. She also taught me the piano and music, and I excelled under her tutorship because she saw something in me. I was always first in her classes as she was the one person in the world who I felt did not see me as a huge problem.

I had concluded that my mother had sent me to this terrible place as punishment for being a bad child. She was ill and my bad behavior had made her worse, so naturally I was a problem. That's the way a child's mind works and it's very hard to shake. Thank God for Sr. Paschal.

The winters were extremely cold. The ground would actually crack as frost covered the playground and children would have chilblains and cold, chapped faces. Girls devised a way to snip the tips off a pair of gloves and wear them all day as they did their schoolwork. Still the windows of the dormitory stayed open. I had the worst colds I have ever had at that school. Mom supplied endless bottles of Hypol, a cod liver oil supplement, to help ease the coughing.

There were happy times and some good friendships were made but I remember the day one of the girls went on the attack.

'You're only here because your parents don't want you,' she snarled.

I laughed and tried to shrug it off, but it cut too close to the bone with me to be easily dismissed as just school girl spite.

Weekends were heaven as Dad picked me up every Friday night to take me home. I would fling myself down the path and jump into his arms and he would gather me up in a bear hug.

'How's my Puss?' he'd ask.

Then I would be blissfully happy. My dad was so handsome and strong with his dark hair, deep brown eyes and beautiful hands. We would drive towards Warburton, stopping at the pub in Woori Yallock on the way. I would sit in the car and do homework until Dad was ready to go home. He was a typical Aussie man in those days, and as the pubs closed in Victoria at six o'clock a man had to have his fill pretty smartly. I swear, the old Pontiac knew its way up the valley on auto-pilot. There was one patch of road called the 'Winding Mile', a very treacherous spot, but Dad was a good driver even with a snoot full. Home was good food and hot showers every day and riding my bike all over, just as I pleased. I wished weekends would never end but all too soon it was Sunday night and I had to go back to the convent.

With me more or less off her hands during the week and her health improving, Mom became very active with the Bush Nursing Hospital in Yarra Junction, a little town about eight miles away. It was the only medical/surgical facility in the area except for the Seventh-day Adventist Sanatorium which did not have an open clinic. She became secretary of the hospital board and her fund raising efforts took her all over the valley. She worked tirelessly for the hospital, staging beauty queen contests and arranging local talent shows to raise money for improving operating facilities and the like. I remember those talent shows mainly because at each one a certain girl would enter and dance the hula. That was her special thing. She must have danced the hula in every contest in the whole of the Upper Yarra Valley.

Mom also grew quite religious and once when I was very ill with an abscess on the ear drum, she prayed me through it. The country doctor had left, saying that unless the thing burst I might not live through the night. She knelt and laid hands on me, praying. I remember being in a sea of pounding pain. Shortly after placing her hands on me, the abscess burst in a flood. I still favor my right ear from that experience.

Another time, the heavy wooden seat of a swing knocked me out and split my head open just above my left eye. Mom poured kerosene on it to kill the germs and then held the edges of the wound together with her hands for hours. She said she did not want to take me to the doctor and have stitches on my face. The scar is very slight today.

Mothers have always been the healers in the first line of defense but I think back then they knew a lot more about natural remedies than do modern mothers. I have certainly come to appreciate the more holistic approaches to health and wellbeing and have made it an area of study in my later life, but I wish I had paid more attention to those early lessons from my mother and grandmother.

One spring, the snow melt was unusually heavy and, compounded by high rainfall, the Yarra River flooded to dangerous levels. The river tore through the valley with a sound like a train rushing towards you. Warburton became an island. No-one could get through to the city and some locals were lost trying to cross the flooded bridges. Of course, we children didn't mind being marooned if it meant no school. I was perfectly happy to miss out! A few years later a dam was built to control the floods and also supply Melbourne with drinking water.

Before the dam was built, the big challenge in spring was to be the first one to swim across the Yarra at the swimming hole. The river moved swiftly in flood and you could easily get sent downstream where it was harder to get out. I became a good swimmer and was always one of the first to cross, even though the water was freezing cold. My swimming lessons consisted of holding on to the bank, crawling on hands and knees in the shallows and one day screwing up the courage to let go and kick! Before I was proficient, Dad would swim me across the river, me clinging to his back like a limpet. Mom hated the water and would never swim.

In summer I spent countless hours with my old blown-up inner tube bumping down the rapids. I would float down the river with my pal Janis Chamley and then came the hard part – the long walk back, wheeling those tubes in front of us. Janis' father worked with Dad at the lumber mill and we were very close friends back then. She was a sweet person and a real animal lover. She went crazy over every single dog we had – I don't think she was allowed to have one.

Dad, Pete and my godfather, Uncle Frank, were accidentally pushed off the road by a logging truck one year and ended up careering straight into the river during the spring floods. Loggers were clearing the forest up stream for the new dam and loaded trucks barreled along the narrow roads which were not always well-maintained. There were many accidents in those days.

Dad's car skidded down the embankment and was submerged so far that only one back tire was in view. Dad and Uncle Frank managed to struggle out of the windows but Pete was stuck in the back seat and was making no move to get out. He was stunned, both by the accident and the temperature of the water. Dad was clinging to the protruding wheel, in shock himself and unable to swim for shore. Uncle Frank, a devout Catholic, invoked the assistance of every saint he could think of and dove down into the icy waters. He dragged Pete out and got him to safety. Then he tried to get Dad to unclasp his hands from the wheel and come to shore too, but Dad was frozen.

They were far from town and the accident was not discovered for some time until a passing truckie stopped to help. Eventually Dad was retrieved from the icy water and they made it home. True to the times, there was no rushing off in an ambulance to hospital for observation or treatment. It was simply a case of go home and have a nice hot cup of tea and you'll feel better.

Christmas Day was usually spent at the house in Warburton. In the best British tradition for a winter Christmas, there would be lots of heavy food to cook and eat in sweltering Australian summer temperatures. This included my grandmother's special 'Plum Dollop', full of sixpences to discover – hopefully without cracking a tooth. Dad had an old caravan which doubled for hunting trips and family holidays. At Christmas time we had a long vacation from school and would pack the caravan, hitch it up to the Pontiac and haul it to the beach, Pete and I bouncing in the back of the car. There on the coast to the west of Melbourne we'd spend sun-drenched days fishing, swimming and playing.

I have always loved the water and in those days the beaches were pristine. I remember one night at the Queenscliff pier seeing squid by the hundreds, all lined up noses to the current as they flashed and changed colors like an electric light show. Like Dad, I loved to go fishing, particularly surf fishing. Dad took us out by day and often Pete and I went flounder fishing with lights at night. We had an old boat nicknamed *The Green Bitch* by my brother. Why the name? Well, it was painted green – of course – and it would never do what it was told! It was contrary. It would fall off the top of the car, spring a leak, get stuck in the mud – you name it. You were lucky to get back alive after you'd been out in that thing.

Back then, the wireless was our connection to the outside world. Disembodied voices brought us dire predictions about epidemics, post-war food supplies, coupons and rationing. Politicians came on the air, promising this and somehow delivering the other. News hour was sacred – Dad would tune into the nightly ABC bulletin and rail about the Prime Minister, Mr. Ben Chifley, and how hard it was to be in business and run the factory in Melbourne. Nevertheless our house was always full of people from the city on the weekends and Mom fed everyone somehow. She was an excellent housekeeper.

The wireless also brought us our entertainment. We were glued to the Australian serials – comedies like *Dad and Dave* and the never ending saga of *Blue Hills*. Music poured out of the wireless too – the new sound of swing had taken over. Mom sported 'The New Look', a fashionable length of dress. I was about seven or eight, doing a reluctant job of dusting one day, when I heard a man singing on the wireless. I liked his voice. It was jaunty and had a swing to it which carried me along.

'Who is that?' I asked Mom curiously.

'Oh, that's Frank Sinatra,' she scoffed. 'He's pretty good but he's always fighting and getting into trouble with women!'

I kept on listening to that voice.

Whenever I'd been asked as a little girl: *What will you be when you grow up?* I had always answered: *A singer!* Maybe one day when I was grown up, I would sing on the radio.

TWO

By Myself

My mother taught piano and singing to the local girls and I was always the pest at the end of the piano, listening and absorbing. She had wanted to be a singer but her parents would not allow their daughter to take up such a scandalous career. I can still hear her singing 'The Old Rugged Cross' and a funny old cowboy song, 'There's A Bridle Hangin' On The Wall'. She had a sweet mezzo soprano voice with good pitch and was one of the minister's favorite vocalists at her local Anglican church.

My dad's only good song was 'You Are My Sunshine', with various made up verses as he never remembered the words. He was of Welsh extraction through his mother's side and sang as only they can do, with his head tilted to one side and a big smile on his face. My brother Pete also had a good voice but was too shy to sing in front of people.

I pleaded with Mom to let me learn to sing but she would not hear of my training until I was sixteen and my voice was developed. I think this was Dame Nellie Melba's belief and Mom was a devotee of hers. In fact she was once offered a training course from Miss Melba but grandmother had said *Absolutely not!* and that was that. I don't think Mom ever got over the disappointment.

So, I was surprised and excited when Mom entered me into a singing contest when I was only eleven. Perhaps she wanted to see for herself whether I had any talent. The Lilydale Eisteddfod was a local competition and I was to sing a number she loved called 'Daddy's Sweetheart', a song of a little girl's love for her daddy. We practiced and rehearsed and all was going well but on the day I came up with a very sore throat and could hardly croak. Mom absolutely panicked.

'Dame Nellie Melba had a sure fire remedy. All the singers use it. We'll have to try that,' she said.

'What is it?' I asked tearfully, seeing my first prize slipping away. Oh, yes, I had already decided I was going to win first prize...

Mom didn't tell me what the miraculous cure was then. We hustled to get ready and arrived at the venue, me coughing and clearing my throat like a chain smoker. I was dolled up in a little floral dress and white shoes with my hair a mass of sausage curls from an uncomfortable night spent in curling rags. It was almost time to go on when Mom produced an egg, cracked it into a glass and held it out to me. There it lay, a glutinous, slippery mass.

'Swallow it, Diana, swallow it down.'

Swallow a raw egg? You're kidding me! I tried to get that egg down, I really did. But I gagged and gagged and with the tears streaming down my face and Mom hovering over me, frantically invoking the authority of Dame Nellie, I decided to be suddenly cured. I went on, sore throat and all, and won the competition. I never tried the raw egg trick again.

Life for me improved markedly the day I became a day scholar at the convent instead of a boarder. The state school bus company had agreed to carry the Catholic girls to Lilydale every day along with the students bound for the government school – a small step forward in Catholic-Protestant relations for conservative 1950s Australia. I remember those days on the bus fondly. The twenty-five mile trip to Lilydale was spent singing all the hits of the day at the tops of our voices. 'Sixteen Tons' and 'Sh-boom' were two I remember and we were always listening to the radio to learn the words of the newest hits. We invented our own sign language, discussed the latest movies on at the cinema in 'Warby' and generally had lots of fun.

The local girls would be sporting the latest fashions while we

Catholic girls would be in our dreaded uniforms. I must say that I really didn't mind the uniforms too much. There seemed to be a kind of safety in all looking alike. Sometimes there was friction on the bus as a few boys traveled with us and were more than happy to stir up a bit of trouble. They would pile into the seats at the back and choose a victim to tease for the duration of the trip. I remember a big local girl called Valerie Tralore almost decking a boy once for a bad remark.

I made fine friendships with other girls. I recall a girl we nicknamed 'Elbows' Pobjoy because she had the sharpest elbows of anybody around and was not afraid to use them. For the life of me I cannot remember her real name. Curiously, there was another girl at the convent with almost the exact same name as me – Deane Trask. She was no relation and although a younger girl than I, the similarity in our names caused no end of confusion at school.

A particularly good friend was Barbara James. She was a constant discipline problem for the nuns and I must say I cheered her on all the way and assisted with the mischief when required. She was funny and resilient and we were 'blood brothers' – or sisters – just like in the cowboy movies. We actually did the deed with an old razor – it is a wonder we were not poisoned. We spent countless hours dreaming about our weddings and swore to be bridesmaids for each other. She was a hopeless romantic and we loved each other dearly.

On Saturday mornings Dad would always rise early and go fishing for trout in the river near home. He'd been after a particularly wily old trout in the stretch behind The Cabaret restaurant for months. Dad always wore an old, tattered Hawaiian shirt, swearing it was a necessary part of the formula for catching this darned fish. He would shush me to total quiet as I watched from the bank. One day he hooked it up and I yelled out with delight. Dad turned to see what I was yelling about and the fish got itself off. Dad was livid – I never heard the end of it. I was barred from watching until I could learn to keep quiet and eventually he caught that pesky trout.

We had a few chickens in the backyard pen as most people did in those days. From time to time we had a rooster and of course it was always very early in the morning that it would wake up and do what roosters do. Dad put up with it for a few months but one early morning after a heavy night at the pub, the crowing began at about 4am and he couldn't stand it a moment longer. I heard Dad tossing in the bed, then he threw back the covers and stormed through the house, growling about the freezing cold and beating his arms to his sides to warm up. I heard a rummaging in the back porch, a fluttering turmoil and bedlam in the hen house, the thumping of his footsteps back to bed and then silence. We were all settling down again when the peace was shattered by the sound of a cock crowing. He had just slain Mom's best hen.

Winter was always a time for bad colds and Mom became alarmed with my condition one year when I had a heavy cough that just wouldn't clear up. When my brother was a baby he had developed spots on the lung and she had taken him up north to the islands off the coast of Queensland to cure him. She was very worried about me and decided to also take me north for a month. No school for a whole month? Sounded good to me.

It was my first time on a plane and I was excited by the whole experience – boarding the aircraft, the hostesses in their uniforms, the bird's-eye view from above.

I flattened my nose to the thick glass of the tiny window, lost in daydreams – a plane could take you anywhere ...

We flew north in several jumps to Mackay in Queensland and then were transferred by boat out to Lindeman Island which is part of the Whitsunday group. The weather was just what the doctor ordered and I quickly improved, the hacking cough disappearing in the tropical heat. We slept in a hut right on the beach and at high tide the water was almost to the door. A coral reef ringed the island, emerging as the tide receded. With a pair of shoes to protect your feet from the razor sharp coral you could walk out and find all the treasures of the reef – huge clams with their soft, multicolored lips, sea cucumbers, brilliant fish, snails and corals of all colors.

One day Mom and I joined a crowd of fellow tourists on a trip a bit further north to the Great Barrier Reef. We travelled on the resort's motor yacht, the *Shangri-La*. The captain said it was a bit late in the month for the trip because of the season and tides but the weather was good and away we went. We reached the edge of the reef, anchored and waited for the tide to go down to where we could walk on the exposed coral. While waiting, we fished from the boat but sharks kept snapping the hooked fish off our lines. We could see their dark shapes circling quite clearly in the pristine water.

After lunch we were ferried in groups by dinghy over the short distance to the now exposed coral. The captain lectured us firmly about listening for the boat's horn.

'When you hear the horn, make straight for the boat, folks,' he instructed. 'The tidal swing is about thirty feet in these parts and we don't want anybody left behind.'

Mom and I wandered way out on the reef, enjoying the sun and the beauty of the magnificent pools and coral formations. We were surrounded by sparkling blue sea, idling the hours away in our own little paradise. The abrupt sounding of the boat's horn startled us out of our reverie and we started picking our way back over the coral. The captain had not exaggerated. The tide had turned in a flash and was beginning to pour back onto the reef at a tremendous clip. Mom and I started back for the dinghy in ankle deep water. By the time we got to the pick up point the water was up to my knees. The dinghy was already full and there were four of us left on the reef.

'Take them and come back for us,' said Mom. The skipper pulled at the oars and away the dinghy went towards the motor launch. The water continued to rise and although we were not in real danger, my blood was certainly pumping a bit faster as the tide crept higher up my legs. The dinghy was heading back for us. The water had reached my hip. I was remembering those sharks. It was then that the magic happened. In a deep pool to my left, edged by a wall of brightly colored coral, a baby whale suddenly breached and turned over, flapping a large fin not forty feet from me. I forgot about sharks and rising tides and just stared. Two hands caught at me. It was the skipper reaching down to haul me up into the boat. The whale sounded and disappeared below the surface.

Later in life I mentioned that incident to a group of disbelievers in Los Angeles and was told that no whales were ever in the Whitsundays. A friend of mine was to dine with the great sea explorer and researcher Jacques Cousteau that night. He'd know if anyone did.

'Ask Mr. Cousteau about it,' I begged. 'Ask him what kind they were.'

The message came back that yes, indeed there were humpback whales in the Whitsundays but they had been hunted almost to the point of extinction. I was saddened greatly to hear it as that experience ranked as one of my greatest memories. Fortunately with intervention the humpback whales are now a common sight again in the protected waters of the Whitsundays.

Too soon our month in the sun on Lindeman Island ended and Mom and I headed back south to Melbourne, healthy once again.

It was about 1950 and another change was in the wind. My parents were becoming dissatisfied with the Lilydale Convent School and decided to enroll me at a school in Melbourne. Mom knew I wasn't very happy at the Convent and she didn't like the extreme emphasis on discipline. The Sisters of Mercy (who had no mercy, I always added in my mind) were not actually a teaching order and it showed. Furthermore, the school didn't continue through to senior classes so I would have to move at some time anyway.

Mom and Dad decided on Presentation Convent in Windsor, an old established suburb closer to the city. The Presentation Sisters were an order dedicated to education and they concentrated on teaching rather than discipline. They had a good reputation with the girls they turned out and still do today.

Despite these positives, Mom was again tearful as she signed me in on my first day. I was nearly eleven years old and I was to be a boarder again, only seeing the family on Sundays. This was the hardest part of the new arrangement; otherwise, I was looking forward to the change. The school was indeed a swankier-looking place with pretty, well laid out gardens and manicured driveways. A small wooden gate allowed entry and sturdy steel gates guarded the drive. Turrets of stone and small paned windows looked out over the facade and the entire compound was encircled with a high brick wall topped with a fringe of nasty looking broken glass shards. I gazed up at those walls – were they supposed to keep us in or others out? I never knew the answer to that one.

A very different educational experience began, including increased exposure to the subject I loved – music. I was to take piano again and was taught by a beautiful little nun called Sr. Andre. She always sat ramrod straight beside me at the instrument and I absorbed her enthusiasm and love of music. She taught me that music has color and showed me feeling and expression.

I was competent at the piano and she said I could go far as a pianist but I knew in my heart of hearts that I would be a singer. The four-hour practice sessions that concert pianists went through every day seemed much too much work for me. I had known from the early age of five that I would be a singer and the fates seemed to be steering me that way. But I loved my lessons with her and received a thorough grounding in music theory that never goes astray for a singer. I wondered how such an obviously talented lady ended up being in a convent teaching us. I never knew the answer to that one either.

One memorable school outing was to hear the Melbourne Symphony Orchestra. That was my first exposure to music performed on a really grand scale and I was entranced – it was magnificent. Orchestral sound can have such an overwhelming effect on the human soul. Music appreciation became one of my favorite studies.

Our days at the Presentation Convent began with 6am Mass followed by breakfast, study, classes, lunch, classes, play, dinner, study hall, rosary and bed. Our routine went round and round, punctuated by tolling bells from the tall bell tower rising above the compound. There was a bell to speak, a bell to stop speaking, a bell to line up for assembly, a bell to go to class, a bell to pray, a bell to stop praying … lots of bells.

Once again I lived in a dormitory overseen by a nun who was like a surrogate mother. Mine was Sr. Lucy. She was Irish, I think, and quite strict but I grew to love her. My dormitory was known as St. Joseph's and I shared it with about twenty girls. I made a few close friends there – Katie Griffith, a really serene girl with a wicked grin (she still has it), Nola O'Loughlin and Mary Darling. On Saturdays we all scrubbed and polished that old dormitory under the watchful eye of Sr. Lucy until it shone. No shirking.

Sr. Concepta was in charge of the choir and all the musical events. I loved the choir and sang 'The Nuns' Chorus' for the school concert one year. Sr. Concepta also taught the Gregorian chants and Latin responses for the Mass. She pedaled that old organ like mad as she conducted with one hand, her robes flapping like the Flying Nun. She really was a fine musician and ruled with a glance that could melt the non-attentive to jelly. In that small chapel early in the morning there was something about those Gregorian Chants combined with the scent of incense in the air that was truly inspiring. I believe we all strove for holiness: some achieved it, others did not.

We all wore a uniform. In winter this was a dark pinafore over a long-sleeved shirt, heavy drawers and stockings, gloves and a reviled hat. I never wear hats to this day. In summer we had a lighter weight uniform but still had to wear the stockings. As we grew, we were encouraged to wear a girdle or what was called a 'Roll On' so as not to be 'uncontrolled'. I think that was the word. Heaven help us if girls were 'uncontrolled'! Anyway, I blame my weak lower back on that blasted girdle.

Somewhere around the middle of my stay at Presentation Convent, a trickle of foreign students started coming in to our school. Following the Second World War, the Australian Federal Government encouraged immigration from Britain and Europe to boost the population and expand the economy. Given the recent threat from Japan so close to the north and the general distrust of Asian people at that time, it was felt that Australia must 'populate or perish'. Displaced people from war affected parts of Europe made up a large proportion of these migrants and a new term entered the language – 'New Australians'. One of these students, an Italian girl, took one look at the girdle she was supposed to put on and flatly refused to wear it. From that day on neither did I unless I was absolutely forced to.

Many 'New Australians' were coming to the school and new languages and ideas were being introduced. Sometimes we would have to coach girls who could not speak a word of English upon arrival. It did not take them long to pick up enough to get by – children know how to survive – although their first weeks must have been terrible.

The education from the Presentation Nuns was broad and thorough. I am an avid reader and I soon perfected the trick of reading a library book propped behind a study text. My favorites were *Black Beauty* and *My Friend Flicka*, along with *Little Women* and earlier all the Enid Blyton novels. Whenever I am in Wyoming I still find my gaze expectantly sweeping the hills looking for Flicka.

We were taught sewing, art and deportment – no pushing and shoving in the lines to Mass – along with the regular subjects. As we were boarders, there was no getting away from the teacher after class so it was better to pay attention and get the job done, then there were no repercussions. On the weekends Mom made the trip down from Warburton to take me home for the night. A lot of the girls were from far out in the country and didn't see their parents or home for months on end. I always felt so bad for them.

So, a few years went by in this fashion. One year my parents traveled overseas, leaving me to spend my Sundays with my Aunt Dolly. Her daughter, my cousin Dorothy, was a lot of fun so that was okay by me. We had many good times together – just two peas in a pod. On returning from their trip, Dad decided to build a house in Brighton, a suburb near the bay, and he took an apartment near my school where we could live until the house was finished. This meant I could be a day scholar again – wonderful! I had my evenings and weekends away from the convent.

The only down side was that the apartment was alongside a large cemetery with a direct view from my window of everything that went on there. Still, it beat a wall topped with broken glass. On the weekends it was back to 'Warby' for the whole family where I could breathe the mountain air. It's funny; I have never been, and never will be, a city girl, but there was a time when the big city lights were all I wanted.

I was about fifteen when I began to notice boys ... *Oh boy!* I would sit out on our front verandah at Warburton listening to the music of the tall trees and dreaming about the man I would marry. I envisaged him with big brown eyes, someone who would understand my very soul. I felt I could almost reach out into the void and touch him. Where was he?

There were the movies at the local Warby cinema – all the cowboy classics, *Lassie Come Home*, *Casablanca*. (I remember being carried out of the cinema when I was younger, screaming and tearful over poor Bambi's misfortunes.) There were also the Saturday night dances at the old Mechanics Hall in Warburton. We girls would get all dolled up in very adult makeup – as much as we could get away with anyhow, before our mothers caught us – and stand along the wall waiting for the local boys to ask us for a dance.

I had set my cap for one particular boy and it took forever to get him to notice me. I had seen him at the swimming hole and he played football with the local team. His name was Johnny and he was a quite a bit older but that didn't bother me. I was smitten. Finally, one night he walked me home after the dance. It was my first kiss and it knocked me for a loop. I fell for him like a rock and had the rest of my life planned out in a flash – wedding, house, children. That summer was magic as we knocked around in his little blue car. I watched him play football and cheered him on madly. I was pretty much his groupie, I suppose. He took me to the drag races and dances and we necked heavily in his car – no real hanky panky, though. I was Johnny's girl. And I was thrilled as only a fifteen-year-old girl can be.

I could only see him on the weekends and there was each long week of school to be endured in between. On the drive back up to Warburton I'd be willing the car to go faster. The trip back to school was always hard as I felt the miles creep between us and the long week stretching ahead.

Inevitably I suppose, the bubble burst. Stories started creeping back. Friends began to talk. He was seeing another girl in town while I was away during the week ... his car was seen parked all night outside someone's house ... he had a thing for older women. There was no end to what I was hearing.

I confronted him and he apologized with tears in his eyes, saying I was his woman and he would never let me down again. I believed him with all my heart – I so wanted to believe him! I thought things could go back to the way they were but very soon it was worse than I could have imagined. Johnny was back to his old tricks running after other women. My mother included. *My mother? He found my mother more desirable than me?*

That was a moment I will never forget – the day I entered the kitchen and, with my own eyes, saw him making up to her. She was in a flutter at his evident interest but I was stunned, watching the little scene unfold as if I had been turned to stone. They heard my footstep and he left abruptly. I asked her what was going on, longing for her to explain away what I thought I had seen but she dismissed me with a wave of her hand.

My world changed in that moment. All my precarious adolescent confidence collapsed under this humiliating betrayal. I was already self conscious about my weight and my looks and this simply confirmed my fears – I wasn't good enough. I can accept now that Johnny was just young and ignorant but the rejection and betrayal I felt then was life changing. You don't easily recover from hurts like that. I refused to talk to my mother about it, blaming her for Johnny's treatment of me. In my confusion and self-doubt I thought she had betrayed me too and I held a grudge against her for a long, long time.

I cried buckets and buckets of tears in those difficult days. I was a teenage girl in the middle of the ordinary ups and downs of life, wondering who I was and where I was going. I'd been cut down by my first love in the cruelest way. On top of that I had a mother to whom I no longer talked and a father who was often away. The break with Mom was a bitter blow as prior to that we'd had a good relationship. I couldn't have been sadder if she had died. I believe the seeds of this unhappy tangle sprang from my parents' marriage.

I knew by now that their relationship was difficult to say the least. As I'd got older I'd realized more and more that in many ways they led separate lives. Dad's absences were legendary. Take his 'business trips' to Sydney for example. Those trips were one of those family 'secrets' we all knew about but never discussed. The truth was my father was no settled family man. He was more what a later generation would have termed a 'party animal'. He would regularly fly up to Sydney 'on business' but the real purpose was to meet up with friends and go partying. Together these guys would let their hair down – frequenting the bars and restaurants, entertaining the showgirls and in general pretending they were still carefree bachelors.

He'd always been a ladies' man, a bad boy. Mom knew all about it – she bore it because she had to. At that time, like many other women in her situation, she had few other options. With no higher education and no career to fall back on, her security lay in staying married to Dad. My childhood was one of tension and undercurrents as I gradually became aware of what was happening. There was antagonism, competition, a continual game of one-up-manship between them as each struggled for a little power over the other.

This did produce its funny moments, proving to me Mom's resilience in the face of what for her must have been a very unhappy, haunted life. My father had arranged an overseas trip with his latest mistress – his secretary – and had booked the tickets in the name of Mr. and Mrs. Trask. Unfortunately for Dad the shipping line rang our home to confirm some details and naturally enough asked for Mrs. Trask. Mom became privy to the plot, confronted Dad with the truth but then calmly packed her bags and went on the trip herself.

'There's a ticket here for Mrs. Trask. I'm Mrs. Trask, so that must mean me!' she declared. 'I could do with a holiday!' Before she left she gave the young woman some advice. 'You're not the first and you won't be the last.'

Looking back I see that my mom lived with a lot of disappointment in her life, not the least of which was the denial of her singing ambitions by her own mother. As a girl she had lived a restricted life, not allowed to choose her own friends or date boys. She had always vowed she would not stop me or my brother from following our dreams. She wanted me to have what she didn't have – clothes, friends, boys, a career – but at the same time she was feeling the loss of her youth and the opportunities she no longer had. She lived vicariously through me and resented it at the same time.

I don't know what went on between Johnny and my mother and I didn't want to know. What I saw was enough. I was out of there. *Give me the big city lights. I'll become that world famous singer she couldn't be. I'll be better than her and better than any of her singing students she brags about. I'll show her – and everyone else – exactly what I can do.*

Rejection was the catalyst that changed my life and drove me out of my beautiful valley. A small tight ball of bitterness was born that day that did not leave me for a long time. I swore to myself never to marry, ever. I became rebellious at school and suddenly completely bored with it. I informed my parents I was leaving at the end of term with the intention of pursuing a singing career. It was time to toughen up, time to stand alone.

'One day everyone in Australia will know my name,' I told my mother coldly. 'I'm going to be famous.'

She just stared at me open mouthed, shaking her head in disbelief.

It was 1956 and my sixteenth birthday. My parents threw a huge party for me, trying to snap me out of my new difficult mood. All my family and friends and my brother's friends came. I was brash and hard, feeling my oats and flirting like mad. We danced all night and kicked up our heels. I would show 'em how to do it.

The Olympics came to Melbourne in November of that year. I sat and bawled tears as white peace doves were released in their hundreds at the Opening Ceremony at the Melbourne Cricket Ground and 'Waltzing Matilda' was sung by a full choir to a slow beat. Thirty years later I would fly from the US to stand in that same stadium and sing 'Waltzing Matilda' to a packed crowd of football fans at the opening of the AFL Grand Final. So much was to happen in between.

Television had become a new part of our lives that year. Dad brought home a clunky box with a small screen in time for the Olympics coverage and we all were glued to the black-and-white images. American shows made up the bulk of our viewing as the Australian television industry had hardly taken off at that stage. One of my favorites quickly became *Leave It to Beaver*, a show which piqued my curiosity about the American way of life and threw my own family into sharp contrast. Like all teens, I longed for understanding and didn't believe I'd find it in my own home. The Cleavers were the perfect family, I thought. *I wish I could find what they had. I will find it and singing will be my ticket.*

The first step was to get myself some training. Around that time I attended a dance at Ziegfeld's Ballroom in Hawthorn, Melbourne that had a big band, a sparkling mirror ball and a great girl singer called Dorothy Baker. I thought she was wonderful. She was slim with dark hair and wore long, soft gloves as she stood up on the stage under the spotlight. She looked like a goddess. I wondered if she would speak to me and I sidled closer as she sang. A small group of fans stood at the edge of the stage watching her and at the end of the song she came across to speak to someone. This was my chance. I signaled to her and she turned to me.

'I love your singing,' I stammered.

'Thank you,' she said.

'I want to be a singer too. Do you know anyone who teaches?' The band was shuffling music in the background, getting ready for the next set.

'There's only one man I know,' said Dorothy. 'His name is Jack White.' She smiled and started to move away.

'Where can I find him?' I called after her.

'In the city. He should be in the phone book,' she answered and turned away to the band leader's summons. I saw her float in her beautiful gown back to her place onstage in the glow of the spotlight.

'One day that will be me,' I vowed to myself as I backed away into the crowd again.

The next day I scoured the phone book and located Mr. Jack White. I copied out the number and stared at it. How much would I have to explain to him over the phone? Would he want to know what experience I'd had? What if he said no? I dialed the number, said a few 'please God' prayers under my breath and waited. A friendly male voice with a foreign accent answered. *American?* I wondered. In a strange way the thought that he might have come from the land of *Leave It to Beaver* gave me confidence. I explained that I wanted to train as a singer and he said he would give me an audition. Easy as that. I put down the phone, hugging myself.

The audition was the following week and I spent the time deciding on songs and practicing in the bathroom. I took the train into the city, located the studio in one of the narrow cobbled back lanes that crisscross Melbourne's city centre and rode the tiny elevator up to the third floor. Jack White turned out to be Canadian, not American – an important distinction I wasn't aware of then! He had a very gentle manner and I loved him immediately. He took me into the audition room, introduced me to his pianist and we got down to business.

'What are you going to sing for me, Diana?'

I pulled out my music and gave it to the pianist. '"Hello Young Lovers".'

'Away you go, then,' said Jack.

I stood where he indicated, gave the pianist a nod and launched into a swing version of the song. At the end I held my breath. Jack started talking. It took a few seconds to realize he was telling me all about the course, so that must mean ...

'I'd like to take you on, Diana.'

'Oh, thank you! Thank you!' I stuttered. I was very excited. He went on to tell me further details about fees and so on. I would need a job to pay for this, was my next thought. I knew Dad didn't think I'd follow through on my dreams. The money side of things was up to me.

I left school and took a variety of odd jobs, mainly secretarial. I flirted with modeling and also put myself through the 'Greta Miers School of Charm' course. My modeling career ended when a greasy little man grabbed a hold of my buttocks in a changing room. I was so shocked that I gave up any idea of modeling from that moment. I do not regret studying with Greta though. She had been a top model in Melbourne and was a very poised, knowledgeable lady. I gained a lot from her advice about how to take a basic wardrobe and make it work a million ways to achieve an understated elegance. Getting in and out of cars, how to carry yourself, 'without your hair done you are never dressed' – these were all useful lessons I still put into practice today. One of my secretarial jobs was with the wholesale division of RCA records. Just a few short years later I would sign with NBC in New York, their parent company. Meantime I was earning a pittance, but enough to pay my voice coach.

Jack was a wonderful teacher. We spent a lot of time at first with breath control, learning skills that would stand me in good stead my whole career. One of my practice songs was 'Moonlight In Vermont' which I sang over endlessly in the bathroom. I realized early that the bathroom is a natural echo chamber where I could listen to myself critically with ease. My dad reckoned I cost him his bladder as I was always in the bathroom and he could never get in. Dad would groan whenever he heard that song after that.

Whenever I came back to Australia in later years to perform, Jack would always come to see me and we'd catch up. He really knew his business and I listened to his advice all along. I asked him once had he ever trained any other singers of note?

'There was never anyone like you, Diana,' he replied.

I accepted the compliment in the spirit it was intended but I happen to know he also trained Helen Reddy. He probably said the same thing to her too.

I'd been working with Jack for about six months when I heard about a new television competition on Channel 7 called *Swallows Parade* backed by the Swallow and Ariel Biscuit Company. Jack encouraged me to enter as the prize was £2,000 for the act of the year. That was a lot of money. Well, I loved their biscuits. Why not give it a try? I entered the competition and Jack prepared me.

Swallows Parade was hosted by a well known announcer by the name of Doug Elliot. There were several heats, all performed before a small live audience seated on ordinary kitchen chairs. The set was small, allowing for just medium and close up shots. A boom mike hovered over my head. This was my first time on television and my knees were shaking.

Everything is a bustle of preparation with cameras, cables and crew everywhere, the heat from the lights is intense, the audience is simmering behind the camera and then, suddenly, a hush falls over the room. All you are aware of is the electronic hum in the air and the little red eye of the camera staring at you. If you're lucky, you will connect with that little red eye as with a lover. You'll leap that distance and enter the home of the viewer.

My first song was 'Embraceable You'. Doug Elliot introduced me, my camera came up and I heard my intro. I looked into that little red eye and sang my heart out. Amazingly, I made that connection that day, my first time in front of a camera. I'll never forget it. I was completely in the moment as I sang that song. While on a break somewhere near the end of the competition, Doug Elliot asked me about my ambitions. I suppose that was the first time I really voiced my desire to try for America. Everyone said that if I went overseas I should try England and that no one went to America, but in my heart I knew that's where my destiny lay. I wanted to find the people like those I'd seen in *Leave It to Beaver*.

The competition was divided into male, female and variety acts. The other female singer of note in the show was none other than Dorothy Baker. For the last round in the competition I sang 'These Foolish Things'. I felt it did not go as well as the first heats.

The final evening arrived and I stood shaking in the line-up as the announcements were made. I heard Doug Elliot's voice announcing Dorothy Baker had won the female section. My stomach dropped. Dorothy was a great singer, I knew that. She deserved to win. But I knew I'd done well too. My heart started pounding. I had this feeling ... could it be...? My hands clenched. I was holding my breath. Doug Elliot was shuffling papers, opening his mouth for the final announcement. And at last it came: 'The overall winner of the inaugural *Swallows Parade* competition is Diana Trask!' I could not believe it. I hugged Dorothy, sincerely believing she was a lot better than me, but I had won!

I began to get jobs around town, mostly by word of mouth. A local promoter, Ron Tudor, the first person to take a chance on me, arranged a recording session in Melbourne for a single. My very first recording was 'Comes Love' on the W&G label with Tommy Davidson and his orchestra. My dear friend Geoff Manion promoted me heavily on his top radio show at 3AW and interviewed me very often, very nicely and generally pushed me on.

One of my first jobs was at a function for New Year's Eve. The master of ceremonies introduced me as 'the girl with the beautiful smile'. That puffed me up no end as I stepped onstage to begin the set with the band. The night wore on and my 'beautiful smile' became more and more pinned on as the liquor flowed and the patrons became unruly. They thought it was funny to throw the snowball decorations from the tables at me. For many years after that I would not work on New Year's Eve. I think I have only performed two other engagements in my whole career on that holiday and they were unchangeable contracts.

A young promoter called Ivan Damian from Adelaide invited me to tour South Australia, performing at concerts and dances. I was thrilled. I was only seventeen and my mother put up some road blocks but I accepted, told her the promoter had a good reputation and said I was going anyway. I wasn't in the mood to be held back by my mother or anyone.

I was picked up in Melbourne and driven all the way to Adelaide, about a 450-mile trip. It was a long, hot drive on single lane country roads; no air-conditioned comfort. I reached Adelaide hot and exhausted but bounced back when I met the band and we went in for rehearsal at the Town Hall where we were to perform a series of midday concerts.

These small bands were generally fun to work with. House bands usually had eight to fourteen guys and they carried stock arrangements for girl singers, so you had to learn the arrangement exactly and do it like the chart said. We packed the Adelaide Town Hall every noontime and traveled round to different dances at night. The band was young and enthusiastic and I learned more each day about crowds and sound.

I liked the concerts best. I was enjoying my newfound freedom away from parents, school and nuns. I was young, the sour taste of rejection was still in my mouth and I was very definitely flirting with my limits. I would eye off the men sitting on the aisle, choose my victim and flounce down from the stage towards some poor fella. Singing 'Fever' in my sexiest voice, I'd move up close and sit on his knee, all sultry eyes and smile. They lapped it up. *Johnny? Johnny who?*

During that trip the legend Louis Armstrong was also performing in Adelaide and I met him backstage after a concert. I was so impressed with his enormous smile and attitude.

'Tune up sharp!' he would holler to his musicians as they prepared to go on. He travelled with a few lead guys of his own, combined with local musos and was a wonderful performer.

In the meantime, I practiced non-stop in the motel bathrooms. I often wonder now about the other patrons of those motels as my practice hours were generally late into the night. I travelled back from Adelaide feeling very experienced and ready for the next challenge.

Back in Melbourne I was getting the occasional gig on a television show. I had no agent, in fact there was no such thing as an agent for the likes of me. I was a very lowly cog in the entertainment machine, getting £5 an appearance. A break came when I was approached by Rod Kinnear, an up-and-coming young producer at Channel 9. He was putting together a show whereby we were to mime the latest songs on the hit parade to the voice of the real recording artist. Maybe they didn't trust the local talent to sing well enough. Anyway, it was kind of bizarre, but a job was a job and it was a good learning experience. It was called *The Astor Show* and one of the funniest moments was when I was dressed up as a sexy hula girl with long black hair trailing down my back. Hey, if that girl from the Upper Yarra Valley can hula her way into the history books, so can I.

'I got an island in the Pacific and everything about it is terrific...' I mouthed as I batted my eyes and gyrated my hips towards the camera.

A bamboo curtain was to lift behind me as I turned. One tiny problem – as the curtain lifted so did my wig. I was hooked like Dad's old trout. With my hair standing on end I continued to mime away while the crew collapsed in hysterical laughter, helpless to assist me. Everything was live in those days and there was nothing they could do. What you saw was what you got.

It was 1958, Australian television was just in its infancy, and its stars were being born. Graham Kennedy hit a home run with his long running variety show *In Melbourne Tonight*. I was lucky enough to get frequent work on *IMT* and was wowed by Graham's wicked wit. I think I even chased after him a bit but to no avail. I learned the basics about upstaging on that show from singing duets with a famous tenor who shall remain nameless. He could manage to take you by the arm or shoulders while gazing into your eyes singing a love song, and ever so easily get you turned around so you ended up with your back to the audience. This would leave you singing to the back wall as he sang out to the front. He wasn't the only performer to try that one on, as I was to discover.

'Panda' Lisner was the glamorous barrel girl on *IMT* and became a great pal of mine. She and Graham had a great line of repartee, fully loaded with double entendre and she played the dumb blonde routine to the hilt. She was anything but dumb and attracted a huge following. I loved her dilly ways ... and her gorgeous shoes. Bert Newton was a terrific young star coming up. There was Ernie Sigley, Val Ruff, Barry Crocker, Barbara Faulds, Patti McGrath, Ted Hamilton, Philip Brady, the Channel 9 dancers and many others commencing memorable careers. They were all stars.

I was home asleep one night at our new house in Brighton when I was awakened at about three in the morning to loud singing outside my second-floor window. I struggled up to see what all the noise was about and there below stood Ernie Sigley and Bert Newton, arms wrapped around each other and singing at the top of their voices...

'I'm so young and you're so old, so Diana, I've been told ... Oh, please stay by me, Diana.'

I was laughing and trying to shush them at the same time as I was afraid Dad would wake up and then for sure I'd be in trouble. They were so crazy and I loved them. Bert had the most irrepressible smile (still does) and Ernie was a trip.

I remember once meeting Isaac Cole, brother of Nat King Cole, at Channel 9. Isaac was a great jazz pianist and singer and had been brought out by Channel 9 to appear on *IMT*. His wife was with him and I glued myself to them, of course, pumping them for all the news on America and telling them how I wanted to try my luck there. They were both very kind and encouraging. Later in the States I met Nat King Cole backstage after his show – he was such a fabulous singer and presence in the industry.

Sometimes silly things hurt the most and for me it was the 'axes and orchids' section of the television papers. Occasionally people would send in harsh criticisms and my heart would drop for every bad one I read about me, especially if it had anything to do with my looks. I fretted and dieted unendingly so that I would be more appealing. I never worried about my voice or the singing, just the look.

At that stage I had no close boyfriends although I went out with a few boys here and there. As the saying goes, *once bitten...* I began to admire men older than myself, looking towards their seasoning and experience. My best friend at the time was Joy Fountain, a stunning blonde model working at Channel 9. She had a beat-up old MG car and we would race round having fun and going to dances. Panda was always a good friend too, very wise and understanding. I was a guest at her home in Las Vegas many years later and she was still the same great girl. Her husband, the talented Jimmy Allan, was always a very loving partner for her.

During this time I saved up for a trip north to Queensland with a friend, one of the Channel 9 dancers, Jenny Adell. We rented an apartment on the beach at Surfers Paradise and then went down to Broadbeach. There was only one hotel in Broadbeach in those days and the beach was wide open and mostly deserted. I spent hours looking out to sea, marveling at the power of the ocean and dreaming about my future.

A jazz band was playing the Corroboree Club, and Jenny and I hung around and got to know the band members. Max Wildman was the band leader. His girlfriend Dixie was with him, not a muso herself but a real jazz buff. Di and Dennis Sindrey were also part of the troupe, great people and still my close friends. Dennis and Di parted company some years later and Dennis moved to Jamaica where he had a great career with the band The Caribs, which became very famous. He is an amazing guitarist. Dennis and Max found out I was a singer and got me up on stage at the Corroboree. Dennis really encouraged me to go for my dreams and still does today, because I find there's always a new dream, a new goal to get excited about.

That was a great holiday. We partied and listened to Jack O' Leary in the beer garden, got sunburned and laughed non-stop. I had just turned eighteen and this was the life. It was there for the first time I saw a singer, Paula Langlands, pour a full bottle of beer onto a heckler's head. I cheered her on; she was great.

My work with *IMT* came to an abrupt end. The rumor was that my father was approached by Channel 9 to buy some sponsorship time for his furniture business. He declined and as a consequence I was dumped. I don't know if that's really what happened – I never got a straight answer out of anyone. Another story I heard was that I was too jazzy, too progressive in my style. I do know that the industry could be cutthroat, even back then. In any event, I had to find work and I decided to try for the next big step – Sydney.

This was a hard decision. Despite my strained relationship with my parents, Melbourne was still my home. I knew nobody in Sydney but many entertainers told me that's where it all happened and I knew I had to go there. I cajoled and wheedled my dad to give me a name as he was often there. In the end he said he would call a friend of his – a doctor – who could possibly put me up for a while. Mom was horrified.

'You're too young to leave home by yourself, Diana!' she argued. 'You're only eighteen! You've had your fun, now it's time to settle down.'

Had my fun? Settle down? Oh, no. I had my sights set on much more than a few gigs with *IMT* and a concert or two in Adelaide. Many people over the years were to echo my mother's words: *You were so young to leave home. It must have been so hard!* Well, yes, in many ways it was. But I had something to prove. And staying at home would have been harder.

THREE

Nightlife

I landed in Sydney with £10 and a telephone number in my pocket. Apprehension filled my heart as the plane circled over the massive harbor town spread out below. The cozy, familiar Melbourne of childhood was far away and, for the moment at least, ambition seemed a poor substitute for familiar faces. No one met me at the airport so I took a cab to the address I had been given, getting my first taste of the sprawling suburbs and bewildering streets of Sydney.

This city is known for its beautiful harbor-front homes in suburbs such as Rose Bay, Double Bay and Point Piper. The doctor and his wife lived in just such a place in Potts Point on the South Shore – a spacious white house surrounded by gardens that sloped gently down to a pool with views to the harbor beyond. The doctor's wife was a real 'Sydneysider' – fashionable and lovely – but I quickly realized the doctor felt a bit put-out by my arrival, although his initial welcome was kind enough.

I was with them for two and a half weeks and the feeling of awkwardness grew every day until it became a real strain to be in his presence. I had no idea what was at the bottom of it until the day he grilled me about my father.

'What's he told you about me?' he asked, his voice sharp with suspicion.

The short answer was 'nothing!' but now I started to put two and two together. All I knew from Dad was that he and my father had met through Dad's 'business trips', those bachelor style excursions we never talked about. I realized from his question that the doctor was nervous. He led a very respectable life with a very respectable wife. He was pompous, rich and particular. And he was afraid I knew too much about him. My presence in the house put him on the back foot and I can only imagine Dad must have twisted his arm to get me an invitation there at all. As it happened, I didn't know any incriminating details about him, and even if I did I had no interest in talking out of turn in front of his wife.

More than anything I just wanted to find a job, get established and be independent of him and everybody. But how? Just arriving in Sydney wasn't enough. I had to find the right doors and somehow make them open for me. Anxious days passed as I wracked my brains trying to work out my next step.

The answer was closer than I realized, in fact it was a casual conversation with the doctor's wife that finally started the ball rolling. She was the complete opposite to her husband – warm and friendly, a real sweetie. I wanted to be useful about the place and one day was helping her empty and clean the pool. She was easy to talk to and we chatted about this and that, about my ambitions and dreams. I found her to be a sympathetic spirit – she had dabbled in theatre in earlier days – and she told me she knew some people at the Channel 7 television station. She also knew a theatrical producer in Sydney by the name of Frank Strain. My antennae went up straight away. Could she please phone and arrange a meeting with him? She promised to try and within days the appointment was set.

Frank Strain was a 'night person', a term I had become familiar with in the entertainment world, so the appointment was made for late afternoon. The day arrived and the morning crept by as I tried to fill in time but I was restless and found it hard to settle on anything. Finally lunch was past and I shut myself in my room to get ready. I dressed very carefully from my limited wardrobe – so much seemed to be riding on this one little hour of conversation. Not only did I want to make a good impression but I wanted to look older than my eighteen years.

The meeting took place at a club he owned and the doctor's wife came with me to make the introduction. I was grateful for her help but I was keen to present myself to Mr. Strain as 'all grown up' and ready to take on the world. He could so easily have given me the polite brush-off as just another 'wannabe' but he turned out to be both wise and kind. After carefully listening to my story he asked me a few questions: *What were my plans? What was I expecting from him? What kind of singer was I?*

My plans were hazy – all I knew was that America was in there somewhere – but the answer to the last question was easy: 'I'm a jazz singer,' was my certain reply.

He was a theatrical producer and so couldn't offer me anything himself but he readily gave me his advice.

'Diana, go to Channel 7 and audition,' he urged, 'and get out and about and talk to all the musicians you can find – they're the ones who know the town.' He gave me a number to call at ATN 7, wished me well and I left feeling buoyed up and on the way.

The timing was right – they were auditioning for a new daytime variety program and if I could get myself there they would give me a hearing. 'Getting there' would present its own hurdles. Sydney is divided by its huge harbor. The Sydney Harbor Bridge, built to link the North and South Shores, was the only way to cross then, other than by boat. The physical distance from the South Shore where the doctor's house was located, to the heart of the city where the action was, meant every trip would be long and expensive. Funds were low but I splurged on a cab across the Bridge and straight to the station's studios on the North Shore – better to arrive on time and unflustered than to battle Sydney public transport on this day of all days. The harbor water was sparkling like diamonds as we crossed the Bridge. Excitement surged in my stomach.

I walked into the studio feeling nervy but confident at the same time because if nothing else, I knew I had the pipes. I *was* a singer! It had always been there right from when I was a kid. I'd just open my mouth and push it on out and I had my successes in Melbourne to prove it. If only I'd had the same confidence in my looks! I didn't have the figure, the wardrobe, the hair or the nails the other girls all seemed to have and I let that play on my insecurities for many years.

I performed a jazzy version of 'Hello Young Lovers', prevailed on one of the musicians – someone I knew slightly from the Queensland trip – to drive me back across the Bridge and then caught public transport the rest of the way to the doctor's house to sit and wait for the call. And within a couple of days it came – they liked me and I landed the job! Confidence was soaring.

Now my routine was one of rehearsing and performing for the daily show and being on tap for any other gig for which the station needed singers. Transport back and forth across town was forever a problem but by getting to know the musicians and begging rides at every turn, I got by. If anyone was going to play any kind of gig anywhere in Sydney I'd cadge a spot in the car and go along too. I wanted to listen and learn all I could.

When I began at Channel 7, I found out that the day after my audition the dining room wall was scrawled all over with the words 'Hire Diana Trask!' It had been scrubbed off by the time I arrived for my first day so I didn't actually see it but I was intrigued – who was my secret fan? When an upset management came asking questions though, all I felt was embarrassment. Everyone was questioned closely and I protested my innocence but I wasn't certain they believed me.

Years later I found out who the real culprit was. Joe Martin, a well-known comic around the traps, had heard me sing in Queensland. He knew I was auditioning and thought he'd help things along. We had many a laugh about that when he revealed the secret years later at dinner one night with my husband and I.

'Why did you do it, Joe?' I asked.

'Station management wouldn't know a star if they fell over one. They needed to be told to hire you,' was the reply.

'My God, Joe, they thought I did it!' I yelped.

He was unrepentant. 'They should have been grateful. It was a work of art!' and we all went into further gales of laughter. Joe was famous for his antics and was well-loved by other entertainers.

The variety show band was about six pieces and the drummer was a young man by the name of Tom Spencer. He was pretty well-known around town as a gifted performer and I admired his talent. On the show one day was a popular psychic, the guest of the day. During a break she amused us by reading palms amongst the cast and crew. She read Tom's hand and then mine.

'You two have a destiny link,' she purred.

Tom and I looked at each other and I am sure he dismissed the idea as quickly as I, thinking 'no way'. She saw our common mistrust.

'Oh yes,' she smiled confidently. 'Tom will be influential for you in later life.'

'As long as it's not marriage and ten children,' I grinned as Tom mimed his horror at the prospect and nearby crew members hooted. She said nothing more, but there must have been something in it because, sure enough, later in life Tom Spencer became my booking agent in Australia and later still I became his son's godmother. Interestingly, another Tom was to come into my story to share my destiny in a much deeper way.

By now the doctor had had enough of me invading his home and disturbing his peace. I appreciated the fact that they had put themselves out for me but after a couple of weeks I could feel him just willing me to leave. But where to go? Rents were high and I was only just keeping my head above water with my earnings from the show and other odd gigs I picked up. My prize money from the *Swallows Parade* competition was tucked away for a rainy day. When the doctor suggested I move out into a low rental house he owned further out of town I jumped at the opportunity. Perhaps if I'd seen it first ...?

My new home was one of a dowdy row of identical brick houses in Marrickville, a suburb southwest of the city, and I hated it on sight. The doctor's clinic was in front and I moved into the dingy shared residence behind. The kitchen was out of the ark, the carpets threadbare, the whole atmosphere dreary and depressing. It was the complete opposite to his harbor-side home. What was he doing running a clinic out of a place like this? Why would he want a practice there? I discovered he owned several rental houses in Marrickville and it was clearly a cash cow for him.

I found myself sharing with about six other girls, all with straight office type jobs and highly suspicious of an entertainer in their midst. They looked at me as if I'd arrived from Mars. There was a skinny girl who had been there the longest and boy, did she lay down the law: when you could cook and when you couldn't, when to use the bathroom and when not, rules about the garbage and the lights.

I spent as little time at the house as possible, hanging around with a growing circle of musician friends every night, some of whom I knew from Melbourne and Queensland and they helped me get along from gig to gig to supplement my work on the variety show. I'm not saying I was easy to live with – I was always coming in late and disturbing them and more than once I lost my key and had to wake up one of the girls to let me in. One night Jack O'Leary, a local singer I'd first met in Broadbeach, saw me home at 5am and ended up perched on the front fence serenading the early morning garbage collectors. This did nothing for my popularity!

I lasted there a month. I clearly remember the day I was standing on a street corner in Marrickville waiting for a bus to take me the long journey into town for work. It was hot, the north wind a blistering, gritty whirl of papers and dust, and here I was stuck at the end of the world waiting for a sweaty, miserable bus. What was I doing there? The despair of living in that place was so strong that I uttered aloud: 'I *cannot* live like this! I've *got* to make it out of here!'

I'm very like my dad in many ways. He was a self-made man and I have his tenacity. He had a saying, culled from his love of football, and I could hear him saying it to me that day: *Diana, you gotta get out of the ruck!* Get out from the huddle and the scrum to a place where you can go for goal.

So it was more of a relief than a shock when my friend the doctor announced soon after that he was moving me on again – this time right out of his life. My unconventional employment and hours clearly kept him awake at night worrying about my morals, my welfare or both. He called me into his office and took me to task. The other girls – no doubt egged on by Miss Skinny – were complaining about my nocturnal comings and goings, he claimed. I disturbed their sleep, I upset the routine of the house and he would not put up with it a moment longer!

In fact he lectured me like I had syphilis and told me I had to leave.

I don't do confrontation. I never have. I don't have the language for it. I learned early on that it's better to stay cool and then hit the ball again when you're ready. Cool indifference is a better way to fight because then you stay above it all. You can analyze the situation and change things if you have to when you're ready. I think this was a protective mechanism from childhood, to help me cope with the daily conflict I witnessed between my parents. Cool indifference can drive other people crazy though, particularly if they're itching for a good fight!

It's funny but often when faced with a situation that could get out of control I become quite British. This very English schoolmarm voice comes out of my mouth, uttering things like 'Would you kindly explain yourself!' I was accosted once by a group of youths in the subway in the States and I turned very British and very frosty. They left me alone.

So I listened in silence to the doctor's rantings, smothering a desire to tell him exactly what I thought of his precious house. Even if I'd wanted to, there was no point fighting the confrontation. But I did have a problem. I had to find a place to live, and fast. He gave me a week to arrange other accommodation and, even though I would finally have to fend for myself in 'big, bad Sydney', I was never so glad to leave a place as that one. I shook the dust off my feet and never looked back. *Diana, you gotta get out of the ruck!*

Dixie, my friend from the Broadbeach holiday, came to my rescue. She and Max were now in Sydney with their band and we had met up again. In another case of great timing, she was looking for a flat mate so we trekked up to the Cross to find a place. Kings Cross was the little Soho of Sydney. It consisted of a main drag terminating in a large crossroads at the top of the hill, hence the name. Every class of society came to the Cross and I tried hard to be cool and not stare at the many different people I encountered on the streets.

Dixie was a good pal and educated me in the ways of the world. She knew the ropes in the Cross as her mom lived nearby and her uncle owned a small shop in the main street. Rooms were cheap so we took a small flat with communal baths down the hall, a tiny cooker in the corner and a steady supply of the most enormous cockroaches I have ever seen. They popped up everywhere and I've been fanatical about them ever since, a fact my family has exploited from time to time. My husband once left a rubber cockroach on our kitchen bench for me to find and I swear I had killed that thing fifty times over before I cottoned on to the 'joke'.

Dixie's family was Greek – warm, voluble and welcoming. Her mom would cook incredible Greek food for us and generally took us under her wing. Dixie worked in the food industry and was also a wonderful cook. She introduced me to hot, hot curry, and whenever we could afford it we would frequent the new Indian restaurants that were appearing in the Cross at that time – it was all very different to the 'meat and three veg' of my Warburton upbringing. It was such an exciting time – I was young, finding my feet in a new city and gathering friends about me who finally understood where I was coming from and shared my dreams.

Less exciting was our landlady – Attila the Hun in another life – who would pound on the door at seven in the morning on sheet changing day. Throwing us out of the stalag to stand in the hall in our pajamas, she would march in armed with rubber gloves and bottles of disinfectant, bent on extermination.

'You lazy people, when do you get up?' she would screech. But we were night people, something only singers, actors and musos ever really understand. Dixie and I were determined to move out of there as soon as we could afford something better.

Brian Syron, a dear friend of Dixie's, came by the flat often. Brian and I clicked at once as he had a wild sense of humor and was very streetwise. His ambition was to be an actor and we talked for many hours, dreaming of our great futures. He became like a dear brother to me, simultaneously trying to protect me and wise me up to the world and its harsher realities. He called me 'The Virgin Queen' and teased me no end.

About five o' clock one evening Brian showed up at our door all in a flap. He had been invited to dinner with one of the richest families in Sydney as a guest of the youngest daughter. Which knife and fork should he use? What if he said the wrong thing? I checked his outfit several times, reassuring him as best I could as he nervously picked at imaginary lint. *Be yourself,* I told him, but he left still in a high state of agitation.

I thought nothing more of it but at about ten the next morning he was on the doorstep again, this time in a fit of uncontrollable laughter. It was half an hour before he calmed down enough to tell me what had happened at the dinner party.

Brian had arrived at the door and been greeted by the butler, George, who ushered him into a formal reception room. The daughter came downstairs and as they sipped their sherry her mother, the Grand Dame, entered in a great swirl of chiffon. Brian was very impressed and even more nervous as they moved into the dining room where George doubled as the waiter.

Over the soup, the Grand Dame inquired of Brian in a very pucker voice what he did for a living. Trying to talk it up, Brian stammered that he was 'in the acting profession'. (He was actually still selling shoes at that time.) This confession she dismissed rather grandly but on the whole the evening was going well, he thought. He hadn't put his foot in it. He was managing the cutlery. *So far, so good*, thought Brian.

The dinner proceeded with the attentive George faithfully plying the Grand Dame with different wines for each course. As the wine flowed, her accent deteriorated and she began to slur her words and lose her place in the conversation. Brian, still trying to create a good impression, was doing his utmost to keep a straight face but was doomed to lose the battle.

Dessert was over and the lady announced, 'Let us adjourn to the drawing room for coffee.'

As she stood to leave the table, her purse clattered to the floor and in bending over to retrieve it, she let go a long, resounding raspberry. Without missing a beat, she turned to George with an imperious glare.

'George, would you kindly stop that!'

Instantly George replied, 'Certainly, Madam, which way did it go?'

That was the last straw for Brian. He was a terrible giggler at the best of times but now he completely lost it. He was helped smartly out of the house by a wooden-faced George who had obviously missed his calling as a stand-up comedian. When Brian told me the story, we laughed till we ached. It was many years later that I attended a performance at Drury Lane Theater in England and was stunned when Brian's story made an appearance in the show! I guess we told that tale one too many times.

I was always on the lookout for different gigs and after a few weeks living with Dixie I auditioned and landed a job at Romano's, an Italian restaurant downtown with a small dance band. The bandleader was an Englishman who tended to be very conservative in style. I was forever harping at him, 'Come *on*, Percy, let's swing!' After awhile he did let his hair down and the band swung.

The good thing about that gig – apart from it being steady work – was a delicious free Italian meal every night. The clientele was pleasant and quite a few well known people came in and out. I remember the Davis Cup was being played in town and all the players came in for dinner. They were kind of yummy and I swooned over them from my spot on the bandstand where I sang my favorite smoky numbers in their direction.

I picked up occasional work singing with the Australian Jazz Quartet on Sunday afternoons at the Sky Lounge in downtown Sydney. The Sky Lounge was a jazz joint and dance hall, filled to the brim with young people. Jazz was in. Terry Wilkinson, Donnie Burrows, Freddie Logan, Errol Buddle, and Dick Healy, all stars in their own right, sat in with 'Spider' and the boys of the AJQ and set the Sky Lounge on fire. 'Spider' was the leader on vibes, an incredible musician, looking for all the world like a spider with his long arms poised above his instrument. He was a great guy, very cool and a gentle soul.

I heard on the grapevine that a new club was opening up – Lee's – and I decided to front up for an audition. I sang what was becoming my signature song, 'My Funny Valentine', for the manager, Johnny Lee. Johnny had heard me around town and he hired me on the spot. I was to be paid around £30 a week to do two production shows a night and work as the band singer as well, six nights a week from 8pm until 3am. Each night we presented two shows with different acts and in between I'd scramble out of one outfit into another and hop back on the bandstand. Lee's quickly caught on and became the 'in' place for Sydney nightclubbers.

I was in my intense phase – I loved to sing the slow, moody ballads and delve into the smoky tones. I could reach out and touch people with that kind of song. People would stop talking and listen when I sang the ballads and I loved that. The upbeat songs they would just talk through.

In many ways I was following my nose when it came to my career. In fact I don't think 'career' was a word I used. I just knew there was a new sound out there and I had to be part of it. It was a sound that was coming out of America – the wild, free, progressive jazz sounds that were like nothing else I'd heard. I wanted to go there and be part of it. Nothing new was coming out of the UK, not until The Beatles, anyway. It was all America.

I listened and learned all I could from observing other performers, looking for their influences and analyzing their style. I was like a sponge. I watched American television shows and idolized stars like Doris Day and Rosemary Clooney. I picked up records of my favorites and listened to their songs over and over, emulating the phrasing, finding out what made these singers tick. Then I had to rework it all for myself, make it mine. Because you had to make it yours in the end. You couldn't be someone else. Whenever I got lost in my career it was because I had forgotten that golden rule and the people I trust would say to me – *Diana, be yourself!*

Sydney was starting to feel like home. I never tired of the sight of this spectacular city, set on the magnificent harbor and crowned by its famous Bridge, affectionately called the 'coat hanger' by Aussies. I tended to see the city at night more than in daylight hours and it was a sparkling beauty then too. I would sleep late and work late, dropping in after my gig to all the after-hours clubs, listening and learning. Musicians would turn up at favorite hangouts after their gigs and I reveled in the impromptu jam sessions that took place. The nightlife was my life, as the song goes, and it was the way I lived.

Sometimes I did miss being the 'outdoor teen' that I'd always been and would arrange to go with Brian to Bondi Beach and spend the day, or take a harbor ferry to Manly. The parks and gardens all around Sydney were beautiful retreats too. I window-shopped the downtown area in my fashionable pointy-toed shoes and traveled mostly in hot, stuffy buses unless I happened to be in the money. Then I would swan around in one of the famous Sydney cabs, playing at being rich and famous.

Whenever I went swimming at Bondi I always kept a wary eye out for sharks, even though nets were placed across the harbor inlets. I had vivid memories of the day when I was fourteen and my cousin Donny saved me from being taken by a shark as we walked in knee-deep water at Portsea in Victoria. Later at that very same beach, the Prime Minister of Australia, Harold Holt, disappeared, presumably taken by a shark. He was never seen again.

Doors suddenly seemed to be opening for me on all sides. I landed some work with ABC radio. The producer of this particular spot was a fan – he had heard me sing at Johnny Lee's club and liked what I did. He put together a radio series called *Diana Trask Sings* which was a lot of fun, mainly because he let me have my head. I did all the big ballads I loved and had a ball. Having my name in the title was pretty good too...

Frank Ifield was also featured on that series. We each had a fifteen-minute segment back to back. Frank was a nice guy and we got to know each other pretty well. He had his career sights set on the UK.

'Diana,' he'd say to me, 'I'm going to England!'

'Frank,' I'd reply, 'I'm going to America!' He did go to England and became a huge star over there.

In Sydney at that time was an American promoter called Lee Gordon who brought all the big talent into Australia. I was thrilled when he approached me about touring with the Australian Jazz Quartet for the *Stan Freberg Show* in New Zealand. Lee Gordon had seen me perform with the AJQ at the Sky Lounge and liked what he heard. He signed me up for my first really professional tour, my biggest adventure so far. *Look at me!* I thought excitedly. *I'm on tour!* A brief road trip to Adelaide just didn't stack up to this.

New Zealand came up from the sea with a spectacular vista of snow-capped mountains. Our plane flew directly over the Alps and into Christchurch, one of my favorite cities. The audiences were warm and responsive but the halls were freezing for me in my skimpy evening dresses.

Maori entertainers joined us on the bill and I loved their huge smiles and strong white teeth. I'd always had a lot of dental work done and I was just entranced with their beautiful teeth. I tasted Tararoa soup and fell in love with the gorgeous green color of the water there. I still have a little music box I purchased on that trip, made of Tararoa shell which plays '*Pokarekare Ana*'. The popular Maori goodbye song 'Now Is The Hour' was poignantly sung during the show in the native tongue.

The excitement of going on my first tour didn't diminish but I discovered that touring is hard work. Our transport was varied and makeshift. One time the whole troupe was piled tightly into a DC3 that took off from a ragged dirt runway. At other times we had long trips in a bus. It was tiring and often uncomfortable and Mrs. Freberg who was traveling with us found it very difficult to organize meals and other essentials. She could not believe that the stores closed at six o'clock and also on Sundays! 'It's the Dark Ages!' she kept saying.

We had a very successful run and then it was back to Sydney and Johnny Lee's. Famous people often dropped by to eat or see the show. Lee Gordon, the American promoter, sometimes took me around with him after I'd finished work and we'd generally go to an all-night eating place called Dennis Wong's. Later Dennis would build the famous 'Chequers' nightclub and later still got himself murdered. He was into a lot of stuff.

When it came to drugs I was an innocent. I didn't know and I didn't want to know. But plenty of it was going on around me. Looking back, I think that musicians and entertainers in general were perhaps more vulnerable to getting involved in the emerging drug culture. The late-night lifestyle, the high energy required to perform night after night, accumulated tiredness – these things may have contributed to the prevalence of drugs in that world. Alongside that was the attitude amongst some in the show business world that drugs were cool. Inevitably these attitudes would spill over into the mainstream population. People who wanted to emulate the supposed hip lifestyle of the showbiz crowd may have seen drugs as just being part of it. I worked with many, many musicians and fellow entertainers over the years who were not into drugs but it was hard not to notice those who were, particularly when I later moved to the States. A similar story was probably unfolding in Sydney at the time but I wasn't as yet aware of the signs. Time spent in Lee Gordon's company opened my eyes a little though.

One night I was with him after work and he stopped off at a private house I hadn't been to before. The door opened as soon as we knocked. Lee had a quiet conversation with the man who then ushered me into a lounge room with a few other people. Lee disappeared out back. Drinks were being served and I waited for Lee, a bit uncomfortable and wondering what was going on. He eventually emerged.

'Let's go,' he said.

He was driving a little erratically but it was very late and fortunately no one was about. We ended up back at his home and I had to help him out of the car to get inside. He promptly collapsed on the divan and went into a deep sleep. Perfect, I thought as I surveyed him. Drugs still didn't cross my mind. I had grown up with the average Australian girl's expectation that guys drink too much, throw up and pass out on dates. Why should Lee Gordon be any different?

What to do? We were at Potts Point, a long, long way from my flat. I checked Lee; he was completely gone. Shrugging philosophically, I let myself out and began the long walk back to the Cross. It was about 5am, dawn was just breaking and there were no taxis about. Just then, down the street came the familiar domestic sound of the milkman jogging along with his horse, dropping milk bottles on the doorsteps as he went. I hailed him as he walked beside his slow pacing horse.

'Can I get a ride back to the Cross?'

'Hop in,' he replied jauntily, 'as long as you don't mind stopping and delivering milk on the way.'

In I hopped and fell asleep to the sound of hooves on the road.

Lee Gordon, like Brian, teased me about my innocence but at the same time protected me. Nothing was ever mentioned between us about that night, or what had caused his collapse, and at the time I had no idea what was happening. But I was uneasy and never went around with him after work again. When the penny finally dropped about what he was into, I was plain frightened. I did not want anything to do with drugs.

When I was a kid I read a book from my dad's library, *Monkey on My Back*. The book told the heart-wrenching story of a man hooked on drugs and how it ruined his life – heavy reading for a ten year old. I determined then never to let the monkey on my back. When later I encountered drugs on a regular basis in the States, I fell back on my detached, indifferent role to see me through any awkward moments.

Some months after my arrival in Sydney I became ill. I was feverish and tired all the time and couldn't get out of bed. Dixie worried and called a doctor who diagnosed glandular fever. She called my mother and my parents flew me home to Melbourne for a couple of weeks to recuperate. I had been running myself down, eating catch as catch can, staying up very late at night and my menses were heavy floods. Basically I'd been burning the candle at both ends trying to make it. I seemed to improve in Melbourne but on returning to Sydney the problem with heavy menses returned. I decided to see another doctor who someone recommended.

Unfortunately he took an attitude towards me that got my back up. He began by asking me what the problem was and where I lived. When I said I lived at the Cross, he immediately thought the worst of me and began right away to lecture me on aborted fetuses and destroyed fallopian tubes. I didn't understand where he was coming from (Brian didn't call me 'The Virgin Queen' for nothing) but went along with the tirade by adopting my best hip attitude of – you guessed it – cool indifference. The louder he got, the cooler I played it.

What happened next was a case of complete miscommunication. He scheduled a D&C operation for me to scrape out the offending tissue said to be causing my condition. My mother flew to Sydney, rigid with condemnation, having obviously decided I had caught some disease or other from sleeping around. She didn't bother asking me about it and wouldn't have believed me anyway – communication between us had not improved – so I went in for a procedure I didn't need. I woke up to the hazy figure of a nurse standing over me.

'We had to cut the hymen,' she said. 'I just wanted you to know.'

I digested that information as the doctor sidled into the room looking far less self-assured than he had back in his office.

'Er, did it ever hurt when you had sex?' he questioned hesitantly.

He must have judged from my expression as I replied, 'But I've never had sex!'

He turned a sickly white and tore out of the room. I never saw him again. In retrospect, a hip attitude is not always the answer when someone is giving you a hard time. A bit of real communication would have been wiser.

Dad came to Sydney on business and dropped by Johnny Lee's club to see me work. Dad was proud of me – I always knew that – but sometimes parents can't help but put their foot in it, in 'your own best interests' of course. I found out later he cornered Johnny one night and told him that I did not have to 'work like this'...

'My daughter is independently wealthy,' he announced. 'She doesn't belong in a place like this. With her talent she could go anywhere.'

'Independently wealthy?' I scoffed when I heard about it. *Really? Could have fooled me!* But Johnny wasn't laughing either. As Dad pushed harder, Johnny got quieter and quieter but the storm was about to break on me.

Next day I was called into Johnny's office. I bounced in, completely unprepared for what happened next. Johnny was standing next to the window with his back to me.

'You're fired,' he said without preamble. I stopped dead in my tracks. This had to be a joke.

'What...what are you talking about?' He turned around and put his hands flat on the desk in front of him.

'You – are – fired,' he repeated slowly. 'Right now. That's it.'

At that point I didn't know what Dad had done and I was completely bewildered. I protested and begged. Johnny had always been very kind to me and treated me fairly but there was no moving him. He was totally insulted.

'Your father said you are too good for this club,' he spat at me and turned his back again.

I was aghast. I stumbled out of there, choked with tears, stomach churning and fighting back nausea. Cool indifference had sure deserted me this time. I remember going into a church where I got down on my knees and prayed and prayed, cried and cried.

This was a disaster. What would I do now? Steady jobs were hard to come by and Lee's was the hottest place in town. It wasn't just the money, it was all my exposure out the window; all my chances to be seen by promoters and picked up for other and better work. It was all gone in an instant. Dad's interference had cost me everything I had worked for and I blamed him bitterly.

I entered into a period of total depression. My friends, Brian and Dixie and others, did their best to counsel and support me. I prayed and cried but nothing seemed to help. Somehow I would have to pick myself up and try again but it seemed so hard.

Gradually that innate tenacity and stubbornness I ironically share with my father flickered back into life. *This is who you are, Diana! Get up! Move onto something else!* If there is a dream or goal I want to achieve, no matter how far in the future, I put it on the wall where I can read it every day. *This is where you're going, Diana. This is what you're going to do. This is what you're going to be.*

I picked myself up and applied to ABC television for work as I had heard they were putting a new show together. Thankfully the producers liked me and I started a weekly gig with a fairly large troupe. The show took off and I was back in work for a while. I remember the makeup person on the show believed in plastering heavy pancake makeup on me and whenever I tried to move my mouth I felt like I was moving through glue as cracks formed on my skin. On replays I looked like a clown. I decided to do my own makeup from then on.

But I soon had more to think about than makeup. Lee Gordon, the American promoter, had spoken to me just before I went on the New Zealand tour.

'I gotta have Australian content to open the show when I bring an act from the States. It's the law. Interested?'

'Yeah, sure,' I said, wondering what act he meant. I had heard nothing more about it. Now he was on the phone again.

'Sinatra's coming. Melbourne and Sydney. I want you to open for him.'

Frank Sinatra! He was a superstar. He was that voice on the radio when I was a little girl. I was absolutely thrilled. Lee had vetted me carefully, seen how the New Zealand tour went and now he was offering me the chance of a lifetime. I was to open Frank Sinatra's March 1959 Melbourne and Sydney shows with two or three songs. But of course there was a problem: the dates crossed with my new television commitment with the ABC. I called the producer to ask him to let me out of a few weeks of the show. I explained that this was an opportunity I couldn't pass up and begged him to help me out. I knew it was short notice but I felt I had no choice. He hit the roof.

'You will never work on the ABC again!' he ranted. 'I will personally see to it!'

I was upset at his attitude but there was no contract and I stood to make £150 on the Sinatra tour. I would also gain national exposure with a top international figure and that was beyond price.

'I'm sorry but I can't make it,' I said firmly and hung up on his furious screaming.

I don't know if the man had extraordinary pull or not but in fact I never did work much for the ABC after that, something I regretted as I believe they are a wonderful cradle for new talent. Their standard is very high and I'm sorry I didn't get to be a part of what they were trying to achieve.

I adored Sinatra's music and was looking forward to watching him and his musicians at work. That was what I loved to do – watch, absorb and learn from the best. I didn't know that much about Frank personally, only that he had a bit of a reputation with the ladies.

During rehearsal in Melbourne, Lee Gordon asked me to go backstage and meet Frank. *Meet Frank Sinatra. In person.* This story was turning out okay until Lee added, 'Frank has been asking, where are the broads?' I didn't know it then but I learned: that was the way Frank spoke, trying to be cute. And, as I was to discover, there *were* generally ladies around – in fact they were supplied. He wasn't intending to insult me but I took it that way and my convent background reared up at once. *I'm a singer, Mr. Sinatra, not some tramp!* I refused the invitation.

'I'll meet him along with everybody else at the show,' I informed Lee.

He grinned at my obvious attitude and smoothed my ruffles. 'Okay, okay, don't get mad.'

So my first meeting with the American superstar was a brief introduction before I went on to perform. The night flew by in a bit of a blur but my strongest memory is of the problems I had with my darned dress – it was a full style, puffed way out with net petticoats and I was worrying the whole time about the view the front row was getting! After my songs I stood in the wings and watched the legend work.

He was very, very good. The venue – the old West Melbourne stadium – was draughty and not particularly glamorous but he held the audience in the palm of his hand. He was savvy to what his audience wanted from him, particularly women, and with his voice he could both seduce them and make them feel sorry for this hurt little boy with the baby blue eyes who was laying his heart bare for them. He never said a word about my performance that night but I know he was there listening and I heard from others that he thought I was good. The only piece of advice he gave me was: *Diana, sing every day.*

We were all staying in the same hotel and after the show that night Frank invited me back to his suite for a nightcap. I agreed, not wanting him to think me really rude. At first it was kind of surreal but show people share a common language and very soon we were chatting easily, mainly generalities but also about my ambitions for America. I was there for fifteen minutes, had one drink which hit me pretty hard, and then got to my feet to leave. Frank walked me to the door and gave me a friendly goodnight kiss. That was it. I went upstairs to bed.

The next day the tabloids screamed that Frank Sinatra had dropped Ava Gardner for me – his marriage to her had ended a couple of years before but he was still embroiled with her and she was actually in Melbourne at the time for the filming of *On The Beach*. And so the paparazzi nightmare began. The press must have been watching the door that night. I remember one guy grabbing me and yelling, 'Did he kiss you, did he kiss you?'

'Well, I suppose so,' I replied naively.

That was all they needed. I had no idea then that the press could be so vindictive, so mindlessly cruel. It was totally bemusing. I felt they were out to get me, to make me out to be a gold digger who would do anything to get ahead. I did not see Frank at all to get his take on what the press was whipping up. I was embarrassed by the whole thing and in fact the tabloids were never mentioned between us. Some years later I spoke to a journalist about that time.

'What were you guys doing?' I said. 'You knew none of it was true.'

'You gotta print something,' was the unconcerned reply.

The Melbourne shows did extremely well and I returned to Sydney for the next leg of the tour. My dear friend Brian helped me get to the venue. We couldn't find a cab and I had no money for one anyway, so we ran down from the Cross to the Sydney Stadium on foot, carrying my new dress and makeup to the show. After fighting our way in – the bouncer did not believe we were in the show – I found out to my dismay that Frank was singing 'My Funny Valentine' that night. I went to Lee Gordon in a state.

'Lee, that's my big number for Sydney,' I pleaded. 'I have to sing it. I have nothing else to replace it!'

'You'll have to talk to the man,' Lee shrugged.

I had only known Frank for a few days and had no idea how he would take a request like this. I was only the support act and it was his show. I gathered my courage and went nervously along to his dressing room. He was sitting on the sofa, drink in hand, talking to the stage manager. They both looked up as I knocked and entered.

'Are you doing "Funny Valentine"?' I blurted out.

'Yes,' he replied.

I must have paled because he asked, 'Why, do you want to do it?'

'Yes,' I stammered. 'It's my signature song around Sydney and I have nothing else rehearsed.'

The stage manager made a noise that meant, 'Who does she think she is telling Sinatra what he does and doesn't sing in his own show!' but Frank was silent a moment. I waited, holding my breath. Then he turned to the stage manager.

'Let the kid do it. She sings it better than I do anyway.'

I stumbled out of there and into the wings where Brian was waiting for me. A quick costume check, a squeeze of the hand and the first notes of my intro started. The electricity in the air was a living thing. I stepped out on the stage and felt a wave of impatience from the audience. They had come to see The Man and here was I, the obligatory Australian content, delaying the moment. I launched into my first song 'Let's Face the Music and Dance' and they sat through it well enough. I glanced a question down into the pit at my conductor, Jack Grimsley. He smiled at me. I gained confidence and away we went into the next number, then my big finale, 'My Funny Valentine'.

It started up high in the back tiers, a sort of rumbling, louder and louder. I thought the building was collapsing. I was scared, not realizing at first that they were starting to stomp. Pretty soon the entire audience was stomping and the whole stadium rocked. They were on their feet yelling and applauding. I will never forget that Australian audience that night in the old stadium. I stumbled off stage into Brian's arms.

'Listen, listen, they love you, they love you!' he cried.

It sank in....they loved me.

It was really happening. Hot on the heels of the Sinatra tour came *The Sammy Davis Jr. Show* touring Sydney, Brisbane and Melbourne and Lee Gordon booked me as opening act. Sammy was an incredible entertainer, in fact I'd say he was even better than Frank because he was an all-rounder. He sang, played piano, danced. I stood rooted in the wings every night watching him work and every time he killed 'em. He was such a courteous man too and a beautiful spirit to work alongside.

The Aussie musicians were excellent but Sammy brought out his own rhythm section from the States as well and they were amazing. I loved and appreciated excellence wherever it came from. These guys took me under their wing and I grilled them about America and the music scene there, hungry for all the information I could get. They were mostly African American of course, a fact that didn't mean much to me at the time. I just responded to the music in them and the kindness they showed me. It wasn't until I actually got to America that I became aware of the race problem so deeply ingrained in American society. I remember once using a drinking fountain on a highway rest stop in Florida and seeing there were two faucets, one labeled 'white' and one labeled 'colored'. I was completely mystified. Why did they have colored water?

In Melbourne the crowd gave me a huge hand and Sammy's tour manager, a great big guy, grabbed me and almost threw me back onto the stage.

'Take your bow, take your bow!' he yelled, and pushed me out through the curtains.

The audience went up again, and as I walked off the manager crowed, 'You gotta learn to take your bow, girl, learn to milk that crowd – they love you!'

It was something I had always been shy about but these guys knew how a crowd works, what a crowd wants. I learned to take my bow.

The experience of touring with Frank and Sammy and the response I'd got from the audiences confirmed my ambitions. I had to go to America and the time was now. When Lee Gordon said he wanted to sign me to a management contract, I was over the moon. His partner in the States, Art Schurgin, would handle my fate and try to sign me to an agency there.

'I'll get myself there,' I told Lee, 'if you manage me when I arrive.'

I'd never had a manager – couldn't afford one. I'd made my own decisions, taken my own chances and stepped on some people's toes along the way as I figured out how the business worked and tried to carve out a piece of it for myself. From the start I had set myself standards from which I refused to budge: never do jingles, never do advertising, never do musical comedy. I wanted to be with the new sound and now I was heading right for the source.

Brian was just as excited as I was. 'Yes, yes!' he screamed when I broke the news, 'and I'm coming too, I'll be there!' I would miss him and Dixie and other dear friends so much in the days to come.

Minor questions like, what will I do for money, how will I live, did come into the mix, but Diana Trask was going to America and that was all! I had my *Swallows Parade* prize money – that would buy my plane ticket and leave a bit in reserve. If worse came to worst, I thought, I'll just come home. I made a mental note to always have enough money held back to buy a return ticket. Being a singer was a hand to mouth existence at times and often I would lie in bed at night saying over and over, *You will not get yourself into debt! You will not get yourself into debt!* I tried hard and was successful with this resolution in Australia but it was to prove a much tougher call when I got to the States.

My parents weren't crazy about the America plan. Mom was convinced I'd be raped and killed and Dad was disappointed because he'd planned to take me on a trip to Europe. I didn't care what they thought – I was going and in their hearts they knew it. They admired my drive, my ability to go for it; in fact Mom once said she wished I was a boy so I could take over Dad's furniture factory. *Hmmm...*

Eventually they came around and we planned for them to see me in the States on their way back home. My friend Di Sindrey decided to accompany my parents to Europe and meet up with me in the States also. She and Dennis had recently divorced and she needed a trip. So, the plan was set.

The preparations to leave seemed endless. There were health requirements to be met, paperwork about this and that. Lee Gordon's accountant interviewed me for a few hours one day. He wanted a record of everything I had earned in Australia for the last two years. This was needed for a tax clearance to leave the country. Luckily I had a habit of writing in a notebook all my gigs and monies earned. I was a bit shy showing my little black book to the accountant as the amounts were very small – £2 here,

£5 there – but he was kind and told me I'd done a good job recording my income.

At last my passport and visa were in my hands and the big adventure was on. Just before I left Sydney I got a surprise phone call. My landlady called me downstairs, grumpy as usual.

'There's some foreign fella on the phone. Calling from overseas. I can't understand a word he's saying,' she grumbled.

I picked up the phone. 'Hello?'

'Hi, baby, this is Frankie.'

'Frankie who?' I answered impatiently.

'Oh, don't be that way, baby,' he whined and then the penny dropped.

'Frank! Oh, my God, it's you! I'm so sorry!' I stuttered as he burst out laughing.

He was ringing to offer me a place to stopover in Los Angeles where I could meet a few people on my way to New York. We had grown to be close friends as we worked together but I had not expected to see him again.

'Who was that?' my curious landlady asked as I rang off.

I couldn't resist. 'Oh, just Frank Sinatra inviting me to stay with him in LA,' I replied airily as I floated back up the stairs. In my experience it's not often you get to score against a landlady.

The invitation added to my mounting excitement as I bought my ticket and packed a far-too-heavy suitcase. The airport was awash with tears as I kissed everyone I ever knew goodbye and boarded a four-engine Qantas Constellation bound for Fiji. I was eighteen and I was leaving everything and everyone I knew behind.

FOUR

Over There

The plane was packed. I was squeezed in between two women in the center row, not even able to take a last glimpse of the coast as Australia dropped behind. The airhostess made me as comfortable as possible and I tried to relax in my seat. I felt a bit numb now that all the rush of preparations and farewells was over. There was nothing to do now but sit as the plane carried me on, hour after hour. My thoughts skated back and forth between what I was leaving and the possibilities ahead.

The first leg was a twelve-hour flight to Nandi in the Fiji Islands and it seemed endless. Eventually we landed, gliding down into a coral-pink tropical evening. As we taxied and prepared to deplane, a beautiful bare-chested native man wheeled in the steps – there was no terminal, only the open tarmac. His lower body was dressed in a *pareau* and he wore flowers in his hair. His skin shone as he greeted us with warm smiles. Memories rose of my tour to New Zealand with the Australian Jazz Quartet and the dazzling smiles of the Maoris. We walked out into the evening, the air scented and soft.

Sitting back on a rise was the hotel that would be our refreshment stop. We walked up the path through lush, tropical gardens, glad to be stretching our legs at last. Showers were available (for a shilling!) or you could just freshen up with a wash. I had a wonderful boiling-hot shower and then joined my companions in the dining room.

Dinner was included in the fare and as I entered, four Fijians with flowered shirts began to set up on the bandstand in the corner. I sat down at the table, expectation rising. Oh, wow! Now I would hear real Fijian music right from the horse's mouth. I held my breath. The band began to play and the lead singer stepped up to the mike. In a heavy accent the lyrics came out...

'One, two, three o'clock, four o'clock rock!'

I listened in dismay. Dinner was also more or less a copy of typical Australian fare so my first Fijian experience was anything but Fijian, except for the beautiful native man who greeted us originally. Back on the plane for the next twelve-hour leg to Hawaii, I slept fitfully throughout the night. It wasn't long before I was heartily wishing I could have afforded one of the full beds to be found in the back of planes in those days.

Arriving in Oahu on a misty morning, we were greeted by girls dressed in traditional hula skirts of grass. They wore leis of highly scented flowers around their necks and flowers shone in their dark hair. As we stepped off the plane, they came forward with a warm welcome and a fresh, white-flowered lei to place around each person's neck. It was like receiving a blessing. We walked across the tarmac towards the old Honolulu Tower Terminal in a cloud of flowery scent.

I asked around and learned that most Aussies on a short budget stayed at the Reef Hotel in Waikiki. I took the bus downtown and was shown into a room facing a lagoon and out to the ocean. One glimpse out of the window at the color of sea, the sky and the brilliant green of tropical plants and I had to be outside. I washed, threw on clean clothes and plunged into two days and two nights of exploring Waikiki. My dad had once been to Hawaii on business and brought home some movie footage of his trip that I had found fascinating. Now I was seeing it for myself.

A few other Aussies were around – I heard their accents in the lobby – but I was happy to spend my time alone. I relaxed on Waikiki's famous beach soaking up the sun, strolled around the lagoon, and window-shopped the hotel precinct. I made one special purchase – a new dress for my arrival in Los Angeles. It was a simple white shift – cool and summery. I loved every minute of it there and Hawaii has remained one of my favorite places in the world. When the time came, I climbed aboard my plane to Los Angeles feeling positive and serene. The days in the sun had filled me with a sense of well-being and I was ready for whatever was next.

I arrived in Los Angeles to a gray, smoggy day. Flying in, the city below us looked large, rambling and unfamiliar. I was used to seeing the neat, red tiled roofs of Australia. The air smelled liked it had all been breathed before and a dank, dreary feeling hung over the city. *Diana Trask, famous singer, arrives in America!* I announced to myself in bracing tones and, summoning my courage, headed for the baggage claim. I retrieved my case, got through customs and found myself in the airport proper.

Crowds of travelers surged and buzzed around me, all with the look of people who knew where they were going. I looked right and left. Frank said he'd send someone to meet me. Now would be a good time for them to show. Just then a smart-looking girl emerged from the melee and summoned me by name.

'Hi, Miss Trask? I'm Marsha, Mr. Sinatra's assistant,' she said. 'I'm here to take you to the house.'

I followed her very gratefully. She whisked me away in a slinky grey car, chatting easily as we wove through the swarming streets and up into the canyons above LA to Frank's house in Topanga Canyon. Through the fog of jet lag I got the impression of subdued luxury. The house seemed spacious and was built over a number of levels. Frank greeted me warmly with a hug and a kiss on both cheeks. Suddenly I found myself getting a bit teary. Maybe it was just tiredness or perhaps a reaction to the strangeness of everything, but here was a familiar face and I just felt so thankful. I tried to tell him but he waved me away, laughing gently.

'Sleep, Diana, sleep. That trip's a killer. We'll talk all you like later.'

He piloted me to the guest quarters. My eyes took in a spotless white bed plump with pillows, soft carpet underfoot and fresh flowers. An adjoining bathroom glittered with tiles and mirrors. A light meal was brought. I ate, unpacked a few things and fell into bed. It had been a long, long trip.

I awoke to sunshine. Frank had breakfast served by the pool and we spent a lazy, restful day swimming and talking. Frank's intention was to introduce me around amongst his friends and with a diary full of dinners and parties it seemed there'd be no shortage of opportunities. Marsha, his secretary, popped in and out planning upcoming events and checking details with her boss. I wondered what she really thought about my presence in the house. *Who is this teenager with Mr. Sinatra? What is she after?* Who knows. Whatever she thought, she was only ever kind and supportive towards me and concerned that I was okay.

That evening Frank was to escort me to dinner with a group of his friends. I showered, carefully applied my makeup, and changed into a dress that I hoped would work. My wardrobe was not extensive – I came with one case and little spare money – but I decided that by sticking to simple black and trying to look as 'Chanel' as possible, I might just pull it off. The floor length mirrors threw back my reflection from every angle. Would I 'do' for Frank Sinatra's world? A convent school upbringing does not encourage you to spend too much time contemplating your appearance but this was my first night in LA, a moment to take stock. A tall, young girl in classic black and heels looked back at me. *Not bad.* I smiled at her for good luck, picked up my purse and went out to join Frank. A limo was pulled up in the drive ready to go.

'You tell me if any of my friends are rude to you in any way, okay?' Frank whispered as we arrived at the club but people generally regarded me with a kind of blasé indifference. They didn't question who I was because I was with Frank. No doubt they speculated amongst themselves about this strange girl from, from ... *hey, where'd they say she's from? Australia? No kidding? What does Frank want with her?* ... but no one asked. Maybe he'd put the word out. I was a bit of a novelty with my Aussie accent and people were superficially polite, but overall I felt invisible to them.

Over time I found the hardcore entertainment world of the West Coast to be pretty vicious. In their own eyes everyone was a 'movie star'- right down to the cab drivers and the bellhops – and demanded to be treated like one. Amongst the big stars a dog-eat-dog mentality ruled and if you didn't speak their language or operate according to their LA code of etiquette you were ruthlessly ignored.

My defense from the beginning was to appear as coolly unconcerned and sophisticated as possible. That first night out with Frank Sinatra I was plunged into a completely different world to the one I knew back home. These people were older, street wise, maybe a bit cynical. They were glamorous, loaded and exclusive. I thanked God for my height – increased further by high heels – and did my best to rise above. One woman, an actress, surprised me by congratulating me on how softly I spoke.

'That's very effective,' she commented, looking at me appraisingly.

Effective? My only reason for speaking softly was to try and avoid being stared at for my accent. She thought I was deliberately taking an angle to gain attention. That's LA.

I might have been tall but I was definitely the youngest person there. The legal drinking age in the States was twenty-one and there I was sampling 'Stinger' cocktails at the bar but when you traveled with Frank Sinatra no one asked for your ID. During the evening his secretary came over and spoke to me quietly.

'How old are you, Diana?' I looked at her.

'I'm eighteen.' She shook her head, concerned for me.

'Very young. You're very young.' The Stingers wiped me out and I don't remember much about the evening after that.

Over the next few days, Frank squired me around to different gatherings. One of these was a birthday party for Janet Leigh at her home and there I was introduced to a lot of names I could not have imagined meeting in my wildest dreams. Tony Curtis was one and he was as charming as I'd pictured him. I enjoyed a nice conversation with him while we watched a rather poor grade of tennis being played on courts adjoining the house. A torso length photograph in the lobby of a nude Janet Leigh came as a shock. She was beautiful but I did wonder why she felt the need to have it on display.

We also attended a party at the Kirk Douglas home with a lot of other names. The conversation was witty and fast, the food and drink plentiful, the dresses of the women gorgeous. And here was I, Diana Trask from Warburton, suddenly catapulted into the society of America's most glittering stars. It was indeed heady living.

During the dinner I went upstairs to use the restroom. I took a wrong turn and ended up near a child's bedroom from where I could hear the sound of crying. I hate it when children are upset so I ventured in and found a little boy sitting on the bed, sobbing his heart out.

'What's the matter?' I crooned, coming closer.

I tried my best to comfort him and told him I would go downstairs and find his mommy. I went in search of Frank and whispered to him about the child upstairs.

'I'll fix it,' he said and had a word with someone. I've often wondered which of the Douglas children I comforted that night.

One night about a week or so after my arrival, Frank and I dined alone at his home. It was nice to be quiet for a while. The parties were fun but I could see it would be easy to be seduced by the names, the glitz and all that went with that lifestyle. I was in America for something more and I couldn't afford to lose sight of that. The meal was over. Frank filled our wine glasses again and looked at me over the rim as he sipped.

'Do you want help or do you want to do it alone?' he asked. 'You just gotta say, baby.'

Frank could have got me anything I wanted just by crooking his little finger – recording contracts, television contracts, any work, any gig, any hotel with any star in the world. He had that kind of pull. I had already made up my mind.

'I want to do it alone,' I told him.

If I'd accepted his offer, how would I ever know if it was really my talent that got me there, having that kind of power behind me? I had some basics in place right from the beginning – I would never trade favors, never lower myself to get ahead. Frank didn't attempt to change my mind. I'm pretty sure he understood my reasons. But just having him make that offer was very special. I think he really had faith in me and that sort of encouragement gives you faith in yourself.

There's no doubt I was heavily attracted to him and times were sweet between us but we both knew we were going nowhere together. We were living in a bubble and I knew it. He was a huge star, a fabulous singer and a wonderful friend to me but my inner heart, still smarting from first love's betrayal, remained wary and cold. I remember him telling me once with a fatalistic shrug: 'I have nothing to say to you. You are eighteen and I am forty.' It was true and I did not fight it.

I was scheduled to be in New York in about a week or so to meet with Art Schurgin, Lee Gordon's partner. I knew no one there and needed a contact so I called up Sammy Davis Jr. who I thought might be there doing some publicity. As it happened he was on his way to Washington D.C. and he invited me to meet up with his troupe. The guys were sightseeing for a day or so and then going on to New York. I accepted as I knew most of them from the Australian tour.

I farewelled Frank and took another interminable flight, this time to Washington. I hooked up with Sammy's group and we went for a marvelous tour of Washington and the capital. With Sammy's entrée I went places the ordinary tourist doesn't get to see. I was in awe of the Whitehouse and the Oval Office and met a few senators, the gruff old Senator Dirkson being the most outstanding. We all had good fun and after a couple of days one of Sammy's road managers drove me down to New York. As we topped the rise entering the city it was an awe-inspiring sight and tears sprang to my eyes. I could not believe I was here!

I checked in to the Warwick Hotel where the troupe was staying and for a couple of days moved along with them, attending the premiere of *Porgy and Bess* in which Sammy was starring. After opening night we were all in the penthouse for cocktails and I could not believe the noise coming up from the traffic below, a continual pounding. My jaw was hitting the ground and I felt like the real country hick.

Too soon the troupe moved on and I had to find a place to live. This was the moment I think I really came down to earth. Money was getting tight so I found myself a very dreary digs in a rundown hotel nearby, terrible but cheap. One little window faced a solid brick wall just a few feet away. There was very little natural light, only what seeped down from the airshaft between the buildings. A small bed and bathroom more or less filled the room, with a tiny cooker in the corner. I could not believe that such a room could be for rent but this was home for now.

I tried to concentrate on the big things and prayed a lot but the room pulled my spirits down and I was subject to crying jags until I fell asleep at night. I got cheap food from automats or bought street food like hotdogs. Everyday living was awful. I had very little money and knew no one. It was June, the summer of 1959, already steamy and humid. Connie Francis and Bobby Darin were on the radio constantly. I turned nineteen all by myself.

There would be a wait for my audition with GAC, the agency Art Schurgin had set up to possibly represent me. I had only met Art once in Australia as he lived in Detroit but Lee Gordon had assured me that Art would be in charge of me in the US. An entertainer has to have a manager and an agent. Your manager gets you an agent and your agent gets you bookings. Then your agent takes the job offer back to your manager to agree on fees and conditions. Both of them cream the top off your earnings. I rang Art Schurgin's office and was told to sit tight, things were moving as fast as possible. I took to wandering the streets, walking around everywhere to fill in time.

I learned the city was well laid out in squares but I was terrified to ride the subway and did not go near it until at least a year after my arrival in New York. I could not believe that people operated at such terrific speed here in America. The first time I tried to use the phone, the very efficient woman asked me about a hundred questions in two seconds. I reeled back across the room in shock, dropping the phone like a hot potato. I couldn't think that fast, let alone answer all the questions she fired at me. Back home I was used to dropping two pennies in the slot and waiting forever.

Everything was big – the roads, the cars, the buildings. The food was big too – big plates, big helpings, wonderful pie desserts. If I didn't watch it I would gain a ton of weight. Broadway was fascinating with all the shows gaudily displayed and lit up in a blaze by night. One day as I was walking along Broadway, I heard an incredible sound coming out of a nondescript dive of a café – the sound of drums played by a jazz genius. I was drawn like a bee to honey and as I edged in to get a better look through the doorway, there was Buddy Rich wailing away on the drum set. I propped against the wall and spent half an hour forgetting my troubles.

At last the day came to audition with GAC. I splurged and took a cab as I did not want to arrive hot and ruffled. I gave the cabbie the address I'd been told and when I arrived I tipped him ten cents. Tipping was not done in Australia and so I thought I was being especially generous. The man actually got out of the cab with the dime in his hand, yelling at me.

'What the hell is this, what is this?' he demanded.

He was a big, heavy man and he advanced towards me on the sidewalk, glaring and yelling. I was confused and scared. I thought he was mad because I gave him a tip at all. It was thought to be an insult at the time in Australia (not so anymore). I believed he was about to hit me but he turned and flung himself back in the cab, steaming away with a screech of tires. I fell back amazed and stumbled away.

If I'd been nervous before, now I was a wreck. I stood staring up at this enormous building like a typical hayseed. *Breathe, Diana, breathe.* The thing was to remain cool – my mantra from long ago. I went through the front door. Took the elevator up. Knocked on the door of GAC's front office. There I was made to wait while I sweated bullets. Finally I was ushered into an inner office to meet Roz Ross.

Roz was a big personality with a big New York accent. She was slim and attractive but whipped out a picture of herself at about three hundred pounds.

'This is what I used to look like,' she smiled. 'I keep it here so I won't ever forget and slide back.'

Her smile was warm and I liked her immediately. She got straight down to business, setting up an audition in front of a few agents in the house so they could hear what I could do. I gave my music to the piano player – 'Hello Young Lovers' and 'Bye Bye Blackbird' – and gave them my best. They seemed bored and inattentive but all the time Roz had a big smile on her face, encouraging me.

That step over, Roz took me firmly under her wing and started to get me gigs. She worked hard and arranged for me to showcase at the Blue Angel in New York, doing two shows a night for a week. The Angel was well known in those days as a launching pad for new talent. It was a tiny room with no band, just a piano. I was lucky; my pianist was Bart Howard, a marvelous songwriter – 'Fly Me To The Moon' was one of his hits. He was very supportive and a wonderfully talented man. On the bill with me at the Angel was Bud and Travis, a terrific duo who did very well later.

Opening night was terrifying. I knew Roz had the audience loaded with agents and producers looking me over. This was the 'Big Apple', the biggest gig I'd ever done. I worried about my program. Was it hip enough for this crowd? Would it show that I could really sing? Frank sent me a cryptic one-word telegram: *Win.* Photographers and stringers from the Australian press were there. My success or failure would certainly be broadcast back home. The sound of my intro brought adrenalin kicking in and effectively conquered my jitters. I was on.

'You did fine,' Roz assured me afterwards as I came offstage in a daze. 'You did great.'

Frank turned up a few nights later with a crowd of hangers-on. He didn't come backstage but I was grateful for his unspoken support.

The reviews from the Blue Angel were good and the bookings started coming.

'You're on the road, girl,' Roz informed me cheerfully.

I'm on the road! I packed my dresses and music arrangements, slammed the door on my little dingy room for good and set off. One of the first gigs was with Lester Lanin, the society bandleader, at some kind of a convention in Dallas. When I arrived, I was informed that Mr. Lanin did not rehearse anything and I was to go on cold.

'No rehearsal?' I stammered, not believing my ears.

'The musicians are all professionals,' was the dismissive reply. 'If your music's in order you've got nothing to worry about.'

I panicked. Not even a talk through? I had never heard of such a thing. It was an unsatisfactory night all round. The crowd was noisy and in a difficult mood as I stepped onstage. I don't think anyone heard anything I sang so it didn't seem to matter anyway. Lester jumped round on the stage with his baton while I was on and I found it all very uncomfortable.

I was kept working on the road with all my baggage and arrangements for a couple of months but financially I was taking a beating. My dresses were long fishtail affairs, sequined and beaded – expensive to buy and to maintain. Arrangements and copying were expensive too and I had to carry music for a fourteen-piece band.

You could easily drop a couple of thousand dollars to get band arrangements done. I would go see an arranger to talk through the music and discuss what I wanted. He would write the arrangements for the various instruments, then a copier would produce all the separate sheets. I could read music well – God bless those nuns – so sometimes to save money I would do all the copying myself using a special paper and ink. The musicians I worked with on the road were not always careful with your music. I'd get the scores back, scribbled over and crumpled, sometimes with pages missing.

With expenses like these adding up, my management was now keeping me afloat. I didn't feel good about it as up until then I had always paid my own way. Now I was going into debt, exactly what I'd sworn back in Australia never to do. Still, I was at last on the way.

Back in New York for a spell, I was invited through Roz Ross at the agency to attend a party honoring Johnny Ray. I couldn't believe I was in the same room as him – he'd long been an idol of mine. There was opportunity for only a few words of conversation with him amongst the press of people but that was enough – I had met Johnny Ray!

Of course I didn't mention the fact that my girlfriends and I were part of the screaming teenage pack in the front row at his concerts in Melbourne just one short year ago in 1958. We were thrilled by the sounds of 'Cry' and of course by his very physical stage presence as he strutted across tearing his clothes off. My euphoria in meeting him was soon eclipsed by the sort of silly mistake that's always waiting around the corner to trip you up – me in particular. Upon leaving, someone reminded me that I had to be up early for a prearranged meeting.

'Okay, knock me up early and I'll be on time,' I replied jauntily, meaning 'wake me up early'.

The whole room went into shocked silence and no one said anything for what seemed like an eternity. I stood there with my mouth open wondering what on earth I'd said wrong. Presently a friend stepped forward and steered me firmly out of the room and onto the balcony.

'Diana, in the US to "knock someone up" means to impregnate them,' he explained kindly.

I was mortified. *Me and my big mouth!* I crawled out of there as fast and as unobtrusively as possible.

While I was back in New York, I returned to the Blue Angel to see the piano player, Bart Howard, who had accompanied my first appearance there. There was a girl on the bill that night who really stood out and I remember commenting to the agent I was with, *Wow, this girl could be big!* So she was and her name was Barbra Streisand.

My first encounter with dope was with a musician backstage at the Angel. He was smoking a joint and the stink sent me reeling.

'What's that you're smoking?' I asked curiously. He looked at me like I was from outer space.

'You want some, baby?' he drawled.

I realized what it was and beat a hasty retreat. I had tried smoking cigarettes when I was about fifteen, one pack only. The taste and smell made me violently ill so that was that, but this was dope and doubly unwelcome to me. Many, many times after that I would be the only straight person in the room, but thankfully no one forced me into trying it.

I met my share of weird and unsavory people hanging around the music scene in New York. One very famous fashion designer coldly offered me an apartment, money, the works if I would move in and be his 'lady'. I did not understand the offer. Wasn't he gay...? What was the point here? I suppose he could clearly see I was finding it hard to make ends meet. He told me I was a very 'strong young woman' when I gently turned him down. Was he kidding?

Roz Ross was working hard on my behalf, getting me gigs and getting me known – the greater my exposure, the better my chances of the 'big break'. I appeared at many lounges around New York including those in the big hotels like the Statler Hilton and the St. Regis, as well as different clubs. The Living Room was a popular club with other celebrities who would drop by late at night – Johnny Carson and Lucille Ball were two I remember. The ceilings were so low there and the smoke so heavy I had to see the doctor everyday to get my throat swabbed. Four or five shows a night there really wore me out. I felt like I never saw the sun.

My dreams were taking shape but in truth I felt very alone, sometimes very lost and often terribly homesick. I felt suspended and out of touch with reality. I missed my active outdoor life and the beautiful fresh air of home. Even though I'd embraced the night life in Sydney, there was still the beach when I wanted it and friends at the end of the day. Here, there was no one who even played tennis, a sport I loved. I would end up slamming a ball at a wall somewhere, trying to work off my restlessness and half understood longings. I'd drifted away from regular religion except for the occasional visit to St. Patrick's Cathedral in New York. When I left Presentation Convent I felt truly 'religioned out' and could not face any more rituals. I felt freer now but my soul was wandering.

The concrete canyons held the heat in like a steam cooker and I would get covered in grit as I walked over to East 48th Street to my new apartment hotel. I would mope around, especially on weekends and holidays as everyone left town for their homes or the beaches. Beverley Wright was a young singer around New York at the time and she took pity on me. She lived in New Jersey with her family and, seeing I was alone so much, invited me home to meet them. I was so grateful – it was really a fantastic break from the hot city life and to be amongst a normal family was restful and healing. They were Italian, all charming, and cooked me the greatest meals. I liked her younger brother and helped him with his homework as we both tried to figure out Edgar Allan Poe. He was about fifteen at the time and told me he wanted to start a band and go overseas to England. I listened with one ear and dismissed the conversation. Later he did go to England and became Gary Wright the rock star, of 'Dream Weaver' fame.

There were a few casual boyfriends. Frank was in the background on and off but there was no one special. The only guys I knew were mostly in the business and had an agenda. Frank called and invited me for a week's stay at his house in Palm Springs. I accepted gratefully as this would be a break from New York and it would be good to see him again. He met me at the airport and we spent a nice week in the desert before I went on to LA to work.

One night we visited the home of a famous songwriter who lived nearby. After drinks the host put on one of Frank's latest albums, clearly thinking he was paying Frank a compliment. Unfortunately his sound system wasn't equal to the task. Frank flew into a rage at the sound emanating from the puny speakers and proceeded to tear the unit right out of the wall. The host just looked on, dumbly accepting the superstar and his temper tantrum. I was embarrassed for the poor man and didn't know where to look. Thankfully we left a short time later, neither of us mentioning what had happened. A couple of times I got a glimpse of this anger lurking beneath the surface of Frank's smooth exterior. I'm not sure if alcohol fueled this incident but it certainly took me by surprise. I'm thankful I was never on the receiving end of one of Frank's tantrums.

Three or four months after my arrival in the States, Mom and Dad and my friend Di Sindrey arrived from Europe. It was so good to see them and we hugged and laughed and cried. They'd had a terrible crossing by sea. The same boat sank a few voyages later and they all commented, 'Good riddance.' We only had a short time together and Mom tearfully implored me to come home with them.

'It'll be Christmas soon, Diana. You can't be away then.'

I felt bad for her but I was determined to stay. 'If things aren't working out within another six months I'll come home,' I promised her.

I didn't mention the fact that funds were critical but I think Dad knew and from time to time I would receive packages of cash carefully wrapped up in letters.

Di decided to stay on for a few weeks with me after Mom and Dad left and I was thrilled. Now I would have someone to talk to who understood where I was coming from, and I don't just mean geographically. People constantly asked me where I came from and when I answered 'Australia' I noticed there was an amazing ignorance about the place.

'Well, you sure learned the language quick!' they often congratulated me. *No comment ...*

I introduced Di to my friends amongst the young entertainers trying to make it in New York. I had the place wired by now and knew musicians everywhere. She was a jazz fanatic and with my contacts I wheedled us in to all kinds of venues. We hung round with Bud and Travis from the Angel and although we had little money between us we had a great time – we were all young and crazy. Someone got us in to some of the wonderful Broadway shows that were on, like *South Pacific* and *Gypsy*. I was able to go backstage and meet Ethel Merman after *Gypsy* and she was wonderful – such a sweet and gentle lady.

It was the era of the bohemians and beatniks, and Di and I went sightseeing in the Village in lower Manhattan in the crisp fall air. The much-heralded hippie era would follow but at that time beatniks were more or less found only in the artsy areas. We would sit and sip coffee at the cafes where insanely dressed, longhaired people would read unintelligible poetry and the audience would snap their fingers instead of applaud – very hip.

It was great to have Di along for company when I traveled to various interstate gigs. I demonstrated to her how I managed to get luggage on board without paying extra. I would approach a business man who was traveling light and ask with my most winning smile if he would check in one of my bags (there were many of them and they were heavy) – that way I avoided extra overweight charges. It worked like a charm many times – God bless all those guys who helped me out. A trick like that wouldn't work today post-9/11 but we were all a lot more trusting then.

Too soon, Di had to return to Australia and I was alone again. I missed her company and our shared history. Every acquaintance or friend in the States, however nice, was new. Winter was closing in and my mood plummeted further. I continued to work and travel, work and travel. On Christmas Day 1959 I woke up in a cold, dumpy hotel in Chicago and sat alone, watching snow fall quietly in huge flakes past a grimy window pane ...

... Snowfall... windows... The past tugged and pulled me back like an insistent child ... Snow was part of my earliest memories. It was 1942 and I was two years old when it snowed right down in the valley at our house in Warburton. I scrambled up onto the old green couch and pressed my nose to the living room window, watching the huge flakes swirling and flying against the glass. There was often snow on the peaks. Our town was the nearest to the surrounding ski resorts and during winter we saw many tourists from Melbourne on their way up the mountain, but it rarely snowed in the valley. I was entranced.

'Look! Birdies!' I yelled excitedly to my mother.

'That's snow,' she explained.

'Snow ...' I tasted the word and pressed my face closer to the beautiful mystery outside the window ...

Now I sat and wept tears for my family so far away in the Australian sunshine. I missed them so badly it was a physical ache, so I splurged and called them via the overseas telephone operator. Their voices, shaky with emotion, sounded distant and crackly on the line. It was a wireless phone so we had to say 'over' at the end of every sentence. Dad could never get the hang of it and it was hard to remember anything you wanted to say. The conversation was tearful, disjointed and unsatisfying. As I hung up, fresh waves of deep homesickness swept over me. It was the loneliest day of my life. It was cold, I was alone, and it was Christmas. What was I doing here?

FIVE

Let Me Hear A Melody

I had no inkling that 1960 was going to be such a huge year for me. So many things were about to unfold, both professionally and personally, that at times I felt like I'd traded my life for someone else's. In terms of my career, Roz Ross was the driving force. She was a magnificent agent and I was so happy to be with her. She had me flying back and forth across the country to endless gigs at all kinds of venues – the Chase Hotel in St. Louis, the Cloister in Chicago, Pierre's in Tulsa, Baker's Lounge in Detroit, the Tudor Arms in Cleveland, El Morocco in Montreal – and really got my name out there. That did not mean I was in the money, though.

One night in the early part of 1960, I was appearing at a rather seedy club in the central states when I noticed a big man sitting in the back through all of my sets. He nursed his drinks and even stayed until the last show. Finally he approached me, introducing himself as Mort Farber, a management lawyer. He said he was interested in me and asked about my legal commitments. A short while later he bought out my contract from Lee Gordon and Art Schurgin and signed me up. I was told I was to have a 'sliding rule contract' which meant he would only take his commission after I reached a good weekly figure. Maybe it sounded all too good to be true – and as it turned out I wasn't any better off – but now I had a real hands-on manager based in New York with good contacts and many famous clients, Johnny Mathis included.

One day soon after that I was back working in Chicago again and having my hair done when I got the phone call that would change everything. The assistant brought the phone over to where I sat in front of the mirror, dripping and disheveled.

'Diana, are you sitting down?'

'Roz, I'm at the hairdresser; of course I'm sitting down! What's wrong?'

'Mitch Miller wants you to do a demo for him!'

'Mitch Miller! Are you sure?' I babbled. Mitch Miller was a star maker. He was the head of A&R – Artists and Repertoire – for Columbia Records and had discovered singers like Tony Bennett, Frankie Laine, Rosemary Clooney and Johnny Mathis. The A&R executive was pivotal in a recording company, deciding which artists and songs the label would record and promote. Mitch was able to hear a certain sound in a voice and then direct how it should go. He had huge influence and a magic touch. If Mitch recorded you, you were on the inside track.

'If he likes you, this could be it,' she sang gleefully and rang off, leaving me in a daze. *Mitch Miller will like me if it's the last thing I do!*

Columbia Records was putting the demo together and I went into a local studio in Chicago and cut a few songs, mentally crossing my fingers. After a nail-biting wait Roz called. I was in! I was to meet with Mitch Miller and very possibly he would sign me to Columbia to do a recording. I flew back to New York in a state of agitation.

Roz, my new manager Mort Farber and I met with Mitch, who was very businesslike and a little scary at first. He said that he liked my singing and was in discussion with Columbia about producing some singles tracks. Art Shurgin had previously arranged a single for me called 'Soldier, Won't You Marry Me' with a small recording company. That had been released in September 1959, just a few months after my arrival in the States but it had not done well so I was very happy at the chance of moving to a top producer with a major company. Mitch's small eyes crinkled as he looked at me, a look I grew to know so very well. 'I'll be in touch with Roz as soon as everything is set up,' he said.

Roz was very excited as we left Mort and Mitch to settle the business. On the ride back to the agency she chattered on about where my career would go from here and how much money could be made. As our taxi pulled up we both had to pitch in and pay him as neither of us had enough cash.

'Meantime, who's got a quarter?' chortled Roz.

Work on the singles began. Mitch called me to his office and took me over to the Tin Pan Alley area, which included the famous Brill Building. Tin Pan Alley was a notable back street in Broadway full of recording and rehearsal studios. It was a hive of musicians, songwriters, A&R guys, all trying out new material and showcasing their songs for producers. We listened to a few songwriters lay out their material and I had my first experience of the way Mitch worked – he had definite ideas and liked to make all the decisions. He didn't like any of those songs.

A few days later he called me again. He'd got hold of a song called 'Long Ago Last Summer' written by Burt Bacharach and Hal David, two of the greatest songwriters in America at that time. The song had been cut from a Kim Novak movie but Mitch thought it was still very good and wanted to use it. Mitch liked to use a studio in downtown Manhattan – formerly a church – where the acoustics were good. The sound was like a kind of natural echo chamber. I liked the idea of recording in an old church – maybe an angel would look over my shoulder.

Mitch took me into the session and we cut 'Long Ago Last Summer'. And we did it *his* way. Mitch had a rhythm theory he always used. He called it 'The Steel Box'. His aim was always to produce a commercial sound, something that audiences would like and buy. His formula combined certain rhythmic patterns from the various instruments – acoustic guitar, bass, cello, whatever it might be – and then he mixed the sound to produce a distinctive aural texture. The artist then came in over the top, singing in a way that complemented his formula. Finally he would add some color with strings or something similar to finish off the mix. If you strayed from the formula he would pull you up with a sharp reprimand. Often he'd get right up in my face and conduct me if I got too swingy like in my jazz days. I hated to be tied down so and found it hard to conform.

'Come back when you feel like doing it my way,' he would say, pointing to the door.

I'd head out, swearing under my breath but come back later ready to knuckle under. In the end I learned so much from him about the sound patterns that work. I liked Mitch immensely. He had small, twinkly eyes that bored into you and a soft beard that he stroked thoughtfully all the time. He was immensely talented and played oboe in the symphony in his spare time. I plunged into the project wholeheartedly.

'Our Language of Love', 'A Guy is a Guy' and 'I'm So Lonesome I Could Cry' were also recorded as singles. This last song was a Hank Williams classic – my first recording of a country song. An omen, maybe? Country music was a complete unknown to me at that stage and the last thing on my mind. The lyrics sure spoke to me at the time, though, as I continued to battle the loneliness that had dogged me since leaving home.

'Long Ago Last Summer' was in the works, due for release in April and who knew where it might lead but for now I still had to earn money. I continued to travel the country working different cities, nearly always alone. My favorite town was Houston, Texas, where I worked a club called the Tidelands. The audiences were great and I met some wonderful people there. Doc Staub was a well-known doctor who frequented the club. He invited me to visit the zoo where he volunteered his time with sick animals. He worked at the Methodist Hospital of Houston and it was through him that I met the great heart surgeon Dr. Denton Cooley.

Denton dropped by the club occasionally along with members of his amateur band, The Heartbeats. Doc Staub arranged for me to mix in with a group of young interns and actually see Denton operate one day. I stood looking down over the operating room with one of Denton's team and watched as the heart was exposed and the awful yellow aneurysm cut out. Denton was like a star on stage as he moved with complete confidence, attended by a multinational group of doctors and students watching his every move. He was astounding. I saw him briefly after the operation and he was studying a book on leprosy of all things, something I was to take an interest in later.

The day I arrived at the Tidelands, Chet Atkins was appearing and I caught his final night. Chet was a country and western singer, the founder of the Nashville crowd and a wonderful guitar player. I knew nothing about country music but I admired his playing even though I thought the show itself was static and lacked New York pizzazz. *The guy is sitting on a stool all night – you call that entertainment?* Everyone stood around afterwards, admiring Chet's performance and talking about how the show had gone. I was quiet.

'So, what did you think of Chet?' said the promoter, turning to me. Now, there was a school of thought in Australia that to be brutally frank was honest and wholesome, especially when asked a direct question.

'Well,' I replied, 'the music was good but the show itself was terrible.'

I was met with a shocked silence. In my own way I was making an honest comment and trying to be constructive but in hindsight I should have just kept my big mouth shut. Chet Atkins was an established star and I was a complete upstart. Chet took the egg on his face stoically but I don't think he ever forgave me for that. I stammered an apology, feeling exactly like that little girl who long ago had put her foot in the wet concrete. It took a few more big mistakes and the patient help of friends before I eventually learned to tread more tactfully.

I worked with Henny Youngman in Chicago – the site of that first dreary, teary Christmas – and there met a young man who used to drop by the club and play cards in the back room with the owner. I was told he was an up and coming publisher. His name? Hugh Hefner. One night after the show he invited me to his home. He seemed very nice but there was something intense and a bit unsettling about him that I couldn't put my finger on – in hindsight, not a man I would have wanted to be close to, although all his bunnies seemed to love him.

In early May my dad came over to visit me again and to make sure I wasn't starving. I took him around the various clubs where I was performing in New York and he was clearly bursting with pride at my recording contract with Columbia, the gigs and the reviews. He particularly approved of the reviewer from *Cash Box Magazine* for this comment: 'Diana Trask is Australia's best export talent to date.' The

Australian press had no trouble getting Dad to talk all about his daughter when he arrived home. They had no trouble making up a lot of stuff too, particularly about how much I was supposed to be earning. Another little thing that caught their attention was a particularly devoted companion of mine at the time, the gorgeous Pepe. Pepe the Chihuahua, that is.

Pepe came to me from a friend I made in Texas about six months after my arrival. He was the tiniest, cheekiest little dog who fitted into my purse and burrowed right under the covers of my bed as I slept. I smuggled him in and out of hotels and aboard planes and he traveled with me for quite a while until finally I decided it was not ideal for him to be cooped up all the time. I gave him to a friend to care for and he was happy but I missed him – he was good company in a lonely hotel room.

Sometimes Mitch would invite me out to eat. We'd talk through ideas and he'd listen to what I had to say, tugging at his beard all the while. I think he wanted to size me up outside of an office setting. He took a personal interest in the lives of all his artists and doled out mostly very wise advice. I think it was also part of his modus operandi – staying in the driver's seat. He liked to know what was going on. When the recording of the singles was finished Mitch took me to celebrate downtown at a little Italian restaurant he liked. He also had a stunning offer to make.

'I've submitted an idea for a television pilot to NBC and I want you to be in it, Diana. Are you interested?'

'Of course,' I gushed. 'I'd love to. What's it about?'

'I have it in front of NBC right now. It'll be based on the idea of those old sing-alongs they used to have at the movie theatres.'

I wasn't sure how this would work and he was purposely a bit evasive. But this was Mitch Miller asking, and that was enough. He was a man who made things happen and I rightly guessed I would soon be 'singing along' with whatever he had planned.

Mitch's scheme soon came to life. NBC had accepted the pilot for his planned sing-along-style show and offered me a contract. Mort Farber brought me in to their office and I was signed up. Also on the show was to be another girl singer, Leslie Uggams, a large male chorus and a troupe of dancers. *Sing Along with Mitch* was born.

Music for the pilot was selected and I was to do a swingy version of 'Waltzing Matilda'. All the music was pre-recorded in our favorite studio with just a five-piece band and the chorus of about twenty five to thirty guys. The sound was great and very clean. I was amazed at Mitch's talent and skill. Then we prepared the show in a large rehearsal studio with no set, just the pre-recorded music and our marks on the floor in chalk. Jimmy Starbuck, a really talented dancer, carefully choreographed us. Our closing signature was to be the entire cast 'singing along', with Mitch himself conducting.

The show was then taped in a studio in Brooklyn which I found a bit hard to get to. Keeping a car in New York was too expensive so the only way to get there was the dreaded subway or a taxi. Funds were still tight so I tried the subway twice – that was enough. It was a long ride at odd hours and I was usually encumbered with wardrobe of some sort or other. There were scary types leaning and sitting round the cars but I was gradually acquiring the New York attitude of 'don't mess with me' and did my best to stare them down, even though I was scared half to death. I still don't like the subway – too much noise and confusion.

The week we taped the pilot Mitch nearly pulled his beard out through tugging it so relentlessly. He was always thinking, always on the watch for little details that might go wrong or could be better. Nothing was left to chance. He was a perfectionist and everyone had to toe the line. At the close of my number Mitch planned for a large boomerang to fly towards the camera. We all thought the show felt good and ran well and we crowded into the control room to see the playback. Mitch was expansive, jovially thumping our director Bill Hobin on the back and confidently predicting success. But what would the critics think?

The pilot aired in May and we all held our breath for the reviews. NBC liked it but when the reviews came out the critics really knocked us – *too schmaltzy, too corny*. Maybe, but audiences know what they like and Mitch knew audiences. He took it in his stride, pulled at his beard some more and worked with NBC to take a chance and contract us for a season of shows.

There was a long anxious wait for the whole troupe while the suits weighed it up but Mitch pulled it off. NBC said 'yes' and once more Mort Farber brought me in to their offices, this time to sign me up to a full twenty-six-week contract.

'This is big, Diana,' said Mort as we rode up in the elevator. 'Prime time television. This is what we've been waiting for.'

I knew it and still couldn't quite believe it. I'd left home just twelve months ago with a pocket full of dreams and some half-baked plans for achieving them. But I hadn't just waited; I'd worked and worked hard. Now the power of prime time American television was about to work its magic on my career.

It would be a few months before *Sing Along with Mitch* moved into full production phase but in the meantime a welcome call came from Australia. It was my former manager, the promoter Lee Gordon.

'Diana, how would you like to come home for a visit?'

'I'd love to,' I said promptly and then quipped, 'are you paying for my ticket?'

'I will if you tour with Pat Boone while you're here.'

Pat Boone. Hmm. I was eager to go home but lukewarm about working with him as I didn't like his style of music at all. But, home was home. The tour was scheduled for July and I packed and flew the long miles to Australia, looking forward to seeing family and friends again and being in familiar territory. It was exciting too, knowing I was coming home 'on top', not with my tail between my legs. I stepped onto the tarmac at Melbourne airport in a chic new green coat and newly tinted bright red hair.

Who's that for? There was a seething press of people, waving and cheering. Photographers were snapping, reporters yelling out, fighting to get closer. *What's going on?* Airport staff were holding them back and trying to hustle me away. *Me? This was for me?* I nearly died. I'd left fourteen months ago as nobody and was being welcomed home as a star. News had been steadily filtering home about my association with Mitch Miller, Columbia and NBC, and Diana Trask was now a household name. The press, ever inventive, had it that I was earning more than the

Prime Minister, Mr. Robert Menzies. According to the newspapers I was already a millionaire. *Really? News to me.*

The airport staff got me off the tarmac and into a room inside the terminal, the press following, and somewhere in the midst Mom and Dad were struggling to reach me. Cameras rolled and I tried to avoid the outright insulting questions of a few, but the general feeling was one of exultation that one of their own had made it big. Mom and Dad were beside themselves fighting through the cameras and crowd to give me a hug. It was extremely stressful for them and Mom nearly fainted from the heat and chaos. They just wanted to see their daughter. None of us had anticipated such a crazy scene. Dad eventually wrangled me out of there and into the car. As we drove out of the airport heading for home we each flopped back and drew huge breaths of relief at the same time.

'Well,' said Dad in his driest tones. 'Welcome home, Diana.' Then we all started laughing.

I had a couple of days with Mom and Dad to get over the jet lag and prepare for the tour. Dad tiptoed around in the mornings making sure my 'beauty sleep' wasn't disturbed and Mom made endless cups of tea.

Mitch had arranged for my single, 'Long Ago Last Summer', to be released in Australia to coordinate with the tour and I sang it to a standing-room-only stadium crowd in Melbourne. Reviews were enthusiastic. I think the critics were surprised at what they both heard and saw. I had slimmed down greatly since Aussie audiences had seen me last – television and New York come down very hard on extra pounds. In fact, I hardly ate anything and sometimes experienced dizziness on stage when pushing for a hard note or holding my breath for a long phrase. I generally just gritted my teeth and worked through it, a habit I continued all through my career.

The tour went well as we moved through three states however I found Mr. Boone a little disdainful, treating me as though he did not like to be around me. I had run into this attitude before in the US. I found that when you were a young female alone and listed your occupation as 'entertainer', you did not always get the benefit of the doubt. I was sometimes treated sleazily and smutty jokes and bad language came my way occasionally but I did not expect an attitude from Mr. Boone. I recall asking him to dance with me one night at an after-show party. It was only a friendly gesture on my part but he backed away as if I'd offered to give him the plague.

After our tour was over, I slipped back to Warburton for a few more days with the family, relaxing and catching up on their news. My brother's wife Marcia gave birth to my dear little niece, Lisa, and she was adorable. It kind of softened the blow of my impending return to the States for my mom. She suffered a lot when I first left home, probably more so because we had not been on good terms at the time. Mom reckoned she could send me messages through the ether and indeed there were times when I would just decide to call out of the blue and she would say, 'I willed you to call!'

My grandmother was like that too. I would drop in unannounced and the tea would be poured on the table.

'I knew you were coming so I poured your tea,' she would say.

My grandmother was a character. She had no phone and no television, preferring to spend her nights with grandfather knitting and listening to the radio. During the war she knitted countless pairs of socks for the troops in Africa. I always tried to imagine what the guys thought when they unwrapped a pair of woolen gray socks with her famous bright red heels and toes. No matter how we all pleaded with her to get a phone she would not, proclaiming that 'some bad person' might get her number and give her a rude phone call. At the opening of the Melbourne show she was uncontrollable. She had never seen me perform in public before and was completely and embarrassingly over the moon. I could see and hear her there in the front row yelling loudly:

'Good on ya, Di, you little beauty! That's my granddaughter!'

Leaving home and fending for yourself forces you to look at your family differently, particularly your parents. You learn to judge them less harshly as you see for yourself how easy it is to make mistakes in life and how few of our decisions are really black and white. Sure there had been tension and difficulty for me growing up because of Mom and Dad's relationship. Yes, they'd both found it hard to adjust to my chosen career path and had at times made life difficult for me because of this – Dad's performance in Johnny Lee's club back in Sydney being the classic example. But coming home and feeling the warmth of their love and welcome, and knowing they were proud of me, meant the world. I think the penny had finally dropped for them that I really *was* a singer, not just marking time until I 'settled down'. There was still some unfinished business between Mom and I but at least we were beginning to understand each other a little better.

I left home again – a much harder parting this time – and flew back to New York, to my commitments and the prospect of *Sing Along*. Lots had been going on behind the scenes while I was away. Mitch and his team of writers and designers had been hard at work and in a couple of months rehearsals for the first season would begin in earnest.

I missed home terribly and was still struggling with the sense that something very essential was missing from my life. On my days off I spent a lot of time lying on the floor, listening over and over to blues singers like Jesse Belvin and Ray Charles. I had come to America thinking I'd find the *Leave It to Beaver* world I'd seen on television during my childhood. I hadn't found it as I'd toured the States back and forth from gig to gig. It definitely wasn't in New York. What exactly was I looking for?

I was overjoyed to receive a phone call from my dear friend Brian Syron who told me he was on his way to New York to study acting with the revered Stella Adler. We were both ecstatic to be together again. I had always thought of him as my protector. In fact, once we were in a theater together in Melbourne when a man in front of us turned around and spat out some nasty names at me. I had to grab Brian and physically hold him back as he just wanted to jump over the seats and take that guy out.

He was always great fun and I loved being with him. He was in awe of Miss Adler and took training with some of the greats like Dustin Hoffman. He was always full of stories about the class and his dumpy apartment where he lived. He took a job as a waiter to make ends meet and showed up one day at my apartment in a fit of hysterics. Apparently he had tripped and spilt hot soup all over a patron, trying to be very suave all the time. They fired him on the spot and all he could do was laugh.

Another time two goons held him up in an alley, demanding all his money. He started to guffaw and spoke out clearly in his best rolling Shakespearean tones: 'My dear man, I am a starving actor. You have the wrong man, believe me. You see this suit?' He turned out the pockets. 'It's rented!' The thugs threw down two dollars and left saying, 'Hey, man, you need this more than us.' Life was always an adventure with Brian.

We took time to see the sights together and even roared down south to Jones Beach near Long Island on a rented motorcycle. When we arrived we looked at each other in dismay – surely *this* was not the beach! I had Australian memories of sparkling Pacific blue water and white sand. The Atlantic coastline was very different, the water more gray in its tints and the sand yellowish-brown. Not that much sand was in view. You could barely see the ground for the bodies spread out in every direction. It was a stinking hot day and I swear every single person in New York was here.

'How will we ever find our towels in this mob if we go swimming?' I worried.

'If they want my towel they can have it,' was Brian's retort. 'Come on!'

We dumped our towels and ran in and I enjoyed the chance to relax and kid around for a while in the sun and the water. I told Brian about the shark at Portsea beach all those years before and he immediately began faking shark attacks and enacting dying scenes for the benefit of nearby swimmers. He had me in stitches. After our swim we mounted the motorbike and scooted back to the big smoke, me clinging on to his back like a terrified papoose.

Travel from gig to gig continued and then one day Mort called me out of the blue, very excited – Twentieth Century Fox wanted me for a screen test. I was skeptical.

'Movies! Are you sure, Mort? I'm a singer, not an actress.'

'Of course you can do it. It's a fantastic opportunity, Diana. That's what we want – opportunities. No other Australian singers are in Hollywood – none. You're to fly to LA and film some songs with them. It'll be easy.'

In spite of Mort's confidence I did not see myself as an actress. Sure I'd been in front of plenty of cameras but I sensed a variety show was very different from movie-making. There were plenty of singers who'd made the transition – Frank was the perfect example – but I wasn't sure if it was for me. Still, it was a new interest and I caught a bit of Mort's excitement and flew out for the test. The powers-that-be liked the material, and Mort signed me to a 'starlet' contract with Twentieth Century Fox.

I was put forward for a few upcoming movies and Mort sent me to a speech coach to try to get rid of my accent but I did not respond very well. The coach tried hard with me but it all felt a little ridiculous as far as I was concerned. I really did not want an American accent although my ear was already adapting to the changes. He also enrolled me with an acting coach, Wynn Handman, and that was much more fun. The classes were a lot like play acting as a child.

What else could they do to change me into an actress? How about my name, for starters? 'Trask,' it seemed, was only used as a name for bad guys in Westerns and Twentieth Century approached me to change it. They had lists of names in categories – good guy, bad guy, studious girl, sexy girl and so on. I bucked at that one and they finally let the idea drop.

I was put up for a screen test for an upcoming movie called *State Fair*, a remake of the Rogers and Hammerstein musical. While I was at the studio lot I ran into Pat Boone who, you guessed it, was cast as the male lead. *Uh oh...* He gave me a formal greeting but I overheard him telling someone that I reminded him of a 'boop girl' with my tight-waisted clothes. It was true that I did wear a waist cincher – a very uncomfortable piece of attire for sure but stylish at the time. I never did work out what his problem was with me.

It was the signal for a rough week, though. My morale was low and I knew I would not get the part. José Ferrer was the director and helped me with the test, reading the lines opposite me. He was a marvelous actor; his eyes changed completely as he read his lines and I believed him implicitly. Not so with my performance.

Over the next twelve months I would be cast in a few things including the television adventure series *Kraft Mystery Theatre*, working alongside Richard Anderson, John Ericson and Jayne Mansfield. I also found myself in a television pilot with Jayne – a really sweet and beautiful girl. The film was a 'whodunit' in which I was quickly killed off with a pair of scissors. A bit prophetic really when I think about my short-lived acting 'career'.

While in Hollywood I once met up with Rod Taylor, a charming fellow Australian, and we went out for a meal together. He seemed to understand the Hollywood scene well and gave me some pointers but it was all double Dutch to me. Acting in movies seemed a tiresome profession with so much down time and waiting between scenes. The producers and directors were supportive, one enthusiast even telling me I was 'like a young Lana Turner'. I certainly didn't feel like it.

I was back in Hollywood attempting to impress Twentieth Century Fox when Roz called to divert me to Chicago before I headed back to New York. She had booked me to appear for a week on the Don McNeill breakfast show, an early morning radio program that attracted a huge, devoted following right through the Midwest.

'Breakfast radio?' I quizzed Roz unenthusiastically. 'Do people actually get up that early to listen to the radio?'

'Don McNeill has an enormous audience,' she said. 'This is a great honor, Diana! Just get up and do it.'

'Okay, okay,' I moaned.

At the airport I found TWA airlines had oversold the plane and my seat was gone. An anxious official apologized. *Would I kindly take a first-class seat instead? Absolutely!* I agreed, looking forward to a bit of unexpected luxury. I settled into my seat and stretched out my legs – this was more like it. And so was that! A sharp-looking guy standing to take a magazine from the rack caught my eye just as the plane taxied out. He was dark-haired, clean cut and exuded magnetism.

'If I ever did get married – which I won't – that is the kind of man I would marry,' I caught myself thinking.

After we took off I saw him move again to the front of the cabin and sit down. In those days, TWA had a lounge in the front of the first class section. I couldn't stop thinking about this guy so I decided to walk forward for another look, pretending to be on the way to the bathroom. To my surprise I found him sitting with a face I knew – Johnny Mathis. Johnny was dealing him a hand of cards and it seemed he'd been asked to join the group to make a foursome. I took the chance that was being offered and walked towards my destiny.

'Johnny, hi, what's happening?' I said cheerily. 'What are you playing?' Johnny stood and greeted me.

'Hey, Diana, good to see you. Why don't you sit and join the game? We're playing Hearts.'

SIX

When I Fall In Love

His name was Thom Ewen. We chatted lightly on the plane, exchanging names and occupations. I found out he worked for the Gillette Corporation and traveled extensively. I learned that he was from a large Irish Catholic family in Connecticut, one of ten children. I noticed that as I spoke he gazed attentively at me. Big brown eyes that seemed endlessly deep observed my every move and I sensed there was something very different about this man. At one point in the conversation my eyes drifted up towards the imaginary walls that seemed to surround me lately.

'They won't come down just by looking at them,' he said.

How did he know what I was thinking? Oh yes, it was 'hearts' all right. Somehow I felt an emotional connection flowing between us and I just knew it was right. Well, destiny may have stepped in but the next move was up to me.

As the plane landed in Chicago, the sky opened up in torrents of rain. I rushed straight to the taxi rank, praying for a cabbie and was lucky enough to grab one. I promised to pay him double if he would wait for me. If there was one thing I knew from experience it was that it is impossible to get a cab in Chicago when it is raining. Then I casually walked over to the baggage claim where Thom stood waiting.

'I have a cab – can I give you a lift?' I suggested offhandedly, my stomach doing flips. The brown eyes locked on.

'Yeah, that would be great.'

I drew a breath and suppressed a mad grin. I was not usually so forward but this man absolutely drew me to him. I knew I wanted to be with him and hoped that a little more time in each other's company might result in a dinner invitation. Chicago traffic in the rain was terrible but I didn't care in the least – anything to prolong our cab ride together. We arrived at my hotel first and Thom was quick to hop out and open my door. He set my bag down for me ... lingered on the sidewalk ... *please, Lord, please!* ... cleared his throat ... and suggested we meet for dinner. *Oh thank you, Lord!!* If he had walked away just then I don't know what I would have done.

We arranged to meet in a couple of hours at a steakhouse restaurant and I watched the cab pull away from the curbside, the air around me fizzing like champagne. I rushed up to my room to shower, change and fret in front of the mirror. *This outfit or this one? This hairstyle or that one? Thom, Thom, Thom ...*

We had a great steak dinner, talking non-stop about everything and nothing. I was on such a high in his company. Every minute confirmed my first gut reaction – Thom was special and with him I felt so alive! Strange is the human heart. At that point when everything seemed to be going so well, a wave of the terrible loneliness I'd felt for so long rose up, overwhelming me. I burst into an embarrassing flood of tears. *Great work, Diana! Tears on a first date. That'll be the end of that.* But Thom didn't let me down.

'Tell me,' he invited gently.

So I did. He listened while I sniffed and mopped my eyes and let everything pour out – the loneliness, the creeping depression, the realization that light seemed to have disappeared from my life. I knew that I'd been retreating behind stiffly-erected defenses, just like my little Cancer the Crab astrological sign. Thom's warmth and kindness broke through that barrier in a second. Something in him called to the real Diana, the part I'd kept carefully hidden from others.

I'd needed to be strong and self-sufficient to tackle a tough world and a tough industry in the States, most of the time dogged by a fear that I was really flying blind. I'd pulled out the positive Diana everyday to impress agents and promoters, travel the length and breadth of the country, work alongside all types and personalities and woo audiences. I couldn't afford to let the negative, vulnerable Diana out. She was there all right, but I'd pushed her down. With Thom I felt safe to be myself. He thawed me out and the flood came. This was both liberating and terrifying but isn't it this kind of trust that makes a relationship real?

I think that was the night he nicknamed me 'Chief Rain in the Face'. All through my life I have tended to tear up whenever I felt overwhelmed. But I sensed a deep need inside of Thom too and as I laid my head on his shoulder I felt like I was home.

For the rest of that magical week in Chicago we were never really apart. I did my radio show appearance each morning, he completed his projects, and the rest of the time we were together. Time flew as we talked and dreamed about sweet nothings as lovers do. I was startled by a call from Frank one day with an invitation to join him in Miami. I really didn't know what to say but finally told him I couldn't come. I didn't tell him I'd met someone, but I'm sure there must have been something in my voice and he sensed that things were changed between us. Too soon the week was over and Thom and I had to part. We said our goodbyes at the airport with embraces and promises to see each other soon.

Back in New York people began to notice a difference in me – I was smiling! Dancing into Roz's office on my first morning back in New York, I saw one eyebrow rise comically.

'What happened to you? Looks like love has come calling.'

I just laughed her off but it was true. Everything seemed different now Thom was in my life – even the New York air seemed fresher!

As soon as he could, Thom flew in from Europe for a few days and we were together again. He was funny and 'out there' and interesting things seemed to happen around him. He talked to everyone on a first-name basis and I mean *everyone*. This was strange to me as I was still the girl raised in Melbourne and had the reserve that goes with it. A British heritage of polite good manners meant not being too familiar too soon. I was still getting used to the more open American culture of immediate friendliness, often misinterpreted by Australians and Brits as being 'brash'. So I was embarrassed at first at Thom's way with everyone he met but he soon teased me out of that. No one was a stranger to Thom.

He also teased me no end because I tended to avoid common things like the subway and had never used a laundromat or the public library, and so he made it his mission to educate me in the American way of life. He thought I had lived in isolation for far too long, meeting and mixing with no one outside the world of entertainment.

'What you need is a lesson on the Common Man, Diana.'

'Oh, yes?' I was suspicious. I was getting to know Thom and his wild sense of humor. He made plans for us to meet in Boston for the weekend. That sounded okay.

'Look, why don't you travel by public bus?' he suggested. 'That way you'll get to meet some average people.'

I dutifully agreed upon the adventure – I must have been in love! – and trekked to the bus station hauling a far-too-heavy suitcase. The bus was noisy, filthy and filled to the brim with every kind of person on the planet. There were drunks, fat mamas, skinny bohemians, crying babies (one very close to me who spat up on everything), every color and creed. The bus reeked of vomit and booze and I thought I was in a nightmare. One thing was for sure: *Leave It to Beaver* did not live here. As we pulled out onto the highway I gazed out of the streaked window and there was Thom driving alongside in a spanking new convertible. I could have killed him as he waved and smiled his big Irish grin. He sped off up the road leaving me to fume all the way to Boston.

I had plenty of time on that wretched bus to rehearse what I'd say to Thom when I caught up with him. Oh, boy, was he going to get it! He strolled up to me at the bus station where I was fighting to recover my suitcase – naturally it had been lost – and took one look at me, his face full of mischief.

'Well, did you get in touch with the Common Man?' he laughed. I gave him a mighty icy reply but he whisked me off for dinner in his flashy new car and by the end of the evening we were laughing about my experience.

I responded to the Irishness of him – the humor, the warmth, the ready forgiveness, the spiritual depth I see in Irish people. He had the power to completely lift my spirits from the shadows where I'd been wandering. As a child I had sat on my Irish step-grandfather's knee – Poppa Cleave – hearing his soft brogue and feeling totally loved. Thom resurrected that feeling of belonging for me. The Irish live life and celebrate death with a cheerful fatalism that defies day-to-day trials.

Thom, twelve years older than I, was a child of the Great Depression and knew privation and hard times. He told me how his Irish grandmother had saved his life by placing him in the warming oven just after he was born, using it like an incubator. His father, whom he adored, died when he was only twelve and he felt abandoned, especially as he did not get on with his eldest brother who was now head of the family. He ran away from home at just thirteen, lied about his age and enlisted in the US Merchant Marines and later in the Canadian Navy. He saw service in World War Two and Korea and had been wounded, spending thirty months in a body cast with the doctors saying he would never walk again. But he did walk again. I was to discover that Thom had a will of iron.

Thom and I took trips here and there to places like Cape Cod where we ate at little Italian restaurants – his favorite. He also loved coffee and hamburgers and pineapple pie but other than that his culinary choices were very limited whereas mine were adventurous. After a while, I began to choose restaurants serving Chinese and other exotic foods. I wanted to see whether he could manage to order anything that even slightly resembled hamburgers and French fries.

We learned a great deal from each other and tended to be madcap at times. He had a great laugh and told lots of funny stories. He is still the only person who can really make me laugh. One of my favorite games we played was to guess the life story of a total stranger seated nearby. Thom's sketches were realistic and funny and probably true. One night we waltzed across Grand Central Station to an imaginary band, much to the surprise of the startled commuters. It was a magic time. The song 'When I Fall In Love' played often on the radio and I dared to think that this man might be the one who would demolish my vow of never getting married.

Meanwhile, work continued for both of us. Thom traveled a lot with his job, and I plunged into *Sing Along* and juggled other appearances as they came up. We got used to tearful farewells and joyous reunions. Soon I was in the routine of rehearsals, costume fittings, studio and tapings. I learned a quick and valuable lesson about punctuality too. After a few tardy arrivals at rehearsal, Mitch upbraided me strongly.

'I'll drop you if you can't learn to be on time,' he warned me in no uncertain terms. 'Hold-ups cost money.'

I quickly changed my ways, buying a reliable alarm clock and giving myself extra time for traffic. I was very punctual after that, a lesson that stayed with me and was well-learned. Mitch was always coming up with new plans and ideas for the show and as time went on the sets and costuming became more elaborate. He and the director, Bill Hobin, worked up some really creative themes. I recall a Cleopatra extravaganza, a Scottish tribute where I sang 'Heather on the Hill' from that beautiful show *Brigadoon*, a Christmas show and so on.

The studio where we taped was absolutely enormous. All the sets for each number were built across the width of the stage floor and the whole troupe could walk out of one set and into another. It took all day to tape a one-hour show and there were surprisingly few takes involved. Of course, we worked our socks off at rehearsals to get it right beforehand. The only downside was the hard concrete floors on which we had to stand and dance. In high heels it was a killer and I had to find a Swedish masseuse in the end to ease the pain in my legs.

The dancing part of it was always my bugbear. Oh my, I was *not* a dancer. The choreographer, Jimmy Starbuck, would teach me the steps, I'd practice and practice and get it right at rehearsal but come taping day something always seemed to go wrong. I'd cover up as best I could but Jimmy always noticed.

'I'm making it as simple as I can, Di!' he'd protest despairingly.

There was plenty of standing around too in between times. The guys in the chorus and the dance troupe were all good fun and we had plenty of laughs. As a whole, the troupe was fairly harmonious although I sensed a slight edginess between Leslie and I, probably because of my bluntness. Her mother traveled with her at all times and was a gorgeous woman who had been in the business herself in earlier days.

Even now I was still doing my own makeup – I'd never forgotten my experience with ABC television in Sydney and the feeling of trying to sing through a mask. The makeup man on *Sing Along*, Joe Cranzano, would follow me around, pleading with me to give him a go.

'Just let me try it, Diana. If you hate it I will never ask again!'

At last I agreed to let him go ahead and was truly impressed with the result – it felt good and looked fabulous. After that I would gratefully sink into his chair for makeup with complete confidence. It was one thing less for me to worry about and besides, what girl doesn't appreciate being pampered? Joe was a lovely guy and the makeup room became a bit of a haven. Sometimes we'd talk and sometimes just be silent while he worked. Usually my head was full of a certain brown-eyed Irishman.

NBC knew they were on a winner with *Sing Along* and threw everything at it. I recall a slight ruckus blew up one time when I was dressed up as a mermaid and a dispute arose as to who would carry me onto the set. The male chorus was supposed to tote me round on stage during the number since my legs were zippered into my mermaid costume. The stagehands assumed they would be the ones to deliver me onto the set in the first place. *Boys, boys – settle!* When it came time to do the number, the guys from the chorus just lifted me up and began carrying me on, ignoring the protests from the stagehands who promptly went on strike. The whole show came to a halt until Mitch took over and negotiated a treaty.

One day we were using children on set for a take – they were there to dance for one of the numbers. The stage manager told the kids they were not to leave the soundstage under any circumstances as we were gathered for the next number. One little girl with big blue eyes was standing next to me and I suddenly locked on to her gaze. Her eyes were growing larger and larger and slowly filling with tears. I had no idea what was wrong but she must have felt that I was sympathetic – we'd played a few games together earlier. I looked down and the poor little mite was standing in a puddle. She just could not hold on any longer.

I was so angry at the embarrassment she was suffering and instantly my mind jumped back to my days at the Lilydale Convent and the little girl in my dormitory who had been continually punished for wetting the bed. I had felt so helpless then but I wasn't now. I called a helper to take the child off set to change and yelled for the stage manager.

'What did you tell that poor little kid?' I snapped. He had no idea what I was talking about so I spelled it out for him. 'They're kids, not robots.'

I threw a glance over at the row of stage mothers on the side, busy knitting and talking. They did not even look up as the child was led off, completely mortified in front of her peers. I grew even angrier – kids are not commodities and the worst kind of 'stage mothers' use their children to fulfill their own dreams.

Thom had met Mitch by now and they seemed to get along okay but I sensed a slight hardening of Mitch's attitude with me. There was a narrowing of the eyes and a tug on the beard. He did not like men around his girl singers. Experience had taught him this could be trouble. Around that time Mitch took me back into the old church studio to cut a full album for Columbia. The company threw their considerable weight behind me and I was elated to be in such esteemed company. The album was to be arranged by Glenn Osser, a well-known musician. I grew to love the old recording studio where angels might be looking over my shoulder.

I fell into the routine of Mitch cutting the backing tracks and overdubbing according to his strict rules. I chaffed a little under those rules as I still favored a jazzier style, but he was adamant. You did things Mitch's way or not at all. The sound that those two men created in that old church was breathtaking. I felt like I was on the bow of a gigantic musical ship floating out into space. The album was simply titled *Diana Trask*, and I prayed Columbia and the fans would like it when it was released.

The Ballantine Beer Company which sponsored *Sing Along* wanted me for a new television commercial. Mort signed me up for the deal and they treated me very well, even inviting me to contribute my ideas to the company board. The board members listened politely and then ignored all my suggestions! So I had to sing and dance (my style of dancing...) in different costumes from around the world.

Dad came over again to visit. Ostensibly he was there on business and to check out how the Aussie America's Cup team was shaping up but really it was to see how I was doing. He always worried about me. He stayed with me for a while in New York and it was so good to have him there. He hated the big city though. In his opinion, the whole of America was just one huge city. Ballantine's heard of his visit and brewed a special can of beer for him with his name on it. He was so knocked out. Thom was travelling then so they didn't get to meet but I told Dad all about 'my Thom' and I think he realized this was something special. Too soon Dad had gone back home again.

I returned to Houston to do another gig at Tidelands where I ran into a couple of Aussie girls who were travelling around. We became friendly and one of the girls, Esther Carp, whose brother I knew back in Melbourne, decided to visit New York. I invited her to bunk in with me. It was so good to have someone from home around and in return for the accommodation Esther became my personal assistant. This was a great help to me as I had grown so much busier. She answered the phone, helped me lug my costumes to the studio and so on.

I was excited when Roz told me she had arranged a meeting with the wonderful Jack Benny. If he liked me I was to appear with him at Harrah's Casino in Lake Tahoe where he had a regular show. We met and clicked immediately – Jack was a genuinely funny person and the kindest man I have ever met. I flew to Lake Tahoe in September during a break between tapings for *Sing Along*. This is a gorgeous part of the world on the border of California and Nevada. Harrah's Casino was sumptuous, set on the shores of the sparkling lake. What an eye-opening place that was. Everything was laid on, from a spacious dressing room complete with wet bar and lounge to my choice of a car placed at my disposal. Mr. Harrah and his wife came personally to my dressing room to meet me and wish me well.

'If there is anything you need, Miss Trask, be sure and let me know,' he warmly insisted. The multi-millionaire was humble and generous – no wonder everyone loved him.

Opening night went well except that I found I was short of breath. I had never worked at this altitude and was huffing after only one song. The stage manager pointed out the oxygen supply available in the wings – it seemed crazy but that's how you got through. After each song I would take a bow, leave the stage briefly and suck on the oxygen mask ready for the next number. The Mary Kaye Trio was on the bill and I enjoyed their music very much. Mary played a big guitar and we would all warm up together in the corridors leading to the stage, hamming it up as we fought over whose turn it was for the oxygen mask.

Jack Benny was divine to work with and I loved him to death. He was like the father everyone wished they had. I was at Harrah's for a week with quite a bit of time to kill and I got interested in watching the people trying their luck in the gaming rooms. I would wander around the tables just watching and listening but one night I thought I'd have a go. I chose the craps table and quickly got glued. I was losing fast when Jack appeared at my side. He covered my losses, took me by the elbow, and gently moved me to a quiet corner. I was feeling embarrassed and silly but he was kindness itself.

'Diana, you have to be careful of the tables,' he cautioned. 'Many entertainers get themselves into trouble and lose all they earn plus they finish up owing the casino. You don't want to end up working for nothing.' It was good advice.

Jack's wife Mary was with him at Lake Tahoe, and during the gig George and Gracie Burns dropped by for a few days. I spent a most hilarious afternoon with Jack and George at the pool one day. It was well known that no one could make Jack Benny laugh except George Burns and that afternoon proved it to me. Jack was helpless the whole time. George was a master of timing and I almost fell into the pool myself, doubled up with the antics of the two of them. George told a long story about a visit to a doctor's office. It wasn't really very funny in itself but the way George told it with frequent cigar pauses made it extremely funny. I don't remember how it came to be that the three of us were alone there that day but I wished I could have taped it for posterity.

Another story I heard about the two of them involved a very grand dinner given by the 'Mayer' third of Metro Goldwyn Mayer. Jeanette MacDonald of *Indian Love Call* fame was in attendance to sing for the guests. She was a true prima donna, deserving of due respect while she sang ... except that George Burns and Jack Benny were amongst the guests.

The story goes that George turned to Jack and said speculatively, 'Jack, wouldn't it be funny if, when Miss MacDonald began to sing, everyone started laughing for no particular reason?'

Just the suggestion was enough. As soon as Miss MacDonald opened her mouth, Jack Benny was doubled up in his seat laughing helplessly while a bewildered singer and guests wondered what on earth was happening. George looked on in innocent surprise, cigar at a rakish tilt. Those two were legends.

Jack and George belonged to the 'old school' of stars. They'd grown up through The Depression and world war, paid their dues in the hard slog of Vaudeville, and paved the way for the next generation of entertainers to have it a little easier. These were the guys who put up with terrible working conditions, little pay and long hours, and slowly wrung some changes out of promoters and bookers. For them, entertainment was meant to uplift others, not just draw attention to you. They tried to pass on some good advice to the up and coming stars: don't throw your weight around; be grateful; treat everyone with respect.

Mel Torme, nicknamed the 'Velvet Fog' by a disc jockey for his smooth jazz sound, was another of the greats with whom I worked at that time. I loved Mel's singing and he was a sweet guy with a big heart. He was a real movie buff too and he took me on my first movie rage on our day off. We went from one movie right into the next, all day and into the night. He told me he co-wrote the musical standard 'The Christmas Song' in New York City on the hottest July day he could ever remember. *Chestnuts roasting on an open fire...* Mel passed away in 1999 and I guess someone is still earning residuals from that song.

Tony Bennett and I did many promotional tours together and I always loved his singing. We would go around with the promoters and get up to do a number wherever we were. He was always the one most in demand.

'What's your secret, Tony?' I asked him half laughing, half serious.

'Just keep producing, Diana, that is the key to this business,' he told me. I believe it. He is still there, handsome and singing better than ever.

On one of those promotional tours I was introduced to the legendary Walt Disney. He stood up as I approached and took my hand courteously. He was tall and angular with a wide smile.

'Such a pleasure to meet you, Diana,' he said.

A pleasure to meet me? Wow ... I was speechless. What a gentleman. Years later I would work quite a bit for the Disney machine both in Disneyland in Anaheim and at Disneyworld in Florida. It was always a pleasant experience as I was treated very well. I never saw Mr. Disney again but his presence was there in the courtesy and spectacular cleanliness of the parks. He left a sparkling ambiance behind him.

And now, no matter where I was, I carried in my heart the spectacular knowledge that Thom was in my life. Meeting him had changed everything for me. I had found the anchor I was looking for here in the States, whereas before my life had seemed adrift. One night towards the end of September, Thom said he would be going overseas for a while and would call me soon. I thought nothing of it except for the pain of not being with him, and saw him off at the airport as usual. He held me tight for a long while. There was a last lingering kiss. A wave goodbye. I heard nothing from him for the next seven months.

At first I thought he'd call any minute and hung by the phone, snapping at Esther, my roommate, if she picked up the phone first. The days turned to weeks and I was getting desperate. Why had I not got his mother's phone number or something else to track him down? I didn't even have a business number or any way to find him. Since meeting him I'd just spent my days in a kind of haze, trusting completely that when he was away from me he would be back soon because we had felt so right together. I still clung to that hope.

Weeks turned to months with no word from Thom and hope diminished. Depression and loneliness were back big time. *Why didn't he call? Where had he gone?* I dragged myself through my work and wandered the streets of New York again. My weight see-sawed and, combined with heavy dieting, my health went downhill. Weight was always an issue on television and I saw a doctor to get help. He gave me some pills but I soon gave them up after it felt like I was floating down Broadway one day. Uppers were routine in the business and even speed was making its appearance amongst the Broadway dancers. A dancer once explained to me that they were asked to put out so much energy every night they felt they could not do it without help. I didn't ever try them – too scared of the monkey.

I had asked Thom to give me something of his to hold close when he was traveling and he had given me a beautiful crucifix that he wore. Now it was the one thing I had of his – that is, until I lost it. *Not that too!* I was beside myself. I scoured the apartment, my clothes, everywhere I could think of. I even posted an ad in the newspaper thinking I must have dropped it in the street. One day about three weeks later Esther came to me beaming, holding out something that glimmered in her fingers. She placed Thom's crucifix in my hands. She had found it wedged underneath my bed. I fell on my knees and thanked God.

But he was gone. I sank into a terrible despair and people began to notice. Whenever I was out of the public eye I was crying. A new nightclub, Basin Street East, had opened across the street from my hotel and I would stand and stare out of my window as celebrities and other notables arrived in stretch limousines to hear stars like Peggy Lee sing there. I couldn't even see them clearly through the tears.

I heard that my single 'Long Ago Last Summer' was doing well back home in Australia. How the lyrics stung. Last summer Thom was with me. Now he was gone. *Life International* magazine published a spread about me in October that year. Dad was visiting again – his third in fifteen months – and the magazine featured a photo of the two of us.

Mort and Roz were very pleased – it was a coup for an Australian singer and the publicity was tremendous but in truth I simply didn't care.

The days and weeks dragged on and I dragged myself along with them, trying to get up and go on. Roz worried about me and sent me to see a counselor friend of hers but what could I tell her? It was an old, old story and it would all sound so stupid and ignorant, gullible and trite. In my own heart I was sure there must be a reason, an explanation, but no one else was going to see it that way. I couldn't talk to anyone about Thom and felt more alone than ever.

At last, though, I began to toughen up inside. Anger came to my rescue. *How dare he do this to me?* I began to feel mean, then mad, then spiteful, then resigned. *That's that. So, okay, I'll find a man with a lot of money and settle for a life of ease. From now on, men get judged strictly by their pocketbook!*

Toughening up meant many things, including using the subway. I put the lessons Thom had taught me to good use and went out and found my way around the city. In those days New Yorkers had a wise kind of tough outer shell and I could feel this attitude stealing over me. Underneath, people were really warm but one had to be glib and untouchable on the outside to survive. Didn't I know this myself from harsh experience? I went to the laundromat and braved the subway wearing my new attitude but I think I was a paper tiger.

Johnny Mathis crooned 'Misty' on the radio and a devastating snowstorm hit the city, dropping twenty-one inches of snow. Esther and I had to walk about three miles through the freezing weather to get to rehearsal. Everything was at a standstill with snow piled high over the tops of cars and the city a complete mess, especially a few days later when it all started to melt. The winter was long and cold and hard.

Christmas was near and I decided I would go to St. Patrick's Cathedral for Midnight Mass. Although I'd abandoned regular worship, I felt the need to recapture something of the certainties of childhood. I needed the comfort of familiar words and rites. It was a frosty night and I stood for a long time in a long line waiting to get in. At some point the realization came that this was a ticketed event and I had no ticket! A wave of utter despair swept through me. Simultaneously, the woman in front turned around and just handed me her tickets and left the line. I broke into tears and saw it as a sign, praying to God to see my Thom again and that he was safe. My heart was desolate.

It was 1961. A New Year blew in on wintery wings, cold and empty. The Maisonette Room was a swanky New York club and Mort Farber got me a booking there.

'I think we need a new act, Diana,' Mort decided. 'Something to really show you off in a different way.'

He engaged a guy to write an act for me – a selection of songs and scripted 'chatter' intended to show a different side of me. Maybe it was the venue – more sophisticated than I was used to – or maybe it was more that I wasn't clear in my own mind what my direction was at that time. Whatever, I couldn't do the material justice. Too much of it was an 'act' and very little of it was me, and I felt unusually nervous and intimidated.

'Do it like Lena Horne,' instructed the producer. 'Just switch on the light before you go on.'

This was a visualization trick I used a lot that was supposed to stop all interference. I would imagine a giant switch that could click me into the mood I needed to be in and leave all else behind. I tried this and it worked a little but confidence had slipped since Thom had vanished from my life. I was received fairly well but I was yet to perfect the skills of audience contact. This didn't come until much later in my career when I learned to let the barriers down and create a genuine connection with the average person in the audience by being myself, not just a 'star'.

Big names were there at the Maisonette Room including rising star Burt Bacharach. A young Sidney Poitier dropped by to see me with a friend. His presence impressed me very much. Frank showed up one night as he passed through the city and we spent a little time together for comfort, feeling somewhat like 'strangers in the night.' Frank was, as ever, a good friend. We didn't say much – I couldn't really talk to him about Thom – but I sensed some sadness in him. He knew about lost love too.

The first season of *Sing Along with Mitch* aired in the States in January and became a hit. And in spite of the critics, we were picked up for a second season. I also recorded another album with Mitch – *Diana Trask on TV* – featuring the *Sing Along* chorus. But the show only really kept me busy three days a week and in my current mood I had too much time on my hands. I still enjoyed *Sing Along* but after a while the weeks of taping became a little routine. I didn't have a clear plan for my future and without Thom I was finding it harder than ever to visualize what I wanted. My career was more of a day-to-day thing where I just let things happen according to which way the wind was blowing.

The winds at NBC were blowing in my favor, though. They liked me and worked with Mort over signing me to a longer-term contract, with *Sing Along* being only a part of the arrangement. David Tebet at NBC was an influential part of this deal. He was always extremely kind to me and gave me endless help and guidance. He had been instrumental in helping other people's careers by dropping the right word in someone's ear and making useful social introductions. He had a career vision for me and was generous in squiring me around to the right places.

I was astounded when he offered me a spot on *The Tonight Show*, hosted by Johnny Carson – it was a fabulous offer but I turned it down. I had been a guest on the show and had seen how slick it was. I didn't feel confident talking in front of a camera and I knew I'd be competing with all kinds of 'showbiz' personalities who were much more glib than I. I wasn't about to risk making a fool of myself. I didn't let on to David Tebet about my real reasons, just thanked him and said it wasn't for me. But it was a sign that things were moving very fast now and I admit I was a bit lost, a twenty-year-old girl with no family nearby to anchor me or keep me centered. New friends and workmates sometimes tried to offer their advice but honestly, they all seemed like strangers speaking another language.

Starring on a hit television show brings the good and the bad to your door. I was being noticed around New York now. My height was always mentioned in reviews and a nickname emerged – 'The Towering Eyeful'. If I went shopping, people would slide their eyes around or look down, trying to be very cool. One little man found out where I shopped and tailed me all over town, even to the point of once taking a seat on an airplane next to me. It was a little scary at times as I was always dodging in and out of doorways trying to shake him. Thank God, I had an excellent doorman at the hotel who kept an eye out and sent the man packing. Eventually I would have to call my grocery orders in to Gristede Bros and they would deliver to my door.

In February, *Time* magazine ran a great article on me, reviewing my career since arriving in the States and praising my first album, *Diana Trask*. Again, Roz told me how pleased I should be.

'Being in *Time* is a big deal,' she urged, trying to cheer me up.

The reviewer was kind and the photographer captured a smiling face but not the emptiness within.

Spring was just breaking into bud when Esther handed me the phone, a peculiar look on her face.

'Someone for you,' she smiled.

It was Thom! My heart leaped painfully.

'Diana, I'm in Boston. Will you come?'

Will I come? Everything was mixed up inside me. Joy and uncertainty, longing and trepidation. *What was going on? What should I do? Will I fly to Boston to meet him?* Of course I would.

I quickly booked a flight and took off in a daze. It was the worst plane ride of my life. The plane practically stood on its ear as vicious side winds slammed into the fuselage. There weren't many passengers and we were all more than a little green as we bumped down. I spent the flight battling airsickness and struggling with my emotions, dying to see Thom and dreading the outcome. *Why had he left me for all this time? Why had he called? What was he going to say?* Thom was on the ground waiting.

My first look at him gave me a real shock. The ruddy Irish complexion was gone. He was very thin and white. I ran to him.

'I'll explain it all, let's go to the hotel,' he said as we embraced.

We talked for the whole weekend. The left ventricle of his heart had collapsed and he was back from overseas to have a risky new procedure at a top hospital in New York. He was to check in to the hospital in two days. The doctors had not given him much of a chance, about six months.

'But, Thom...' I was so confused by this time. I knew he loved me, I had always been sure, so why had he left? Why complete silence for seven long months? I couldn't just pick up where we had left off without knowing. He sat me down and told me the story.

'I'm married, Di,' he said. 'We're separated.'

I let that sink in.

'It was a mistake. We got married in a hurry and found out we didn't have a lot in common. We haven't actually spent that much time together. Things have never been very happy between us.'

'Children?'

'Two.'

I stared at him, digesting this information. He took hold of my hands and tried to explain what had been happening for him in the last seven months. Basically he decided he had to step back from me in order to think through his situation. Divorce was serious and he agonized over the children. He knew I was Catholic too and worried about the status of our marriage should we take that step. Thom's marriage had taken place in a Registry Office and so in the eyes of the Church was not a Sacrament, not valid. If we were to marry he would have to seek the Church's permission. Things as they stood were messy. Conflicting arguments had chased themselves inside his head for months as he tried to decide what was best for everyone. It was life-threatening illness that crystallized his decision – whatever time was left he wanted to spend it with me.

My head was spinning. *Marriage ... children ... dying?* I took a breath.

'You should have told me sooner.'

'I didn't know how. I thought it would be better if I just got out of your life.'

'It was not better!' I told him, bursting into tears. 'I thought you were never coming back! Don't ever leave me like that again!'

He held me close and stroked my hair.

'I never will, baby,' he promised.

I made up my mind. Thom was my best chance at real happiness – I knew that right from the start – and I would always be there for him. We belonged together, no matter what was in store, and we would take our chances together. We would go through the hospital thing and live for the moment.

I had commitments in New York. We flew back together, taking comfort in each other's company and trying not to think about what lay ahead. I was in the last part of my *Sing Along* season as Thom went in for the procedure. I remember singing 'I'm Sitting on Top of the World' as he lay fighting for his life. *Don't tell me Diana Trask can't act,* I told myself grimly as I smiled and sang. I visited whenever I could but when he was moved out of town to recuperate we only had phone contact. After several weeks and against all odds he made it through, and as soon as he could travel we were together again – our 'six months' had begun.

Meanwhile, back in Australia, my parents were planning a big party to celebrate my twenty-first birthday. Twenty-one is hailed as a person's coming of age in Australia and is generally celebrated by the whole family. *Sing Along* had started airing there in April and was a big hit. Mom and Dad were glued to the set whenever it was on, our tenuous contact over the long miles. Now they were so excited about my coming home and if it hadn't been for leaving Thom, the break away from the stresses and strains of the last months would have been welcome. I hated leaving him but I couldn't possibly stay away. Thom and I had decided to get married if things worked out but for the time being we kept the news a secret.

'Don't disappear while I'm gone,' I told him half seriously as he saw me off at the airport.

'Every time you look in the mirror I'll be there,' he responded and home I flew to Australia.

I had told Dad about 'my Thom' when he was last over and I must have continued to refer to him enthusiastically in my letters. As usual, Dad could not resist telling a friend who told a friend who told a friend... Reporters infiltrated his club, got friendly and started him talking about me. My dear father, completely unaware that he was being mined for information, told his new 'friends' all about me and 'my Thom'.

When I stepped off the plane in Melbourne, the press was there in force with a barrage of questions and speculations about Thom. Interest in me had increased exponentially with the success of *Sing Along*, the coverage in *Time* and *Life* and the release of my first album, *Diana Trask*, in May, but throw in a romance and the press goes absolutely mad. Wild stories about Thom were rampant – one even claimed he was an astronaut!

This was all meat for my old friend Graham Kennedy, host of the late night television show *In Melbourne Tonight*, who quipped on air: 'Wouldn't it be funny if 'My Thom' turned out to be a cat?' I thought that was quite funny but the press's continual hounding of me was not. *Woman's Day* magazine came to the party too, publishing a cover story to celebrate my twenty-first birthday. I had once told my mother that everyone in Australia would know my name and it was true. Equally now, they all knew Thom's, the front page of the *Sun* newspaper announcing that Thom would be seeking an annulment in order to marry me. The whole situation was unbelievable.

Mom and Dad threw me a great birthday party at my godmother's reception place in Kew, and Brian, back in Australia, showed up as a wonderful surprise. We hugged and kissed and the photographers who had crashed the party snapped madly. Now, supposedly, there was another man in my life! Oh my ... !

Brian had of course met Thom in the States and was over the moon for me. Brian had been such a soul mate for years that I felt totally blessed when he and Thom clicked straight away and became great mates. It would have been terrible if they hadn't got along. Of course, it helped that they shared the same insane sense of humor. We three of us shared many, many laughs over the years – the kind of laughter when you fall down absolutely helpless. Dear Brian passed away in 1993 and I still miss him.

Graham Kennedy and Bert Newton also made an appearance at the party as the cameras popped. I waltzed with my dad as he sang along with the tune, making up the words as usual. During the evening I took Mom and Dad aside and told them that Thom and I wanted to get married. They took it well but I could see the concern in their eyes. The rumor mill had done its work on them. He was married. He was a divorcee. He was American. I reassured them as best I could.

'Wait 'til you meet him,' I begged. 'He's funny and kind and wonderful.'

I didn't fill them in on Thom's state of health – that was still just between us and I didn't want it getting out. I also shared my wedding news with my godmother, Eileen. She blessed me without reservation and that felt so good. Somehow, of course, the conversations got out and soon everyone knew I was going to get married.

I flew back to the US and returned to work but things were changing once more. Mitch seemed to lean on me harder than usual, becoming more and more adamant about every aspect of my performance. I had been prepared to do everything his way at the start because I was new and ready to learn but it's not in my nature to buckle under all the time. I had my own ideas and my own style and I was starting to feel stifled and manipulated. I retreated into my aloof, detached mode – something I knew people really hated – but I used it to deal with difficult situations then. I withdrew from Mitch and became hard to get along with.

In July I got a call to go to Washington and fly down to Vice President Johnson's ranch in Austin, Texas. A group of us were to entertain the President of Pakistan at the time, Ayub Khan. I arrived at the military airport in Washington and was standing nervously amongst a group of military types waiting to board Air Force Two. Whenever I get nervous I tend to chatter, and I was nervous now as the big plane came into view. I turned to see a man standing quietly next to me, dressed in what looked like an air force uniform. I was never any good at identifying uniforms or ranks, especially in the US.

'So, what kind of plane do you fly?' I asked him brightly.

He stopped for a minute and replied rather slowly, 'Well, I do have a small plane I fly from time to time.'

I stared at him in confusion for a moment. An aide sidled quickly on the scene and took my arm.

'Miss Trask, I would like you to meet the Chairman of the Joint Chiefs of Staff of the United States of America,' he said pointedly.

I took that one in, ready to sink. In confusion I spun round, looking for a diversion and found it in a tall man in a large cowboy hat who was striding towards me.

'Here comes a big Texan,' I piped.

The 'big Texan' came right up to me with a big grin and took my hand. The aide introduced him to me.

'Miss Trask, the Vice President of the United States.'

O-*kay!*

The Vice President shook my hand and said graciously, 'Oh yes, Diana, I've heard about you.' *Heard? Heard? What has he heard? That I have a big mouth?*

I boarded the plane determined to keep my mouth shut from that moment but that didn't last – there was too much to get excited about during that weekend. Everything – the ranch, the entertainment, the food – was big, Texas big. Ladybird Johnson greeted me kindly and impressed me with her polite and intelligent questions about Australia. This great lady left behind a wonderful heritage with her passion for the beautification of American towns and cities and she also raised awareness about protecting old buildings and natural landscapes. She spoke a simple message: we can't keep trashing America.

There was a wonderful candlelight dinner for fifty out by the pool that night, the tables dressed in white linen and the guests entertained by strolling Mexican singers and musicians. The girl singer had long, shiny, jet-black hair dressed in the traditional way and wore an intricately detailed campesina outfit. The singing was beautiful and I have loved Mexican voices ever since. Later in life I traveled in South and Central America and learned Spanish and still believe the Mexican singers and their music are the best in the Spanish field.

I performed out by the swimming pool with just the piano for accompaniment and a full moon riding above. My number, appropriately

THE VICE PRESIDENT
WASHINGTON

July 19, 1961

Dear Diana:

The LBJ Ranch was certainly improved
by the pretty red-head from Australia this weekend. You "boomeranged" all the guests, i.e.,
we hope you will return.

The President of Pakistan told me how
much he enjoyed the evening where you starred
by the swimming pool. Lady Bird and I thank
you so much for contributing your fine talent and
sweet presence to the event.

Sincerely,

Lyndon B. Johnson

Miss Diana Trask
Middletown Hotel
48th Street
New York City, New York

400G, The Sheraton Park
Washington 8, D.C.
July 19, 1961

Dear Diana:

What is the range of our boomerang?
I'm torn between hanging it on the wall in
the rec room of our new house in Washington
and using it in the wide open spaces of
Texas. Thank you for the momento of your
country, but most of all thank you for
adding so much to the success of our dinner
for President Ayub. All the guests enjoyed you,
but I think you will be interested to know you
made a special hit with our honor guest.
President Ayub mentioned particularly how
much he enjoyed you.

With appreciation and best wishes.

Sincerely,

Lady Bird Johnson

Mrs. Lyndon B. Johnson

enough, was 'Blue Moon' for which I wore a blue gown accentuated by a soft blue spotlight – very romantic. I was a little shocked when Ayub Khan stood up in the middle of the show and walked out with the Vice President trailing after him. One never knows with politicians who or what grabs their attention or why. It was a memorable few days culminating in a wonderful Sunday barbecue with everything laid on.

Back in New York, things were no better between Mitch and I and the time had come to re-sign contracts.

Mort Farber thought I should get a raise. I was happy enough with the money I was getting but at his suggestion I agreed for him to try. He took it to NBC who took it up with Mitch. Mitch hit the roof.

'If she feels that way, she can work somewhere else!'

Mort was flabbergasted. Knowing Mitch, I was less surprised. I had one more show to do and tried to approach him about changing his mind but he was legendary when he was ticked off and the upshot was I was dropped from *Sing Along*. I thought back to when Johnny Lee dumped me from his club back in Sydney. Then I was devastated. Now I just shrugged.

I still had a contract with NBC, which put them in a bind, but the whole episode confirmed a lot of things for me. Like Mitch, but for different reasons, I decided it was all over. A mentor's job is to nurture you and help you grow but then they have to let you step up. Mitch didn't like that I was ready to step up. So I felt some sadness that this era had come to an end but no regret. I had other irons in the fire and was ready to move on. Thom had obtained a divorce by now and so we decided to go back to Australia and get married. He was thirty-three and I was twenty-one.

I went to the bank and withdrew enough money from my joint account with my manager to buy a wedding dress and a ticket home. I shopped on Fifth Avenue for my dress and, in trying to avoid the avid questions of the assistants, made what was surely the fastest selection by any bride anywhere. I was in and out of there in a trice. Brian, back at school in New York, was to mail the dress to me in Australia after the alterations were done.

I suddenly could not wait to get out of New York. I threw a bash at my apartment and invited all my pals and the troupe from the show. We partied long and loud, doing the twist all night. Next day Thom and I jumped in a car and took the legendary Route 66 all the way across the country to California. I had not told my management or Roz or anyone who ran my life in New York that I was leaving. I felt as if everyone had been using me – Mort, Roz, Mitch. Someone was making money from all the hours I worked and it sure wasn't me. Rebellion was uppermost. This was my life and I would decide.

SEVEN

Here Comes The Bride

Thom knew the country well and as the beautiful scenery and different states rolled by I was overjoyed to finally see America this way. The diversity of the land and the people lifted my spirits every day as we passed slowly west. Here at last was the *Leave It to Beaver* country I'd imagined for so long. I was humbled and excited and awed.

We stopped by Lake Tahoe where my dear friend Jack Benny was appearing. He was his usual lovely self, announcing from the stage that we were engaged. I thought about the one and only time he was ever even slightly annoyed with me, when I forgot to wear a ring that was the punch line in a sketch. I was supposed to kiss him whilst singing 'Mr. Wonderful' and then faint in his arms, whereupon he would pull out a jeweler's loupe and examine the ring on my finger. It usually got a huge laugh except this one time when I had forgotten to put the blasted ring on. I remembered just as we kissed and I stiffened in his arms.

'I forgot the ring,' I whispered.

'Shit!' he said under his breath. 'Okay, ladies and gentlemen ...' He explained the joke to the audience but it fell flat and I walked off awkwardly. He went on smoothly with the rest of the show but he was annoyed with me that night. Not so this meeting and he was indeed Mr. Wonderful to us.

Thom and I boarded a Qantas flight in LA bound for Hawaii and took a short break there, staying at the Hilton. Martin Denny was playing there and we went to the show. He saw me in the audience and suddenly announced from the stage that we were newlyweds! That is when it hit the fan. The press was on us like locusts but what was worse, a newspaper stringer from Australia happened to be in the audience too and he must have set to work right away. We didn't correct Martin, as it would have been very embarrassing for him but just tried to pass it off. Little did we know of the firestorm that would soon begin brewing at home.

We stopped briefly in Sydney and, more or less as a favor, appeared on a late-night television show there. I remember I sang 'Stardust'. As things turned out later, that appearance would come back to haunt me. The press had not been too bad in Sydney so we were completely unprepared for the circus that greeted us in Melbourne.

We stepped off the plane to be greeted by a mass of photographers and reporters all trying to muscle in closer and get a comment. Thom in particular was besieged with questions, most of which were designed to put him in a bad light. 'How do you like Australian girls?' was one pointed question I heard shouted out.

I could see my family in the back, crowded out by the press and desperately waving at us. We tried to get a few steps nearer to them, dodging cameras and reporters. Finally we got close and I had to introduce my fiancé to my family in the midst of this melee. It was awful.

The press made an issue out of everything – Thom's previous marriage, his age, the fact that he was American. I was portrayed as the little princess and he the evil, foreign vanquisher. Evidently the press had decided I should have come home engaged to some millionaire or a big star at the very least. Who was Thom Ewen? We'd robbed them of a big story and there was no way we could win with them. If it hadn't been so serious for us it would have been funny.

We retreated to my parents' house for a few weeks, staying with the family and trying to calm down. The phone rang off the wall day and night. Poor Mom and Dad were very stressed. At first Dad tried to answer the reporters' questions but he soon learned about the trap of one-liners. Pretty soon he became known as 'No Comment Trask', having learned that his every word was likely to be repeated and taken right out of context. My family was not used to this kind of harassment and did not know how to deal with it. We closed ranks and even with the members of the press that had been kindly, we learned to say nothing or else we would be some front-page sensation again.

Christmas was approaching. We planned to get married on the 6th December and so went to our parish priest in Warburton, Fr. Cerini, a well-known, saintly man, to arrange our nuptials. Even in this we were baulked. The press, of course, had got hold of the story of the wedding announcement in Hawaii and insistently reported we were already married. Now this would have to be investigated by the Church before our union could be sanctioned. We were stunned – all we wanted to do was get married! We agreed to the Church looking into it, changed the wedding date to January 6th, and buckled down to weather the incessant barrage from the press which greeted any new angle with enthusiasm.

The devil's advocate appointed by the Church was a Fr. Ahern in Melbourne. We explained the situation to him but he believed we had staged the whole thing as a publicity stunt. He was skeptical of our claims that it was all due to the press going crazy in search of a story. Perhaps he needed a lesson in how persistent and difficult the press can be?

We suggested that all phone calls regarding our marriage be referred to his office. He agreed but after three days of his phone ringing non-stop and reporters pursuing him day and night, his tone changed and Fr. Ahern bowed right out. Years later I spoke frankly with a member of the press from those days and he told me that if he had nothing to run with that week he would just make up a story about Diana Trask.

'It was a favorite sport,' he shrugged.

Fr. Cerini now suggested that we go to see Archbishop Mannix, a highly regarded cleric worldwide. An appointment was made and he received us graciously. He was of medium height with piercing blue eyes that looked into your very soul. He reviewed the situation carefully.

We were not married in Las Vegas or any other place? *No.* We were both Catholic? *Yes.* And Thom's marriage had not been in the Church? *No.* The Archbishop took his time. At last he said there was no reason we could not have the ceremony if all we said was the truth, but how was he to know if it was the truth? Would we sign a paper requiting the marriage if at a later date a marriage certificate was produced, be it from a Church or a Civil Authority? *Yes, yes.* We gladly signed the paper, he blessed us kindly and at last all was set to go ahead.

In Warburton all the townsfolk and family friends were eager to meet 'Diana's Yank'. He charmed them all and was a huge hit at the local pub where he was staying, the Alpine Retreat. Mom had thawed out fairly fast but Grandmother was a harder nut to crack. She had listened to his jokes and fun and been the subject of his teasing. He would ask her if she had ever been to Tasmania?

'I was born in Tasmania,' she would reply.

A minute or two would pass and Thom would ask her again, 'Have you ever been to Tasmania, Nanna?'

She would look at him like he was an imbecile and repeat loudly, 'I was born in Tasmania.'

This went on all weekend. Later in the afternoon I caught her alone sitting on the front verandah.

'What do you think of my Yank, Nanna?' I asked.

'Well,' she considered carefully, 'I reckon you gotta take what he says with a grain of salt.'

Christmas passed with the usual family celebrations, the New Year – 1962 – came in and January 6th drew nearer. Wedding preparations had reached fever pitch. My wedding dress arrived from New York, a long simple dress with three quarter sleeves. I was on tenterhooks until it was safely hanging in my closet, picturing it lost in transit and having to get married in whatever came to hand.

One day I came across my father tinkering with something in the garage. He looked up and saw me, called me over and then hesitated. Like Nanna, he had taken his time weighing Thom up.

'Di, are you sure you want to go through with this? Are you sure this man is right for you?' he questioned. I gave him a hug.

'Quite sure,' I replied. He thought about it for a moment.

'Well, at least it won't be bloody boring,' was his comment as he turned back to his job.

My old friend Di Sindrey was to be the bridesmaid along with my godmother's little daughters who were to be my handmaidens in white dresses with pink roses in their hair. Di arrived and we hugged and kissed and talked long into the night. The wedding was to take place in the tiny timber Sacred Heart Church in Warburton where I had been baptized for the second time. Fr. Cerini would conduct the ceremony and I would carry water lilies, my favorite flower. Dad ordered them especially to be flown in from Queensland.

The Seventh-day Adventists loaned us a pedal organ for the day; singing was organized; Eileen Eveley, a parishioner and friend, decorated the tiny church; dresses and suits were ready. We just didn't plan on all the uninvited guests.

The day dawned hot and sticky, a true January day in Australia. You can tell a scorcher is coming before you even step outside – the world is wrapped in stillness and the sky stretches high and far, filled with hard, pure light. A minute to take it in; a moment of lying quiet, breathing in the eucalyptus scented air of my childhood home in Warburton, Victoria. And now the next adventure: I was to marry my Thom at last! I sprang out of bed and the final preparations began.

The wedding was to be at 11 but by 6am reporters began banging on the front door. They were faced down by a very irate father of the bride who all but slammed the door off its hinges. At the Alpine Retreat Thom was besieged by members of the press, some of whom even followed him into the bathroom.

I helped my little flower girls get ready and then donned my bridal gown and veil. Di Sindrey was looking beautiful in off-white silk; my mom in pretty pink. A long black car was waiting at the foot of the steps and my dad took my arm as we drove up to the church at La La. I thought nothing could shock me anymore but as we approached I was rocked to see about three thousand people pressing round the tiny church. They were a packed, noisy group with television vans, mobile cameras, cables and reporters everywhere. Someone had even propped ladders up against the church windows and people were hanging inside. People were pushing and running as the police made a cordon for Dad and I to pass through.

I had been too busy with last-minute things to attend the usual wedding rehearsal and now I was, in true showbiz form, winging it! I had placed myself on Dad's left side but he grasped my elbow firmly and steered me to his other arm.

'Are you sure this is right, Dad?' I whispered as we threaded our way through the melee.

'I was at the rehearsal, you weren't,' he retorted as he maneuvered us into our starting positions inside the door of the church.

The music sounded and off we went down the little aisle, my flower girls strewing rose petals before me. The church was packed to capacity and breathlessly hot. My brother Pete was best man and waited at the altar with Thom looking so handsome. Thom later told me he felt like an observer in a dream at that moment as I came towards him. Pete had to give him a push to remind him to move. They stepped forward as my dad and I arrived at the communion rail. Dad in turn gave me a little shove towards Thom and we turned and looked at each other.

I was feeling fairly serene but I would be glad when the whole thing was over. I promised to 'Love, honor and cherish'. I did not include 'Obey' as I believed that was a very tall order and I probably would not be too good at it. It was a high Mass and I remember sweat dripping off Fr. Cerini's considerable nose onto the Bible as he read the vows. At last there was the kiss and the Grand Bridal March rang out as we started back down the aisle.

I faltered as I passed the pew where Barbara James sat. Did she remember the vow we had taken as children to be bridesmaids for each other? *Probably not...* I passed on. Years later I asked her if she had remembered those long-ago blood sister promises. She had. We hugged as I apologized and she laughed it off but I still felt bad. I wish I had honored that old promise.

As we reached the outside of the church, clapping and cheers went up as the Aussie crowd yelled encouragement and good wishes. I felt deeply emotional as Thom and I were swept towards the limo on a wave of goodwill. We sank back thankfully, the crowd surged forward, waved us off and we left for Melbourne where the reception was to take place at my godmother Eileen's reception centre.

Back at the church the family had a hard time getting to their cars and through the crowd. Someone picked my father's pocket and he was heartbroken, not for the money but for a letter in his wallet which he held dear – the one I had written him as a small child, asking for a kitten.

We were starving hungry and stopped to buy a Kit Kat candy bar, our first meal together as husband and wife. There was one other thing I wanted to do before the partying and the speeches began. We called in at Presentation Convent in Windsor to see the nuns who had been such a big part of my early life. They 'ooh-ed' and 'ahh-ed' and we drank a cup of tea with them in their front parlor. Sr. Lucy was smiling broadly and I thought I saw a tear in her eye as we left. They had been instrumental in my early training and I guess I wanted them to know that no matter what they might see or hear in the press about Thom and I, we took our marriage seriously and had always tried to do the right thing.

The reception was a wonderful night with mainly extended family and some close friends celebrating in a quiet way. The only hitch was a photographer friend of mine who got himself drunk as a skunk. My godmother had made all the arrangements, including keeping the press away, so the relentless scrutiny was relaxed for a little while. The loquacious Fr. Heffey, assistant to Fr. Cerini, gave a wonderful speech, as did my brother Pete and my new husband. I danced a waltz with my dad as I had on my twenty-first birthday.

After the meal and all the speeches, we prepared to leave on our honeymoon. I changed into a dull-gold dress, up went my bouquet and guess who caught it? Barbara. My parents saw us off and we took my mother's car for a three-week trip up the East coast. We had really made no plans. We just wanted to drive and get away from the madness for a while. The press was not about to oblige us, though.

Our first night was spent in a Melbourne motel. We laughed a little about our wedding night as we had both bought sleeping apparel that suited the moment. I slipped on a white frothy thing and Thom disappeared into the bathroom, appearing thirty seconds later in a white silk pajama set. I was speechless as in all the time I had known him he had never owned a set of pajamas, preferring to sleep as God made him. As he entered the room, he lifted up his arms and posed ...

'How do I look?' he preened.

At that point his pants fell straight off onto the floor. Never known to have hips, those pants fell right down and that is where they stayed.

After hours of driving northeast we arrived at sunset in the little fishing town of Eden on the East coast. The road there winds down from the hills towards the town and as we rounded the last bend we could see the ocean glowing in the evening light. January is the main summer vacation season in Australia when schools are closed for an extended Christmas/New Year break. The town was full of holidaymakers and the only accommodation left was one tiny room at a standard Australian hotel. Well, how bad could it be? We took the key and looked inside. Memories of my first dingy room in New York were forcibly brought to mind. There was a dusty window, a washstand and a tiny bed strangely located in a corner underneath the hotel's main staircase. There was nowhere else and we were too tired to drive further that night. It would have to do.

We ate in the dining room, served by a cranky waitress who made us feel very uncomfortable. Obviously they had been reading the papers up here and had decided we weren't respectable. Later we squeezed into the tiny bed as hotel patrons pounded up and down the wooden stairs all night directly over our heads. There was not much sleep to be had and next day saw us up bright and early, driving on up the coast.

It was 1962 and things were different in Australia then, particularly as you moved away from the cities – much less sophisticated. You got plain food and plain service. Meals were served on a strict timetable, dining rooms closed promptly, shops closed for lunch everywhere. My Yank could not get over it.

'But what happens if you get hungry in the middle of the night?' he would ask, shaking his head.

One day when we stopped for lunch I decided to introduce Thom to the good ol' Aussie meat pie. Well, something was definitely wrong with those pies and it wasn't long before we both felt decidedly ill. We would be driving along when suddenly brakes would screech and both doors would fly open as our outraged stomachs hurled up their contents onto the roadside. Not exactly one of our more romantic moments.

I suggested we should go to the Hume Weir on the Murray River in northern Victoria, one of my family's favorite holiday sites. I had many wonderful memories of camping holidays there as a child. Dad, the fisherman, would catch very large landlocked trout which we would barbecue over an open fire. Those were wonderful days and I thought Thom would like the area but we had no sooner arrived at the Weir than the press found out and were on our tail. We had a run in with a pushy photographer and discovered we had been dubbed 'The Battling Ewens' in the newspapers. That was probably accurate as by that stage we were in no mood for the constant invasions.

We wandered back down south towards Gippsland in southeast Victoria – an area of beautiful unspoiled beaches and lakes. Thom thought we could rent a caravan and find a quiet place there near the lakes. This turned out to be a great idea. We found a spot to set up camp and people left us alone at last. In fact some of the other campers were even a little protective of us. The area was lovely and peaceful and we enjoyed our first quiet time together since our wedding. It became clear though that it was not time for me to be the little wife and do the washing – imagine my dismay when all Thom's underclothes came out bright yellow. No one told me the water was artesian!

I had a little 'incident' with the car one day. I didn't stop quite soon enough and ended up 'leaning' it against the side of the caravan which got pushed right in. Thom teased me for days.

'What are we going to tell the man who rented us the caravan?' he laughed. 'Oh, sorry, she just *leaned* the car against it?'

We met up with a group of young people who had a boat and were down water-skiing on the lakes. They were a group of 'cow cockies' – small scale dairy farmers – from Gippsland; all local footballers and strong, young farming guys full of fun. They were holidaying with their wives and girlfriends and had a fast ski boat which they liked to jump-start off the sand dunes and zoom down into the lake. One couple, Marie and Jim Summers, became firm, long-lasting friends of ours through the years.

Thom took to the skis and learned in one day, so everyone decided we should ski down the lake about five miles to the town of Metung for the day. These waters are a breeding ground for baby sharks so we were warned it was not a good idea to fall off. It was fine going down but on the way back when Thom and I were criss-crossing and playing around, I fell off. My ski towline snapped and snagged around Thom's ankle, wrapping around it and breaking one of his skis in two. Now I was in the water and he was balancing on one ski.

He was holding his leg with the broken ski up out of the water and had no option but to stay like that or be dragged behind the boat. He was not an expert as yet but gamely hung on. The couple towing us were in love and too busy looking into each other's eyes to turn back to watch us. I was yelling and screaming, thinking of those hungry baby sharks, and so was Thom, but it was a good mile further on before this couple finally turned and checked on us. The boat pulled up in a hurry, Thom clambered in and then they all rushed back to haul me out of the water.

We were young and laughed the whole thing off and turned our attention to more important things – dinner. We made plans to go to the Metung pub and a large group of us had a fun night talking and laughing about everything and nothing. A band set up after dinner and my new husband grabbed my hand.

'Come and dance, Mrs. Ewen,' he said and pulled me up. The others joined us and the tiny dance floor quickly filled up. I made a face at Thom – the music was pretty stiff and boring.

'Follow my lead, Mrs. Ewen,' he whispered in my ear and next second had launched into his version of the Twist, the new hit dance that was huge in New York. Soon we were all twisting and the band was getting left way behind. The music stopped. The band leader, highly insulted, instructed us very haughtily not to dance that way in his establishment. I guess he was of the school that thought Rock and Roll was way too sexual. Thom and the other guys in our group were less than impressed and made it known. Someone called the police and of course the press showed up.

It was a melee as the footballers were set to take on the press, the police and the band. We girls were trying to restrain the guys who stood as a body, refusing to budge. We got out of there eventually without blood on the floor, the bandleader huffing away in agitation. The next day the headlines screamed, 'The Battling Ewens are at It Again'.

We moved on, ambling across country for a few more days. We called in to Jim and Marie's farm in Gippsland – they were back home by now – and happily milked their cows and met their animals. By week's end we were back in Melbourne.

We returned to find Dad had suffered a kind of nervous breakdown. He had collapsed two days after the wedding and was very weak and disoriented. The stress of the last few weeks battling the press and hearing the publicity about Thom and I had been too much for him. Mom was in distress and very worried. We were upset to be even partly the cause of the problem and wondered what would be best to do. Perhaps we should go back to the States and let things settle down?

We had thought about staying in Australia but I still had contracts back in the US and we finally agreed we should go back. Our return tickets were running out anyway so we went ahead and completed the requirements for getting my green card in the US. Dad seemed to improve a little and Mom was coping but it would be quite a long time before Dad was really well again.

Part of the green card regulations involved a thorough health check, and as the doctor took X-rays and did the usual tests he peered closely at me over his glasses.

'I've checked your tests and they are slightly irregular. Is it possible that you are pregnant?'

I blushed from the bottoms of my pointy-toed shoes. 'No, I don't think so,' I said hotly.

I was hoping this was not so as I was remembering some of those rough falls I'd had on the water skis recently. I got out of there as fast as possible and ran outside to tell Thom what the doctor had said.

'Well, darlin', we'll just have to wait and see.'

He took my arm and helped me into the car, smiling from ear to ear. I did not say anything to my parents and two days later we flew back to the US.

EIGHT

Baby Love, My Baby Love

Thom's grin grew wider in the coming weeks when my mornings were made uneasy by strange nausea. He made an appointment for me with an obstetrician – oh yes, we were pregnant! I was pleased but Thom was completely ecstatic. I did wish we'd had a little more time together to catch our breaths before babies came along, but it was not to be.

We were back in New York by now and I'd had to face the music with Mort Farber and Roz Ross, both of whom felt hurt by my protracted 'absence without leave' in Australia. For them, my marriage had come out of the blue and they were very cool when I explained where I had been the past weeks. It was a very uncomfortable interview and I didn't think it a good moment to mention morning sickness. Meantime, a movie audition had come up and I dutifully went along. I read for the producers but gave enough away for them to guess I was pregnant.

'Thank you for coming, Ms. Trask,' they said politely. 'And good luck.'

My management was not so polite when I eventually revealed my condition. Silence filled the room and frustration filled their faces. I was sorry to let them down. Roz and Mort had worked hard on my behalf (not to mention their own) and I suppose they thought I was completely thankless. But there was not much I could do about it. How can you beat Mother Nature? Besides, Thom and I were happy and to me that was the most important thing. I had a right to a life of my own.

For sure, I was to be out of the entertainment picture for a while and we had to settle what we would do next. Thom had retired from his job at Gillette before we were married, trying to step back from the stressful life he had been living and he decided California could be the place to try for work. We packed up and made the move and after trying a few jobs here and there he found a niche with the Anheuser-Busch beer company. We purchased a nice little white house in Huntington Beach and settled in to wait for the big moment when our baby would arrive.

Thom's health had improved and he was enjoying his job; I was relishing being away from the stale air of New York and making a home for my little family. The only hitch was the paycheck problem. The company paid Thom by computer-typed checks and I'd never seen one before. I thought they were advertisements and threw them out just as soon as they came in. After about six weeks of no pay Thom called up to find out what was happening.

'Can't think what the problem is,' said his boss. 'Don't worry, Thom, I'll send your money by courier straight away.'

The replacement paychecks duly arrived and the truth came out. Thom did not know what to do with me when I told him I had been regularly throwing his money out with the trash.

'You what?' he yelled.

'Well, why don't they look like ordinary checks?' I pouted.

'Because they are computer generated!' he fumed.

I know he wanted to add the word 'dummy' to that statement but to his credit he did not.

I didn't have a car of my own when I first came to the States but sometimes show-business friends lent me an MG or Porsche to take out for a spin which I didn't mind at all. I have to admit I was a bit reckless in those early years, like many young kids are. I tended to drive like a whirlwind. It worried Thom.

'Diana, you're going to kill yourself,' he told me seriously. I knew he was right and being married and pregnant certainly prompted me to become more cautious. I was still having my 'Australian moments', though, as I called them. One day I was making a left turn in my car and for a second I thought I was back home where you drive on the opposite side of the road. It was high drive time and I pulled into the center of the road, propping for the turn as we do in Australia. Instantly, the traffic snarled up behind me and the biggest cop I have ever seen blew his whistle and headed on over. I cringed in the seat, paralyzed, not knowing which way to go. A large head was thrust through my window.

'Lady, where in the hell do you think you are?'

'Australia,' I croaked. He held up an arm and cleared me a way out.

'Waal, ma'am, THIS is California!' he yelled disgustedly.

The months passed and my tummy grew enormous as I felt life stir inside. I knew very little about pregnancy and birth but Mom had taught me basic nutrition and I was determined to give my baby the best chance. I had been dieting for years but now I ate everything in sight that I deemed healthy. I refused to take pills for headaches and even had my tooth filled without anesthetic. The drill hammered my brains but it was worth it. Dental drills have always been hard for me. My ears are very sensitive, even to the point of being able to hear the high-pitched alarms in stores used to identify shoplifters.

I was nervous as the weeks went by and called on Thom's mom, Helen, in Connecticut. I figured after ten kids she should know a thing or two.

'There's nothing to it,' she assured me.

I felt marginally better after this blithe statement. All this time I had heard nothing from my management in New York. From being one of their daily cares and concerns it was as if I had dropped right off the planet. The Australian press hadn't forgotten about us, though. Back home, reporters claiming to be friends of mine were still pumping my dad for any information about me. One day I opened the door of our house in Huntington Beach to a guy introducing himself as an 'old friend of your father's' who was 'just passing though' and clearly hoped to be invited in. They were relentless.

We talked about Thom's children by his first marriage. He hadn't seen them in some months and now that we were settled it seemed right for him to claim some regular time with them and try to build a relationship. They lived fairly close by with their mother and after some negotiations they came to us for a few visits. Thom's little girl, Dale, was then about seven and Tommy was a cute, blonde five-year-old whom we nicknamed Boo. I loved having them around.

Unfortunately their mother was not very interested in cooperating to make the visits smooth, and in the end we felt it was just too hard on them. After a period of tears and heartache we pulled back from their lives and tried to let time do its healing.

My own time approached. Mom and Dad were coming over from Australia to be with me and I couldn't wait for their arrival. I really needed my parents with me. They were as nervous as I was, but they did their best to comfort me and took over the domestic front as I waddled uncomfortably around and saw to the packing of my case for hospital.

At about eleven one night as I lay down I felt a strange sensation – I was in labor! In no time Mom and Thom had inserted me in the car and the three of us were heading for LA to the hospital. Dad stayed at home to hold the fort and pray – he could never stomach hospitals. It was a drive of about forty-five minutes and Thom drove at breakneck speed all the way. Not knowing what to expect I was carrying on with every contraction.

'It's coming, it's coming!' I moaned.

This was not only highly distracting for the driver but, as it turned out, completely inaccurate. It was to be a long, long night. There was a heavy fog on the road and visibility was bad. A cop pulled us over about halfway there and, after taking in the situation, gave us the classic sitcom escort to the hospital, siren screaming.

Once again I was winging it. I had not taken any classes on childbirth – my doctor did not even suggest there was such a thing – so I didn't know what to do or what to expect. I had been to the library and done some reading; that was all. Information and resources for pregnant mothers were not so readily available then and I am amazed now as I look back at my ignorance.

I guess I thought women were supposed to have a natural knowledge of these things, having delivered children for thousands of years without the benefit of childbirth classes. Not my thinking these days! If it had not been for a wonderful nurse at the hospital I don't know what I would have done. She looked at me and my obvious terror, kindly laying her hand on mine.

'Is this your first time, honey?'

I nodded furiously.

'Look, just puff like this when the pain starts.'

She puffed in and out to show me how and checked me as I puffed all through the night while Mom and Thom paced the floor.

Baby was presenting in a posterior position and not coming easily. The doctor showed up after a few very tough hours and told me he was concerned the baby was in distress. I was given something for the pain and dived headlong into blessed oblivion.

Morning dawned and I woke to see a beautiful little boy next to me who looked exactly like my dad, with huge shoulders and a barrel chest, and big blue eyes like his paternal grandmother. It's a funny thing – Thom and I had both decided long before we ever met that 'Shawn' would be the perfect name for a son. So our beautiful boy was named Shawn Thomas, and Thom and I held him and gloated over him with wonder. Our world was changed forever. At just under eight pounds he seemed so tiny to me that I was scared to touch him. Coming from a large family and being a dad already, Thom knew the ropes. When we brought Shawnie home he took on bathing and changing duties until I felt more confident. Brian flew out from New York to be godfather when Shawn was baptized.

Mom and Dad were going to be with us for a few more weeks to lend a hand. Dad also had some business contacts to chase up in Georgia and Thom had some time off work.

'Let's go camping!' suggested my unstoppable husband. 'Let's get some fresh air into this baby's lungs.'

Why not? Shawnie was growing like a weed and had a sunny disposition. Mom would come with us – it was a wonderful idea. Thom rented a camper to slip on the back of our truck and when Shawn was only ten days old we piled everything in and drove to Yosemite.

The fall weather was perfect and the air beautifully clear. Breathtaking scenery surrounded us. I loved being out of doors, just cuddling Shawn and drinking in the beauty all around. From the cliff above the campground a spectacular cascade of water fell in a constant spray of mist and every night the rangers lit a bonfire at the top and tossed it over in a firefall of flames. It was a spectacular sight.

I was still getting the hang of nursing Shawn. He tended to fall asleep when he should be feeding and I had plenty of milk. The tame deer around the camping ground picked up the smell and would follow me around sniffing expectantly. The couple near us warned me about bears too.

'Wrap up all your foodstuffs carefully, honey. Bears can even open a closed car trunk to get at food.'

I listened, wide eyed, and sure enough one night as I stumbled out of my bunk at 2am to feed Shawn, I suddenly heard a snuffling sound outside the camper. I hurriedly warmed some formula and propped it in Shawnie's mouth with a diaper to hold it in place then jumped in behind Thom, holding my breasts hard up against his back.

'What are you doing?' he mumbled sleepily.

'Just wrapping up my foodstuffs.'

That bear would have to go through Thom first to get at me. Next morning as we went outside we saw a food cooler burst open and lying on the bank of the creek behind us, empty contents strewn about.

Back at Huntington Beach the baby was thriving. I had got into the swing of feeding and caring for Shawn, managing the house, being a wife and mother, cashing the checks. I was also slimming down to work weight.

'Call him,' said Thom.

'Do you think?'

'It can't hurt.'

I picked up the phone and put it down. Picked it up and put it down. *Call him. Just call and see. Maybe he's relented by now.* I picked up the phone and called.

'Mitch? It's Diana.'

But Mitch was cold and non-committal. The next season of *Sing Along* was already set in concrete. He had nothing for me.

'No problem, Mitch,' I said, at my most detached and unconcerned.

Silence.

'Why didn't you tell me you were pregnant, maybe I could have helped.'

I glanced across the room and saw my beautiful baby peacefully sucking his thumb in his sleep. I felt a chill.

What did he mean? Why was my baby such a problem?

I slowly hung up the phone. I had always loved and admired Mitch but we did not speak again for a long, long time.

David Tebet from NBC phoned about that time. He congratulated me on the baby and then told me nicely that NBC would be dropping my contract. He said that technically I had broken my contract by appearing without their permission on that television talk show in Sydney when Thom and I flew home to be married.

'Our lawyers saw it as a breach,' he explained regretfully.

I was sad but not very surprised. I hung up the phone with a mental shrug. Another door closed.

Trouble comes in threes, they say. My manager, Mort, was on the phone asking for money. He said I still owed him. Thom weighed in on that conversation. He knew how low a percentage I actually ended up with when I was working for Mort. I was lucky if I walked away with five percent after everyone took their piece of pie. He pointed out in no uncertain terms that I had no intention of paying Mort for the privilege of working for him. Mort dropped it and that was that.

When I got married and fell pregnant they all considered I had walked out forever. I didn't see it that way but to them I had thrown it back in their faces. They wrote me off. It took a while for that to sink in. I knew they were sore but I thought a little time would mend fences and gradually we'd look for other opportunities. Not so. My management team clearly wanted to be rid of me, so I obliged. My contracts were terminated and I gave up any further idea of show business.

But I needed to do something. I needed mental stimulation and purpose – other than changing diapers – and decided returning to school might be the answer. I enrolled at Orange Coast College to study a psychology course and went along for a while, really liking the health classes the best and the interaction with the other students. However managing school and baby all at once turned out to be harder than I'd thought so regretfully I opted to give up higher education for the time being. It would be a long, long time before I went back.

Thom was doing very well at the brewery and we were asked to move to San Diego for him to take a higher position. It was a good financial move but once again Thom was away traveling a lot. This left me at home by myself with the baby and I began feeling lonely and isolated. I'm not a good 'alone' person and it was a long rough week without Thom. Shawn was just beginning to crawl and he was beautiful and kept me 'busy', yet in another sense I didn't know what to do with myself and couldn't see what I was achieving.

It's the dilemma all of us working moms face – I loved my family deeply but I missed my work and, yes, I missed the spotlight. The sudden stop from rehearsing, performing and touring was hard to take. I worried about my voice too – I didn't want it deteriorating through lack of use. At the same time I knew I wanted to have another child, and as soon as we moved to San Diego we started trying for another little one. A little brother or sister for Shawn would be perfect. New dreams had taken precedence over old for the moment.

San Diego was growing on me with its beautiful beaches and pleasant surroundings, and the warm climate was great for Thom's health. Our 'six months' had stretched out but his prognosis was still hanging over us. Weekends were so happy when Thom came home and we were together. We lived in a tract house – a subdivision – on the top of the rolling hills that surround the area. Thom worried about me during the week when he was away so we went along to the dog pound where we found a beautiful black Belgian Shepherd. He was ours immediately and took over the job of guarding Shawn in an instant. He was so intelligent and we named him 'Aussie'.

Mom had raised us to have dogs outside and much to Aussie's chagrin, he was put firmly out the door at night. That was until we had a prowler. I was alone in the house one night and Aussie was barking like mad out the back. I fetched him inside, afraid he would wake everyone up. He patrolled the house, deaf to my requests about where he was and wasn't allowed to go, and finally settled at the foot of the bed. He was too big to argue with so there he stayed. Three nights later I heard a prowler in the back yard as he ran into the washing I had on the line. Aussie curled his lip and posted himself near the door. I went back to bed feeling quite secure. I would not have liked to run into Aussie in a bad mood, even in the daylight.

Jack Ayling rang me out of the blue. He was a friend from Australia who wrote for a television guide there. He wanted to do a follow up on me and interview other stars as well while in the States.

'Come and stay with us, Jack,' I urged and was so happy to see him when he arrived. I still experienced feelings of homesickness from time to time and any friend from Australia was welcome. We showed him around San Diego and caught up on all the news from home. It wasn't long before I confided to Jack how I was feeling.

'I feel so let down,' I told him. 'My management's gone, my exposure's gone. It's like Diana Trask was never here. Show business was my focus for so long and now I'm left right out of the mainstream.'

'Why don't you come back to Australia and perform there?' Jack encouraged. 'I think you'll find there's a demand. I'm sure you'd do well.'

'I don't have any management, remember?'

'Thom could give it a try.'

This was a new idea. I'd left home to make a career in America. I hadn't contemplated returning to Australia to revive it. Thom and I mulled it over. Jack Ayling knew television in Australia. He could see there was a gap to be filled where performers who had left and made it big overseas could be brought back to perform in the country of their birth – he felt there was story to be told.

Thom's health was still a concern and financially he was doing so well with Anheuser-Busch – better than I had performed as a corporate wife anyhow. I'd been called nicely onto the carpet by the senior executive's wife and talked to because I'd ordered the opposition's beer at a function and had favored the wrong horse at the races. I needed to toe the line! Try as I might, my heart was not in it and the old resentment of being restricted bubbled underneath. Thom knew I was struggling and was prepared to give it all up for me, to make me happy.

We called Mom and Dad. Did they think it was a good idea to come back to Australia? How was Dad? What should we do? They said Thom's health came first and they would love us to come home. After talking around and around the issues for weeks we made the decision.

Thom resigned from his job, resisting great offers from the company to stay. We did have cause to regret this later, especially when things got tough, but for now Australia was our goal. We packed up the house, found a new home for Aussie aboard a tuna fishing boat with an old seafarer who loved him immediately, and headed for Australia. It was November 1963 and I was about three months into my second pregnancy.

Once again we faced a press barrage but this time they showed a little more respect. Our plan was to stay with Mom and Dad for a while, find employment for Thom and somewhere to live ready for the arrival of baby number two. When we were settled and I was back in shape we would tackle the show business possibilities. Thom began the search but no doors opened for him easily. It seems people still remembered us as the 'Battling Ewens' and Thom, the vanquisher. We started to wonder if we had made a big mistake. Thom picked up some odd jobs but we were still with my parents as the baby's due date grew closer. We were fast asleep one morning when Mom woke us up, pounding up the stairs.

'The president had been shot!' she said in an alarmed voice.

We sprang out of bed and turned on the television. We agonized through the day like so many others and prayed for his survival but the news came through that he was dead. It was a terrible time. People were so shocked – it was impossible to take it in. When Vice President Johnson was quickly sworn in as president I thought of my time at his ranch in Austin, Texas and prayed for him.

Living at home was hard on us after being accustomed to our husband and wife time so we bought an old Volkswagen camper and took off on the weekends. The old camper did not have a strong engine and if we traveled into the wind it could only crank up to about fifteen miles an hour. We loved our freedom though and had a wonderful time exploring national parks and other beauty spots.

One memorable visit was to Cowes on Phillip Island, just southeast of Melbourne, to see the fairy penguins come in from the sea to their nests on the shore. A whole visitor program has been established now with specific observation points, but in those days the access to the beach was unrestricted. One spotlight lit up a section of the shore as the little birds landed. We arrived late on the headland, parking haphazardly where we could, and walked through the dune grasses to the beach, picking our way by torchlight. It was pitch black and even with our torch we almost tripped a couple of times as fat babies stood at the edge of their burrows mewing loudly as they tried to steer their parents to the nest. Other watchers were scattered around the dunes too, flashlights waiting for the nightly 'penguin parade'.

Suddenly out of the water popped a tiny figure dressed like a maître'd which shook itself and waddled up the beach. Soon, hundreds of penguins were making their way towards their chirping babies. Shawn was enchanted. We trod carefully back through the night, passing noisily reunited families on either side. By the next morning the parents were gone, headed back out to sea, and the babies were curled up in their burrows.

We rented a rustic house in Doncaster, an eastern suburb of Melbourne, with a couple of rambling acres around it. The house was timber and would be very cold in the Melbourne winter, so we installed gas heating in the main areas and reworked a lot of the house to make it useable for us. We felled some pine trees – Thom was impressed that I knew how – and bought goats to clear the wild blackberries that tumbled all over.

The oldest goat, Matilda, was very cantankerous as only goats can be and succeeded in head-butting me several times. Hanging the washing was now a dangerous sport as Matilda liked to trap you on the back porch. We gave her away after she pinned Shawn down in a ditch in an attempt to butt him. He was just a tot and when I saw she was after him I waddled screaming towards them. I grabbed that old goat by the horns as it turned on me and was sidestepping at quite a rate as she tried to get at me. I was as mad as fire but suddenly not afraid of being butted anymore.

An incident with a magpie terrified me, though. It happened when our second baby was a few months old. I had put him on a blanket in the shade near the verandah, safely (as I thought) in the play pen. I was nearby doing chores of some kind. Something made me look up and there on the side of the play pen was a huge magpie looking intently at my little one. Into my mind flashed stories Mom had told me about crows and magpies taking out the eyes of lambs. That bird was so close to my little lamb!

The bird looked at the baby, up at me, and back at the baby.

'Don't you go near that baby!' I threatened, starting towards them. The bird took off and lazily flapped up into a tree. I had nightmares about that for years afterwards and still think with dread of what might have happened.

Being a second-time-mom had in no way calmed my fears about the impending birth. Shawn's delivery had been tough and I wasn't looking forward to a repeat. I had selected a doctor and on the very first visit he saw straight through my carefully constructed bravado and treated me like any other anxious pregnant woman.

The pregnancy was fine until the end. Like Shawn, Baby just did not want to arrive and I felt like I was in slow labor for weeks. My sister-in-law delivered her third little daughter very quickly a few weeks before me and I was wishing my delivery would soon be over too. I 'ooh-ed' and 'aah-ed' over Samantha, my new little niece, and hoped I too would have a girl. I sometimes babysat my other two nieces, Melanie and Lisa, and loved the little girls so much.

Our second son, Patrick Joseph, arrived in Melbourne on the 7th of May 1964, two weeks late by my count. My family was overjoyed, all except Dad who reckoned I ought to stop having babies so fast. The delivery was once again a very hard posterior presentation but at least I was awake and Thom was with me. Wishing for a girl went away as soon as I saw Patrick's tiny face. He looked like a little prune.

We had a big baptism and party, and my dear granny stuffed ten shillings in Patrick's diaper as she held him in the rocking chair. Our baby was a dear little guy with large, soft, brown eyes like his dad. My grandmother died shortly after but not before rocking her latest grandchild again on her sickbed.

We bought another dog, a German Shepherd we named Judy Garland Van Ness Ewen – what a handle. I was beginning to practice vocalizing again and Judy would sit outside the bathroom door and howl her little heart out – not sure if that was applause or the other. She loved Shawn and watched him devotedly in the yard as he played. One day I caught them both going out the gate onto the road. I grabbed Judy and shook her, telling her not to let the baby onto the road. She got the message.

A few days later I watched through the window as Shawn once more headed for the gate. Judy grabbed his rompers and threw him on the ground. Shawn got up and tried for the gate again. Judy threw him on the ground. Now Shawn was furious and as he tried his luck a third time, only to be thwarted by the faithful Judy, he reached over and bit that dog on the neck with all his might. Poor Judy howled and leapt back to a safe distance but still she placed herself between Shawn and the gate. It was a case of Boy Wins the Battle but Loses the War.

We both wanted to give show business another go and with his characteristic energy and drive, Thom now undertook to manage my career himself. I got back into shape fairly quickly, physically and vocally, and Thom cast around for opportunities. He set up a meeting with Colin

Bednall, the boss at television station GTV 9 in Melbourne, whom I knew from my time early on with the show *In Melbourne Tonight*.

While this was in the pipeline, I was delighted to be asked to open the very first transmission of a new television station in Australia in August 1964 – ATV0, or Channel Ten as it became known. The station was launched with a variety show called *This Is It* and I sang a version of 'Hey Look Me Over', the lyrics altered to suit the occasion.

The meeting with Mr. Bednall of GTV9 took place. He was open to suggestions and Thom proceeded to sell him his idea.

'*The Di Trask Show*. Musical numbers, a dance troupe, Diana as host,' suggested Thom.

After a bit of to and fro they agreed on the general concept and terms. Colin Bednall could suggest no-one who could produce something along the lines Thom was describing so Thom said he would be producer. Brian Phillis was brought in as director. I would be the host and cover the music which would be overdubbed. Taping would be done on Sundays as that was the only day the Channel 9 studios were free.

Mr. Bednall agreed to a budget and a pilot and we nervously put our best foot forward. While tending to the boys and the house I now had a head full of plans and schemes for *The Di Trask Show*. I had learned a lot from Mitch – now was the time to put it into practice as I planned the musical side of the show.

I had seen *The Dinah Shore Show* and had observed the way her warm personality worked upon guests and audiences alike. She came down the camera to her audience with such friendliness and I admired the way she handled segues from one musical number to another. She had great poise and this was the kind of style I tried to emulate but I think she won hands down. Years later I would appear on her talk show and I took the opportunity to tell her how I had taken her for a role model at that time.

A choreographer was hired for the pilot and he enthusiastically created an ambitious opening dance for me that began at GTV 9's front door and continued all the way back to the studio ... *hmm, I don't think so.* Recalling my dancing efforts on *Sing Along*, I hastily put an end to that little dream. I would be fine during rehearsal but get a camera on me and that would be that.

I turned to the 'Steel Box' theory I'd learned from Mitch, carefully choosing the material and aiming for the best sound possible. We used the whole studio for the sets, the Channel 9 band played, the lighting guy worked miracles. We began with a splash, featuring a group of Australian Army men marching to *Sound Off*.

The pilot aired in 1965 and we held our breaths for the reaction. It was good! The show was picked up and we were set to do the series. We celebrated with a big party at our house, inviting all the crowd from GTV 9. Australian entertainment legends Bert Newton and Patti McGrath were among the guests – their first date, they told me. In no time they fell in love and were later married.

The Di Trask Show was hailed as being fresh and imaginative as we stretched our budget to the max with our Sunday crew, going for the best television we could muster. Lots of stars were born on that show. Our director Brian Phillis went on to be the lead cameraman on *The Red Skelton Show* and one of our floor cable guys, Peter Faiman, also won fame in later years as director of the movie *Crocodile Dundee*. We showcased the talents of many Australian greats and up-and-coming greats, including Johnny Farnham, who later became the top male singer in Australia with a magical voice and a sweet personality.

Our closer was an all-Irish show with live sheep and goats on-set – right up Thom's alley, as he is a pure Irishman. It fairly rollicked along and I felt so proud of what we had achieved. Thom and I crossed our fingers that we would go on to do another series.

It was the first time Thom and I had worked together as partners and I admired the way he plunged so confidently into this completely new industry. I briefly deluded myself that I was at last in the driver's seat, remembering the many times in the US I'd had to bite my tongue and conform. Driver's seat? I don't think so. I still had a producer telling me what to do! Thom didn't back off from telling me what he thought. He was one hundred percent truthful and didn't hesitate – *do this, don't do that*. Still, I appreciated it – it's not always possible for a performer to judge how things look from the front. He would be up in the control room during taping, keeping an eagle eye on everything. He really relished being in control of our destiny. Whatever the outcome, we were out there having a go.

At series end we took a break and visited the Great Barrier Reef and the islands of the Whitsunday Passage while the boys stayed with my parents. Thom and I enjoyed an idyllic holiday swimming and snorkeling the closer reefs. Strange and beautiful creatures abounded, dangerous sharks and deep, multicolored coral canyons alive with sea life. We swam in T-shirts to protect us from small stinging coral spawns in the water. I was always the last to come out.

We met a happy crowd, amongst them Deidre and Doc O' Dowd and Keith and Colleen Plant, and we remained friends with them all. Too soon our holiday ended and we returned to Melbourne to find out that for budgetary reasons *The Di Trask Show* was not to be picked up for a second run. The program had sold all around Australia and in that sense was a success, but in the mid Sixties Australian television was still in its infancy. Perhaps the program was a little ambitious for that time. We had been strictly monitored budget-wise and although most weeks came in under budget there was not a big enough market, sponsors were few and production companies fewer.

We took the news as philosophically as possible. At least we had tried. GTV 9 did offer me some work in another capacity but Thom and I had decided that we wanted to work together. We loved living in Australia but there seemed to be a limited future for us there. We considered going out on the land and even sent enquiries to a land dealer in the north. On asking about the rainfall he replied that they got very little.

'Remember when Noah built that ark and it rained a lot?' he wrote back. 'Well, we got about an inch and a half in that deal,' he joked.

It seemed inevitable that we would return to the US. Having learned the ropes in Australia, Thom felt ready to try his hand as my manager in the States. It was a gamble, but after nearly three years trying to make it in Australia the decision was made.

It seemed a cock-eyed thing to do with a toddler and an active three-year-old to manage, but we decided to travel back to the States by sea. We took the P&O liner *Canberra* with stopovers at New Zealand and Rarotonga on the way to Hawaii and Vancouver and finally Los Angeles – about a three-week voyage.

At fourteen months, Paddy was just toddling and had a penchant to vanish if you took your eyes off him. All the workmen on the ship were Indian and called him 'Little Sahib'. One day he wandered out of my range and I couldn't find him anywhere. I was in a flat panic, imagining him overboard and food for sharks as I ran full tilt along the deck. Within a couple of minutes I found him safe and sound but covered with white paint. He was surrounded by a group of laughing workmen who told me that Little Sahib was only trying to help them paint.

We dropped anchor outside the harbor at Rarotonga as the ship was too big to enter. Locals paddled out to greet us wearing their grass skirts – men, women and children. They were welcomed aboard and were to sing and dance for us in the main salon. The kids were all sitting cross-legged in the front watching the show when I saw a little island boy plop down beside Paddy. From somewhere underneath his grass skirt he carefully hauled out a package of Wrigley's chewing gum and offered a stick to Paddy. In the international language of children Paddy just accepted the gum and chewed away happily, not at all phased at being approached by a child of a different nationality or, indeed, one dressed in a grass skirt. Later the troupe clambered aboard their canoes and paddled back to their island, singing happy island songs as they went.

The trip was long and sometimes very boring and when we at last arrived in Hawaii we went straight to McDonald's and ordered six Big Macs and three milkshakes. Thom's main complaint about the food in Australia at that time was that there were no American hamburgers. He had maintained a one-man search for a decent hamburger there and had been known to drive forty miles out of the way if he saw American hamburgers advertised anywhere.

As we were nearing Vancouver, measles broke out amongst the children aboard. We watched our kids closely and I suspected that

Patrick was sickening, but we needed to get to Los Angeles so, to avoid any possible quarantine hassles, we disembarked without mentioning anything and drove fast. Paddy began a fever the night we arrived in LA and sure enough next day he was covered with spots and a little later Shawn was too. We kept them in a darkened room and nursed them for a week or so.

Thom cast around the agencies in LA but without any luck. Finally we decided to return to the East coast to Connecticut, his home state, to start all over again. We bought a camper and piled the kids in and drove across the country once more, this time traveling the southern route. Money was tight and Thom – ever resourceful – hired on to a sign company in LA before we left, selling signs along the way.

The trip was beautiful once again, the deserts and canyons reflecting the changing colors of the sun from sunrise through sunset. Traveling across the country in this way was an entirely different experience to working and traveling when all I saw was the inside of smoky clubs, hotels and airports. We stopped in Las Vegas. It was the first time I'd been here and tears sprang unexpectedly to my eyes as the city appeared out of the desert darkness, ablaze with lights. I didn't know it then, but the lights of Las Vegas would become very familiar in just a few short years.

When we reached Connecticut we bunked in for a while with Thom's favorite sister, Dutchie. She was wonderful to us and I hoped I could repay the family one day. We had discussed our future during the long miles driving across the country and had both decided that the music business still held the best shot for us. We wondered if we could possibly resuscitate my career again in New York.

Four years had passed since my time on the Mitch Miller show and my name was cold as ice – things change fast in the Big Apple – but Thom was determined to try. Through his brother, he got a job driving trucks by night and by day he donned a suit and pounded the agencies. He was exhausted most of the time and weight just fell off him. I worried constantly but he was always upbeat and positive.

It was the late sixties and the music field was changing drastically every day. I was out of the mainstream and it became apparent that I would have to reinvent myself in some way if there was to be any chance of getting back in. The options coming from the agencies seemed to be soft rock or blue-eyed soul, but I could not see myself pursuing either. Thom put his thinking hat on while we began a few gigs like cruise ships and small time venues. We rented a beautiful little house near a lake upstate. While the kids napped and Thom was working I taught myself the guitar and tried my hand at writing songs. I wrote little songs for the kids and simple songs about life, and one special song about Thom called 'Little Bit'.

Things were in turmoil in the US. The civil rights movement was at its height and Martin Luther King was a prime figure on the news. Riots broke out in California and Detroit and people were scared. The only African American people I knew were entertainers and I had admired their knowledge and skill greatly as many a night I had stood in the wings and watched these pro entertainers tear up the house. The average African American was a bit of a mystery to me though as they were rarely seen on simple things like toothpaste ads. Serious change was on the way and good people of both colors who died in the fray were paying the price.

One day Thom returned home from his truck-driving shift. Through his tiredness I sensed a new intention in him.

'Here, listen to this,' he said, sitting me down and switching on the radio.

He tuned it to a music station playing hard country and I thought it was possibly the worst music I had ever heard. Thom had picked it up on the truck radio while out driving.

'What do you think, darlin'?' he asked me. The hillbilly twang dinned in my ears.

'It's horrible.'

'Not all of it. Listen some more.'

I got that he was trying to tell me something else and tried again. Over the next few days I listened carefully, particularly to the lyrics. I could feel certain artists move me and I could see the music was simple and from the heart. I thought of my attempts at song writing, my 'simple songs', my song for Thom written from the heart.

'You could sing country, Di,' Thom said earnestly.

In trying to resurrect my career, Thom had spoken at length and persistently with many agents in New York, especially one named Bobby Brenner. Bobby had contacts in Nashville. I had read about The South and Nashville. I remembered seeing Chet Atkins play at Tidelands and how his country style 'show' had left me cold. But I knew nothing of how life really was there.

Bobby Brenner gave Thom a name and a contact in Nashville and life was about to change for us again. In spite of Thom's confidence in me, I had no idea if I could sing country music. To me it was all pure Americana but I was willing to give it a go. Once again we packed up the babies and the dog in our old camper and took to the road. This time we turned south towards Nashville, Tennessee.

NINE

Climb Every Mountain

As we drifted south, the scenery changed and softened. It was early fall and the road was barred with the flying shadows of huge old trees as we passed. There was no interstate all the way in those days, just the 'country roads' John Denver was later to sing about so eloquently. This was 1967 and we listened to country music on the radio as we passed through the Shenandoah Valley and ran down along the Smoky Mountains.

I had learned the history of the American Revolution when I attended Orange County College for that brief time in California, but it was not the same history story I had learned in the more British-oriented schools in Australia. In those books the American revolutionaries were regarded as upstarts and criminals, not the brave stouthearted men of Virginia and Kentucky. Strange how history changes depending on who is wielding the pen. I had also read that the Appalachias were home to immigrants from Ireland and Scotland much like the immigrants of Australia. I had heard that quilt patterns were preserved in Latin and faithfully reproduced by the women who lived in these mountains. As I listened to hard country and bluegrass music, I could recognize links to the old Irish and Scottish music I had heard in Australia as a child.

Our arrival in Nashville wasn't very promising. We were almost there when the truck started overheating. Thom pulled over. Steam was pouring out from under the hood and Thom lifted it up and gave the radiator top a tiny turn. Instantly boiling steam poured out, scalding his arm and face. I screamed and dived for ice from our camper refrigerator and then drove us back towards a hospital sign I had seen a few minutes earlier. I found the Lebanon hospital – just eight miles from where we would eventually live – and Thom was treated for the burn. We spent a few days in a motel quietly nursing him through the pain.

Nashville itself was a slight disappointment. It wasn't a pretty city then but rather a collection of buildings stuck on a rise. It is well situated though, with the Columbia River flowing at its foot. Folks were genteel and I felt at home with the Southern manners reminiscent of my Australian upbringing. I loved the scents and the accent, punctuated with lots of characteristic *y'all* and *come back and see me, y'hear*? Given the racial tensions of the time, the city seemed balanced and secure and I noticed none of the strains we had felt in Connecticut. The town seemed sleepy and soaked in tradition and I felt safe there.

We were to meet with Bob Neal, a country booking agent who operated with his son, Sonny, and his wife who worked the front desk. The family was so charming and gentle – it was a huge change from the push and shove I had faced in New York and Hollywood.

Bob took us on and arranged for us to meet with Buddy Killen, a young mogul of the country music publishing and recording scene. He and his partners ran Tree Music and it had been Buddy's good fortune to discover Roger Miller and his magic pen. They were doing very well and didn't need me but consented to meet and talk.

Thom and I walked into Tree Music to meet a young, tall, good-looking man with an inquisitive attitude and a deep Southern accent – Buddy's partner, Jack Stapp. Jack was an impeccably groomed man and gave the impression of being the brains of the outfit. The whole time I knew Jack I don't think I ever saw a hair out of place.

Tree Music was housed in a rambling building on the famous Music Row and many writers, known and unknown, hung around the back in their mini recording studio. The front office buzzed with activity as singers and writers rubbed shoulders with their latest efforts, all honing their skills. The Grand Ole Opry was mentioned often – *What was that?* I wondered – and various recording studios where the greats were recording right then. I immediately felt that exciting things were happening here and sensed it would be good to be part of it.

Buddy asked to hear what I had written and I shyly hauled out my little songs, one of which he liked – my song about Thom, 'Little Bit'. He agreed to seek a label that would be interested in me and told me he would get material together for a single. We were thrilled but at the same time I was still really intimidated by the genre. I needed to hear, see and learn a whole lot more.

During our first week in Nashville we were invited to attend the mysterious Grand Ole Opry and that's where my real initiation into country happened. I learned that it was a long-running radio show and landmark venue. We approached the stately red-brick building and were amazed to see the hundreds of people queuing to get in. We paid at the little ticket booth in the front of the theatre and as I peeked inside, the ticket-taker was surrounded with stacks of crinkled one-dollar bills.

Inside, the house was buzzing. The audience was packed in the lower floor and overhead in a large balcony. Our seats were down front and we inched along the row of hard wooden benches, much like church pews. The stage was dressed as a barnyard scene, a few musicians wandered around. A man loped casually onto the set and picked up a fiddle, cradled it. It was Roy Acuff and the audience let loose their approval in a yell that raised the roof. His band melted on stage and they launched straight into 'The Wabash Cannonball'. Imperceptibly the show had started.

Roy was the host of the show, which was broadcast live, and stars appeared for one or two numbers with the bands changing in the background, depending who was on. I saw there was a basic core of musicians, but lead men and singers strolled on and off with no particular fuss and it all seemed incredibly laid back and casual.

I sat entranced as backup people, children and families sat around the stage, all seeming to obey some unseen stage director. The musicians were often family groups like the Osborne Brothers singing 'Rubeee, Oh Ruby'. Archie Campbell killed the house with 'Big Red', a song about an 'ornery' rooster, and smiles were plastered on our faces. The audience was extremely enthusiastic and supportive of the artists. It crossed my mind that if I was to be in show business at all this was a wonderful atmosphere to bring kids into.

I fell in love with the steel guitar and the bluegrass banjo that night. Flatt and Scruggs toned through their numbers and I had never seen or heard such close harmonies and pickin'. Fingers flew over instruments with careless brilliance and it was not until later that I noticed that there was not a real drum set anywhere to be seen. The whole evening had been acoustic with no lack of toe tapping and percussion. The concert ended with the fans going wild. Thom and I looked at each other. This was truly great; we had made the right decision coming here. 'Country Roads' had indeed brought us home.

It was October and we attended the Country Music Deejay Fan Festival. Fans and deejays came from all over the country and there were constant showcases, crowds and events for three or four days. We sat up high in the bleachers of the auditorium as awards were handed out for top songs and the stars made it their business to be very present. There was nonstop entertainment: Ernest Tubb, Loretta Lynn, Faron Young, Porter Waggoner and a young Dolly Parton in her extreme costumes to mention just a few. Record companies jockeyed for their stars, and stars jockeyed for songs; fans jockeyed to meet the stars and it was all very exciting. Most of all, I felt the music was real and honest and indeed music from the heart of America.

We rented a little house in Mt. Juliet and commuted the twenty minutes to Nashville. Big, soft oak and black walnut trees surrounded us and I had a little garden that I tended lovingly when I had time. Fall colors quilted the countryside and the lightning bugs I'd had grown to love found spots to hide for the coming winter.

Buddy found a recording company to put down our first session and we went in with four songs, one of which was 'Little Bit'. Sonny Neal thought it was a hit even before we recorded but I was very nervous. I knew I didn't really understand the finer points of country yet.

When we were finished, I took home the tracks and listened to them over and over. My instinct told me it just wasn't right. I sounded like a parody of the real thing, not hitting the mark at all. The more I listened the worse I felt. In tears I finally called Buddy and begged him to hold the tapes. He listened in silence.

'What's the problem?' he asked.

'I sound so phony,' I sobbed. 'I don't want to sound like that.'

'Tell you what, I'll listen again. I'll let you know.'

I hung up, trembling. I did not want to come across as a fake with my first attempt at this pure, true sound. The music demanded more and I demanded it of myself. It *had* to be right. Buddy *couldn't* release the single as it was. I walked the floor until he called back.

'Okay, Di, let's do this,' he said. 'Come on down to the studio and work with the songwriters and sing their demos for awhile 'til you get comfortable and we'll try again later.'

Thank you, Lord. Now I was a demo singer for Tree International. Now maybe I could get the feel of what I was meant to be doing.

I hung a round the studio most days and sang anything that was thrown at me. Tom Casassa was the engineer at Tree and we became good friends. Later, in July of 1969, we would all sit on the floor at his house with our combined kids to watch Neil Armstrong walk on the moon, an amazing event. With Tom C.'s help I tried hard to absorb the nuances of the country style, like learning to bend the notes, but it was difficult. I likened this process to my early days when I spent hours analyzing jazz and how the best singers worked their material. In both styles there was a similar kind of freedom within the parameters of the sound.

I studied George Jones (a hero), Willie Nelson, Johnny Cash, Waylon Jennings – they were all so good at it. There were not too many girls singers that I really liked. They seemed very nasal to me except for Dolly, whose voice had a sweet, pure quality, and Patsy Cline, who was a powerhouse. She had passed on before I got to Nashville but she was still remembered and loved by the community.

The Neal Agency started me out doing country gigs. Oh boy, what a shock! This was definitely learning the country business from the ground up. We assembled a band when and where we could and Thom and I traveled The South most weekends. I was restricted to singing songs the band members knew, as rehearsal generally was not an option, so I glued myself to the radio and learned all the standards.

Audiences accepted me well enough but they weren't knocked out either. I knew I could do better and my ambition centered on having my own band. From that base I'd be able to sing the songs that showcased my voice best and ultimately produce a better show.

After about six months in the back room, Buddy decided to try recording me again. I was in a much better place now and eager to give it a try. We searched the catalog for an oldie but a goodie, and he came up with a Roger Miller song called 'Lock, Stock and Teardrops'. I sang it over and over around the house until even little Paddy was word perfect. Recording day came and my nerves were jumping. I so needed this to turn out well.

I'd traveled a long way to arrive at this point. Musically it was a complete departure from my beginnings in Australia, the jazz I'd loved, and the *Sing Along* era in the States. Geographically I'd covered thousands of miles traveling, touring and searching for work both before and after marriage. Personally I'd climbed some mountains and stumbled along my share of rocky paths. Here in Nashville, Thom and I had found home, friends and fresh air, and I'd been offered a second chance at making it in the fickle world of entertainment. We recorded the song. Buddy was pleased. I was cautiously hopeful.

It was 1968 and meantime the boys were growing and thriving and had commenced at kindergarten and pre-school. It was getting close to spring one day when Shawn was in a petulant mood. He announced loudly that he was running away. I stayed calm and held my breath.

'Okay, there's the door, go on,' I said and watched him march out of the kitchen onto the back porch.

When he reached the patio he slowed down and stopped at the edge, gazing out over the fields. Tall grass rose higher than his head and the fields rolled out towards the woods in back. He scuffed his boots on the concrete a while and then marched back into the kitchen.

'I'm running away right after lunch,' he proclaimed. Oh me, just like a man.

Thom and I took off for a tour of US military bases in Germany right after the recording session and we didn't learn what happened with the song until we called Nashville a few weeks later. 'Lock, Stock and Teardrops' was a hit and I was number 33 on the charts of the top 100 country hits! I was on cloud nine as Thom and I hugged each other and shed a tear. I was on the charts! Maybe all the hard work really was going to pay off.

It was on that tour of Germany one night that I struck a very tough audience. The troops were mostly young men between eighteen and twenty, all shipping out for Vietnam the next day. They were in a scared, noisy mood and to make things worse the opening act, a comic, had not shown up. The booker was backstage wringing his hands when, on the spur of the moment, I volunteered Thom as a fill in. Thom has always been the jokester, teasing and making everyone laugh, so I thought this would be a good fit. I also thought that maybe if he had a taste of the stage he would not take it all so lightly.

I walked casually up to him. 'Hey, babe, the comic didn't show so I volunteered your services. Do twenty minutes, will ya?' His mouth fell open.

'What! What am I going to say, I have no act!' he blurted.

'Oh, just tell a few of those jokes that make everyone laugh,' I returned.

'But ... but.'

'Too late, you're on,' I chuckled.

I watched him for a little while as he warmed them up with a Don Rickles impersonation and a few stories. They were laughing and in a good mood as I took the stage. They had loved him. Thom retired to the back of the room and, as the story goes, the booker sidled up to him with an offer for the next weekend.

'How about coming back? I don't care for the girl singer but I really like you.'

Serves me right. That was the last time I booked Thom.

Now that we were on the charts, we worked to put together a band. We signed up an experienced lead man called Charlie Harris, who had worked on the road with Ray Price, and he brought three other guys along to form the group: Dave Owens on bass, drummer Bob Collins and Jack Watkins playing steel guitar. Charlie was a fantastic singer in his own right and often received a standing ovation even before I set foot onstage. The guys were great and we called ourselves Diana Trask and the V.I.P.s.

We went on the road playing the honky tonk circuit, country dancehalls and the 'Buckets of Blood' as they were called – very rough venues where the patrons were not afraid of throwing things like beer bottles at the entertainers. I was amazed when I saw the couples take to the floor in the dance halls. In tall hats, cowboy boots and tight pants they would slide along with their heads close together and their butts a mile apart in strange V-shaped formations. Sometimes I felt like I was on a different planet.

We traveled the country in cars and other setups, even a stretch limo at one stage, but finally Thom and I opted to travel apart from the guys in a small camper while they took the limo. At least this way I could prepare some homemade food every so often as the food at truck stops and country cafes wore thin pretty fast. The miles were long and we would be out on the road for a week to ten days at a time, often traveling long distances between gigs. Later, as the name grew, we would restrict our travel to less than three hundred miles between jobs but at the start it wasn't uncommon to travel five hundred miles a day.

We got word from Australia that my parents were coming over for a visit. It was close to summer here and cold 'down under', so it suited them well and they were bursting to see Paddy and Shawn. We had taken a two-week gig in Halifax, Nova Scotia, and thought we'd show Mom and Dad the real America on the way up to Canada. We rented a trailer that slept six and hitched it to my old Caddy ready to go. Mom and Dad arrived exhausted after their long trip and thought we were joking when we broke the news.

'We're leaving for Nova Scotia tomorrow.'

To their credit they did not turn around and go home but gritted their teeth, did their wash, then loaded up with us once more, although I think Dad did moan and groan a little.

As we traveled north, Dad could not believe what he was seeing. The open country and the ever-changing scenery amazed him. Up until then all he knew of the States was big cities. America was just concrete in his view. At the various stops he would jump out of the car and try to talk to people along the way. They reacted with great hospitality but with his broad Aussie accent they had a hard time understanding him.

'Where's the pub?' he would ask. They would gaze back, sorting it out.

'Where can a man get a snort?' he insisted. Silence or a bemused scratching of heads.

'I'll be glad when we get to Canada and people speak the Queen's bloody English,' he would grumble to us back in the car.

The day came when we crossed the border and made our first stop for gas in Canada. Dad immediately jumped out of the car and bore down on the young kid pumping gas.

'Where's the pub, mate? A man needs a drink.'

The kid mumbled something and walked into the office. I happened to be close on his heels on my way to the ladies' room as he spoke to his boss.

'You better get out here and talk to this guy,' he said. 'These Americans are getting worse and worse – I can't understand a thing that guy said.'

The gig in Canada was, to put it nicely, different. It was a small restaurant-type club and the opening act was a pickpocket. The guy showed how he could get your valuables or wallet out of your pocket in a few seconds, not to mention your watch. My heart dropped when I saw the 'band' – a trombone, a violinist and a snare drummer. How was that supposed to work? I was singing a mix of country and pop and couldn't for the life of me see how I could possibly pull it off.

The owner had a dry cleaning business, was a new promoter, and was constantly complaining that he wanted audience participation. I did not know what to do or how to do it – it was a nightmare. Out of desperation I asked a patron one night to join me onstage and be my backup singer. I teased him along and believe it or not the show went well. I learned a thing or two on that gig: not to be scared to include the audience in the show and to watch my wallet carefully if ever someone bumped into me. One good thing, we got free dry cleaning.

Back in Nashville, Buddy Killen decided to take my sound in a slightly different direction. We had just recorded a song written by Joe Tex called 'Hold On To What You Got'. It was not strictly a country song, more like a soul song, but it was being played on the radio. How would it be received? I was not from the heart of America, I was not singing a strictly country song – what would happen?

That week I was making my first appearance at the Grand Ole Opry with 'Hold On To What You Got' as my debut number. There's nothing like jumping in at the deep end. Right away I caused waves when I asked for a hand mike. In country music no one used a hand mike in those days but I liked the freedom it gave me and knew it would add to my confidence. One of the backup musicians handed me his mike. Roy Acuff introduced me as I stepped out on stage.

'Here's a little girl from Down Under, ladies and gentlemen, and she can sure sing. I am very happy to introduce Miss Diana Trask!'

Thom and the boys were there. I knew Thom would be holding his breath for me, willing it to go well. I took a deep breath and launched in. Roy had stepped to the side, fiddle in hand, facing back at me. As I got to the falsetto part of the song I heard a rumble of applause begin from the audience. I had never heard of an audience applauding in the middle of a song but they just started in and didn't stop. Roy sidled closer and was about a foot away from me in the end, staring into my face like he was mesmerized. The crowd went up and Roy was hooting and hollering. I walked off in a daze.

Usually in gigs like that, the other entertainers mill around backstage killing time and waiting their turn. I remember glancing over to the wings during my number and noticing a lineup all staring at me.

It wasn't long before girl singers dropped their 'stand in one place and sing' routine and were all using hand mikes unless they were playing instruments.

I remember being warmly welcomed to the country music world by Dolly Parton that night. She cut a startling figure with her costumes and curves and her trademark hair, but mostly I was struck by her shining personality and sensed a reflective person underneath with a tender heart.

Following up our hit with 'Hold On', Buddy released an album written by Joe Tex and titled 'Miss Country Soul'. It did well and I was busy with promotional tours. In Baltimore I was slated to talk to a deejay with a great following. As we arrived at the radio station, we noted this was a station that featured soul music.

'I wonder if they're expecting an African American?' I muttered to Thom.

The jock, an African American himself, ushered us into the studio and covered his shock well at my countenance. As the hour went by he warmed to me and I to him. We both relaxed, joking around, and I had a great time.

'You really are Miss Country Soul,' he enthused and the name stuck.

We bought a better camper and painted the logo 'Miss Country Soul' on the side. Imagine my surprise when I heard that Jeannie Seeley, another singer, claimed the name for herself and was thinking about suing me over the right to use it. I was initially upset but soon dismissed it. Let the fans sort out who was the most soulful if that was the question. Soon after the whole name thing just fizzled out anyway.

Time passed. I became friendly with all the top writers at Tree: Bobby Braddock, Curley Putman, Red Lane, all writing furiously as country music was starting to make waves and hits were emerging. The war raged in Vietnam and evening television was terrible as images of wounded soldiers and burned-out villages were beamed into our homes every night. Riots were breaking out in Los Angeles as African Americans sought to find a place for themselves in the American fabric. Rock and roll was still king but folks were growing open to the idea that old-style pop and country could be mixed and give birth to a new crossover sound. I was one of the first singers to carry on where Patsy Cline left off. She was a country singer with a pop feel. I think if she had lived she would have been the biggest star of the times.

Our dates were increasing and we were gaining recognition and popularity with disc jockeys, getting good play throughout the South and West and even some in the eastern states. The most powerful deejay in the South was located in Nashville – Ralph Emery, a cigar chompin' man with a profound knowledge of every star in the business right down to their home telephone numbers.

I have noted that cigar smokers use their cigars in a variety of ways. There is the 'roller and puffer' and the 'chomper and mouth-mover'. George Burns was a 'roller and puffer', using inhalation as a stage wait then moving his cigar to his hands. Ralph Emery was a 'chomper and mouth mover', stowing his cigar on the side of his mouth after a healthy chomp, then asking a question and taking a few puffs as the person answered. His show was aired at night from WSM radio that sat atop a hill in Nashville and he had a huge audience around the country.

I was booked for an interview with Ralph at the station and was treated very nicely by him. Everyone seemed to know each other and the atmosphere was easy as Ralph played the top hits of the day plus the songs of whichever guests were sitting in with him that night. He played my latest record and then, cigar tucked in the corner of his mouth, asked the question:

'Diana, why do you want to be in country music?'

There was a wait. He regarded me coolly as I tried to explain my feelings about family atmosphere and how the soul of the music here had touched me. My previous career stints were well known and there was a tendency for some in the industry to distrust my motives. Was I here just to horn my way in and rip them off? I was a pop singer really, not Western, not from the South, not country. I didn't remind them that I was from so far south – Australia – that it was ridiculous. The question reminded me that I was still to earn my place here.

Following the idea of creating country-pop crossover hits, Buddy thought it would be cool to record my version of the Patsy Cline song 'I Fall To Pieces'. The movers and shakers in the industry saw that country music in fact needed to come out of the country and get into the mainstream where the real music dollars were. The music scene was constantly changing as recording companies tried to expand and the 'western' part of country and western was dropped from the vernacular. Hard country and bluegrass would always have a place but it was hoped a broader audience could be attracted to a modified sound. A separation had begun between hard country, crossover country and bluegrass as a smattering of interest outside Nashville worked on the scene.

I juggled my appearances with being a mom and a wife. Our main problem was babysitters and we begged friends to help take up the slack. The school year was very hard to organize and I longed for help from family but they were in Australia or Connecticut. The kids were with us as much as possible and joined the other children who sat onstage at the Opry.

Thom and I always toured together. We became known as 'Salt and Pepper' – if you see him, you see her. He was kept busy organizing musicians, keeping his ear to the ground for new opportunities, looking for new songs and recording possibilities. He was a networker before the term was even invented.

He came home one night full of news. A package was being put together by a guy called Buddy Lee and there was a chance we could be included. The only downside was we would have to leave the Neal Agency and sign with Buddy. I liked the Neals very much and they had been good to us in so many ways from the time our old camper had first pulled up in Nashville, but as always, change was in the wind.

TEN

Family Tradition

Buddy Lee had come out of the wrestling world. He was an enormous man who seemed to constantly find it hard to breathe – whether this was due to his size or old injuries I never found out. He was the manager of a then very skinny, jumpy young kid called Hank Williams, Jr., son of the legend Hank Williams, Sr. Buddy's plan was to tour with Hank Jr. starring and me closing the opening half of the show.

It was my second year in Nashville and we would have to sign with him and agree to do a free showcase for the visiting bookers that were to attend the upcoming DeeJay Convention. I knew Hank Williams, Sr.'s status in the business – think of hits like 'Your Cheatin' Heart' and 'Hey Good Lookin'' – and I had a feeling the son would do very well too. Thom had good reason to be excited about the prospect of our being part of this new venture.

We rehearsed a program of latest hit covers and performed the show to a packed, smoky house. It was very well received. Buddy Lee was the man behind the scenes and heads nodded together throughout the night as the business was done. We walked away from that showcase with a full year of bookings in hand. The *Hank Williams Jr. Show* was on the road.

It was a very strong lineup. We had The Four Guys to open, a terrific foursome of virile-looking guys with a great sound. The songwriter Merle Kilgore was the emcee – he wrote 'The Ring of Fire' amongst many others – and I closed the first half. We were backed by Hank's fabulous band plus what remained of Hank Sr.'s original band, The Drifting Cowboys. Hank Jr. was a very talented singer and musician. His hands were never idle – some kind of an instrument was always on the go. He was a gifted writer as well, just like his father. There must have been something in the genes or, as it goes in a song he wrote, it was 'just a family tradition''.

Thom and I commenced the tour traveling in Hank's big bus that had been transformed into a luxurious affair with comfortable seating and lighting and sleeping compartments for the band. Everyone was congenial but I was aware of being the only female on board. We stopped at hotels in all the different towns but I had the feeling maybe the guys could not relax with me around all the time and I needed a bit of 'girl space' for myself too.

Next time out, Thom and I took our own snazzed-up camper. Now we could carry the kids with us and have a spot to lounge and relax between sets. Most of us traveled in such a fashion, pulling up beside each other behind the stage or sometimes in the fields and using our conveyances as dressing rooms and retreats from the heat or rain.

Life with the 'Hank Show' was a trip. Summer was coming and it was a constant parade of outdoor venues and county and state fairs. I think I must have been to every town and every fair in the States. The show was certainly doing the business for us, as both Hank and I had records in the charts most of the time. There were many memorable gigs. One was the Frontier Days rodeo in Cheyenne, Wyoming. The arena was huge and featured a pit dug out in the center for photographers and press. American Indians danced to traditional music in beautiful costumes and my favorite event, bull riding, spilled into the ring with its rough and tumble.

At night a portable stage was hauled by tractor into the middle of the riding ring and there we would perform in the glare of huge spotlights. There were no wings in which to stand and wait so I had to walk across the open space in the dark just before I was announced. On opening night I stepped gingerly across the ring, uneventfully as I thought.

'Ladies and gentlemen – here she is with her latest hits, please welcome Miss Country Soul!'

I stepped into the pool of lights, my gorgeous silver lame boots winking and glittering, and there, sure enough, was a big glob of bull droppings firmly glued to my heel. The show goes on. My wardrobe was fairly simple in those days – short skirts and boots in shiny materials. Other girls tended to wear spangled Western-style shirts and pants or, like Dolly, were spangled all over. Heavy glitter was not my thing; I found it uncomfortable to work in but I must say it looked good and was entertaining to see on the other ladies.

I made a vow early on that I would never do a performance or wear any costume on stage that would make my sons or husband uncomfortable. It was important for them and for my own dignity, but I also saw it as part of my responsibility to represent Australia well.

We played that rodeo for a few days and one particular night I was standing near the bullpens with Thom and the kids when we both looked up – where was Patrick? We had both started running when a cowboy grabbed Thom by the arm.

'Take it easy man, look over there.'

He pointed toward the bullpen. There was my six-year-old Paddy. He had slipped through the slatted fence and was patting the head of an enormous bull that slobbered and snorted, pawing the ground. About ten other bulls in the pen towered over Paddy, not really crowding him, but oh so big. Every bull had its head up watching the scene. My heart was in my mouth. The cowboy spoke quietly in Thom's ear.

'Just move slowly. That bull doesn't like people much. Just call to your son in a quiet voice.' Thom took a cautious step forward.

'Son, come on, we have to go,' Thom called, his voice very calm and low.

Patrick looked up and started moving towards us. The bulls parted around him as he came through like a little Moses parting the Red Sea.

'Goodbye, bullies, see you later,' he told them as he headed for the fence and started clambering out.

One leg, one arm ... he was through! My legs were like jelly and as I ran to him I didn't know whether to hug him or tan his bottom. In the end we gave him a good swat on the backside and a good talking to about never leaving us or going off alone. We pointed out how dangerous the bulls were – in fact, our helpful cowboy told us this one was a killer – but I don't think Patrick has ever met an animal that he saw as a threat. The boys were given a lot of free reign at the fairs as security kept a general eye on them and they rode the rides for free. We drilled it into them to stay together and report back to us often. They were especially good after the bull incident.

Hank's musicians were headed up by a family member, Lamar Morris. He was a truly great lead man and I respected all of the players greatly. One day the piano player taught me the number system that is used in Nashville. This enables chords to be played in any key, numbered one through eight. It very cleverly cuts down on arrangements and rehearsals and many a night I have heard the number to my songs called out softly behind me as musicians unfamiliar with my songs numbered their way through, following the lead man.

We were traveling through the heart of the America I had dreamed about as a teenage girl watching television. I was amazed at the good people we came across, their hospitality and their unbelievable skills and talents. The animal shows were wonderful with farmers and their children and wives devotedly brushing and grooming their beloved animals. Children raised sheep, pigs or goats and proudly displayed them before the local judges.

I especially loved the ladies' craft and cooking displays – pies, jams, the largest vegetable contests, quilts and all kinds of food. The fresh corn in Iowa was indescribably delicious, dripping with fresh farm butter. I watched the tractor pulls open-mouthed – the loads were unbelievable. Sometimes horses were used for these demonstrations, their handlers whispering in their ears. Our audiences were large, supportive and enthusiastic. In contrast to the club audiences of New York, I felt a much stronger connection to country music audiences. They knew who you were and followed your music. They let you into their world and felt a part of yours.

Country music in general was a much less cutthroat, more supportive world than the Pop scene I'd been familiar with. A pop star is usually surrounded by people – management and handlers – who prevent the fans from getting any real contact. Not so with country. Audience contact was essential, and the whooping and hollering and applause that would begin in the middle of your song was an uplifting experience for me. I also liked the way country music honored its seniors, and its values overall were more conservative.

We appeared at many types of outdoor venues including the odd racetrack. These were not my favorite as the audience, seated in the stands across the width of the track, felt much too far away from the stage. This particular night a terrible rainstorm hit and the track was reduced to a mud pit in no time. The rain abated towards the end of the show and the crowd pushed forward across the track to get closer and shake our hands.

One fan got more of me than he bargained for. As I reached down with my hand outstretched, my center of gravity shifted and I lost my balance. It was like a slow-motion movie. I was toppling off the stage from six feet up – right towards him! I could hear screaming and sensed the band members rushing towards me. There was nothing I could do to prevent the landing and my admirer ended up flat on his back in deep mud with me sprawled on top of him. The crowd erupted in laughter as I dragged myself out of the mud and squelched off unceremoniously to the camper. I didn't have much sympathy left for him – I needed it for myself – but I bet he didn't forget the incident either.

Sometimes the fans were a little over the top. After a midday show in the summer heat I remember running offstage, soaked to the skin with sweat as usual. I pushed open the camper door, stripping my dripping clothes off as I went through to the little bathroom to get a towel. As I reached the back of the camper I turned round just about nude and got the shock of my life. A woman had followed me inside right to the bathroom and was standing there gawking, autograph book in hand. This was audience contact taken a little too far! I don't know who was more embarrassed. I always locked the door after that.

Hank's performances were getting better and better as he gained confidence and stature. Thom and I got along well with him and he was a good person. The kids loved Hank too – he was kind to them, taking time to talk to them and be interested.

Some months later he took the whole cast to dinner for his twenty-first birthday celebration. That night he inherited a twenty one million dollar fortune from his father's song catalog.

Sometimes our package joined with other road shows and we played a super large venue. On one occasion we joined with 'The Killer', Jerry Lee Lewis, to play a few nights. The show was packed and Hank was pleased as he watched Jerry from the wings, Paddy and Shawn each perched on a knee.

During that gig there was plenty of entertainment backstage too. A 'battle of the bands' was taking place, and I don't mean the musical kind. It was more about which band was the toughest and the strongest – a kind of macho-man thing. Jerry Lee, 'The Killer', was really into it, boasting at every breath how tough his bodyguard was while the guy stood round posing and flexing his muscles. Everyone was getting tired of it as Jerry went on and on and we tried to avoid his dressing room if possible.

Our bass player, Charlie, was a real quiet guy who just stood leaning on his amp listening to the tirade for days, sizing things up. One day as we were all standing round hearing once more how tough the bodyguard was, Charlie just walked right up to the guy and flattened him with one knockout punch. We all fell back as Jerry Lee stood over the unconscious man.

'You are fired, fired, fired!' he screamed over and over.

I was still taking bookings on my own account and would sometimes work with an existing band or headliner. Arthur Godfrey, a well-loved old-timer of radio and television, was one. I worked several times with him in New York and in Reno. He had a personal plane and would fly us to gigs – a step up from the camper. He claimed to have once had a close encounter with an UFO while in that plane. He seemed sincere about the encounter, but who knows?

We appeared at The Nugget in Sparks, Nevada, which is famous for its 'Circus Room' that featured live elephants. My dressing room was right next to the elephants' holding area. I was a little shaken when I realized the alarming bulge coming and going in the toilet wall was Bertha the African elephant leaning her weight against the other side.

As I was standing with the trainer one day, Bertha reached over and grabbed me by the wrist. I have never felt such strength and yet she was gentle. There was no resisting however as she pulled me over towards a cupboard in the corner behind her massive body.

'What do I do?' I babbled at the trainer.

'Just go with her,' he said. 'She wants something sweet. Do you have anything sweet in your bag?' I scrabbled around in the depths. Why is it that you can never find what you want in your bag when you need it? Comb, lipstick, handkerchief ... my fingers closed on a package of chewing gum.

'I have this!' I squeaked.

'Okay, just get it out and give it to her,' he said quietly.

I fumbled the paper wrapping off and finally extracted the gum. She was getting more and more interested as I nervously held it towards her inquiring trunk. She took it daintily but then it dropped to the floor. She shifted around looking for the gum and one huge dinner plate of a foot stepped on it. Up came the foot, Bertha's trunk patiently picked off the gum and placed it in her mouth and she began chewing placidly.

In the meantime she had let me go and I edged to a safe distance (behind the trainer!) from where I watched her, fascinated. She swayed slightly, regarding me with small eyes. I wonder what would have happened if I did not have that gum? The hotel management asked me to ride out sitting on her trunk for the opening of the show. Apparently she would rear up and walk out on her hind legs with some hapless person sitting in the curl of her trunk. So I'd shared my gum with Bertha – that did not make us best buddies. I declined.

Travel arrangements with our own band were causing problems. A couple of times confusion about destination meant that Thom and I would arrive in one town and the band would turn up in a town of the same name but in a different state! One memorable night in Alabama I had to go on alone with no band at all.

'Thom? The band's not here, Thom!'

'Pretend you're singing in the bathroom, darlin'.'

'Perfect.'

That night I sang completely a cappella to a capacity-arena audience. They sat extremely quietly and listened to every syllable. You could have heard the proverbial pin drop. The other artists on the bill were knocked out that I even attempted it. It was amazing but I didn't want to repeat the experience.

'I think we need a bus,' said Thom as we thankfully wrapped up that night.

So Thom went shopping and came home with a used Greyhound bus that we fitted out to suit us. In a short space of time we put together bunks for the band and a separate compartment for me at the back. We had 'Diana Trask and the V.I.P.s' painted on the side.

Now we were a package and joined all the other entertainers out there hauling down the road. Bins underneath were loaded with sound equipment and boxes of recordings we sold at the gigs. We took the lead there from the various gospel groups on the road that had been selling from their buses for years. I had two rules for the bus: no drugs and no bad language.

One very funny bus story sticks in my mind. A new musician, Mickey, was traveling with us and no one had got around to explaining the lever in the restroom. Thom was driving at the time and he noticed a very nice convertible alongside us on the highway. The couple driving had the top back and they were enjoying the beautiful day. He was an older gentleman looking pretty happy with life and seated beside him was a much younger, plunging-neckline blonde.

'Nice car,' said Thom slewing around in his seat as he passed them.

'Eyes on the road, honey,' I returned as I registered the blonde's assets.

The convertible fell back behind us just as Mickey entered the rest room. A minute later we all saw the car coming alongside, horn tooting and the driver gesturing madly with a closed fist. The windshield wipers were going non-stop trying to dislodge blue toilet paper and other debris that now covered the front of the car. Something unpleasant was sticking to the guy's hair ... Mickey, curious about the lever, had mistakenly released the toilet's giant size holding tank and emptied the contents onto the car behind. There was nothing we could do but laugh but the couple in the car did not think it was very funny I am sure.

'Don't touch the lever, Mickey!' entered our vocabulary from that point.

The venues, if we were not with Hank, were generally smaller and more rustic. Some were very rough. One such place had a very tough patronage and as we pulled up Bob, my drummer, flashed a knife he had slipped from his boot. He was of proud American Indian heritage and one did not ask whether he was armed or not – he generally was. We always put him in charge of the cash collected from our gigs as we were sometimes out for weeks at a time and had quite a collection of bills on board. Lots of gigs were paid for in cash in those days.

The guys were very protective of me, especially onstage. Thom was usually busy taking care of the staging and front of house while the boys and I did the shows. Dave, my bass man, was a very hefty guy and very slow to anger, but if he reached a point it was better not to mess with him. Sometimes at rehearsal when things were getting testy I'd just ask, 'What key do *you* want to do it in, Dave?' and not argue the point. If rough people or dancers got too close to me on the stage he would move to the full extension of his bass cord and glare at them. Then he'd back up to me and whisper loudly.

'Do you want me to take care of it, Diana?'

'No thanks, Dave,' I'd say brightly, crossing my fingers that he'd simmer down. 'I think it's okay!'

Our little troupe went on tour in Alaska. It was white, white, white.It snowed every day and was colder than I'd imagined possible. We were playing Elmendorf Air Base in Anchorage and staying downtown. After a few days I was really suffering with 'cabin fever' as they call it up there, a feeling of suffocation from the constant whiteness everywhere.

When not performing we entertained ourselves. With Thom that often took the form of practical jokes. Charlie and the rest of the band were always inventing ways of saving money on the road so as to have more to take home to their wives back in Nashville or to buy a drink at the bar. Charlie had perfected the art of making a toasted cheese sandwich on a steam iron. He would turn it upside down over a metal garbage bin and toast away. Another trick the guys came up with was to hang their groceries outside the window like in a freezer.

Thom found out about the window freezer thing and got hold of a tall extension ladder from somewhere. He climbed up the side of the building – a very dangerous ascent in freezing weather – and reached their rooms. He bagged their groceries, all but the milk, and left a note saying 'Thank You' and signed 'The Abominable Snowman.'

A furor broke out when the theft was discovered, Bob and Charlie accusing everyone except the guilty party. Did we really think there was an Abominable Snowman? How tall was this guy anyway? Thom stirred the pot, saying solemnly that he had heard of such things before. They shook their heads suspiciously. Was nothing safe? It was all very funny. Oh yes, we were bored with the snow. Thom gave the guys a bonus at the end of the gig to offset their losses. He never told them that he was the culprit. The band was a kickin' group.

Many times out on the road we discovered the incredible hospitality of our fans. Once a gentleman offered us accommodation at his guesthouse in Nebraska as there was nowhere else comfortable to stay in the area. We drove out to his place after the show and out of the dark emerged the big gates we'd been told about – the ones we had to be sure to close, for what reason we didn't know. We duly closed them behind us, were welcomed to a comfortable luxury cabin, and all fell into bed.

Early next morning we woke to a yell from one of the musicians. He had woken and pulled up the blind to be confronted with the shaggy head of a buffalo.

'It really is home on the range,' he quipped.

The area around the house was a veritable private zoo of American animals fenced in behind that gate we had sworn to shut. Buffalo, deer and others, almost tame, wandered freely around the property that was dotted with manmade lakes. We all had a great time there for a few days and the kids enjoyed the canoes and animals. We all especially enjoyed the peace and quiet.

We would be on the road for weeks at a time and I missed my little boys when they couldn't travel with us because of school. They were with a family near to our home and were safe but I wanted to be there too. Best was when we had down time and the house and family would get back together and somehow back on track. Bruises were tended, hugs were given and family memories were made. Babysitting was just an awful continuing problem for us and for the boys. We tried live-in babysitters, college students, local families, even a Mexican couple living in with us but it was always unsatisfactory.

Summers were the best when school was out and the boys could come with us. Sometimes the band members brought their wives and girlfriends with us *en troupe* and that was wonderful as we all mixed in. I learned to keep out of the way when couples were having their spats, though. Touring had its downside of too little personal space at times and it was always good to get back home to peace and privacy. I loved those summers – long, light-filled evenings, kids running around, meals outdoors. But one day I overheard Patrick in conversation with another little boy.

'Do you like having your mother being a star or would you rather have a regular mother?' queried junior reporter.

Paddy thought about it for a minute.

'I think I would rather have a regular mother,' he said seriously. My heart broke.

Always missing my family in Australia as well, we took a booking back home to see them all. I tried to make it home every eighteen months or so. My brother Peter lived fairly close to my parents with his wife and four children. This was a help for Mom and Dad but I missed Pete and Marcia and their family too.

I was set to appear at Sydney clubs and approached the booking with some trepidation as this time I would be singing my new style, crossover country. The last time the folks in Sydney had heard me I was known as a pop singer or for my work on *Sing Along* and *The Di Trask Show*. This tour I would deliver a real surprise. I hastily put together some arrangements, mixing my original repertoire – songs like 'Unforgettable' and 'Dear Heart' – with my latest Country hits. We opened to a full house at a top Sydney club.

That night didn't quite hit the mark. I knew what I was driving for and I was the first to do it – country music with a Big Band feel. But in my mind the sound wasn't quite right yet and the 'feel' wasn't there. It would come later. The Sydney crowd received me politely but I sensed they were puzzled – especially when I hit them with 'Harper Valley PTA'. They viewed me like a work-in-progress, which is probably pretty accurate. I could only hope most of my fans would stick it out to the end of the experiment. Predictably, the booker hit the roof.

'What the hell was that! What are you doing?'

I tried to explain my new direction but he was definitely not happy. I noticed during that tour my audience was changing. News had spread that I was singing Hank Williams and Patsy Cline. New faces and fans of country began to take the place of old fans as some dropped off.

I had no idea what kind of following country music had in Australia at that time but I was soon to learn. Stars like my friend Reg Lindsay and Slim Dusty had been slogging down the country road for years but had not made it to the slicker downtown clubs as yet. But their fans knew. I learned that Aboriginal Australians were staunch supporters of country and they turned up in force at my shows, sitting down front in large smiling groups. Crowd numbers were good despite my new direction but old friends left, shaking their heads in dismay.

Some people were in shock but it was like Buddy Killen back in Nashville used to say, 'Diana, you can't hide a hit.'

More than ever I felt it was time to move on completely from the old material and go with the new.

We had left my tearful mother and father in Melbourne again and were to catch our international flight from Sydney later in the day. In our rush to get out of the cab at Sydney airport I somehow missed my carry on bag. We fronted up at the ticket stand to discover that my bag with tickets and passports, all our cash and checks and ID had disappeared with the cab. It was about three o'clock on a Sunday afternoon. Thom and I stared at each other, speechless. What in heck would we do now? Suddenly a man stepped towards us.

'I'm Harry Devereaux,' he said, shaking Thom's hand. 'It's Miss Trask, isn't it?' he added, with a friendly nod to me. 'I run the duty free store here – a fellow American,' he explained, smiling. 'Can I help?'

Thom and I thanked him profusely, explaining our predicament.

'How about you come back to my apartment? We can call around the taxi companies and track down your bag.'

We trailed after him out of the airport like two lost children, piled ourselves and our baggage in his car and he took us back to his home. He sat us down with a drink and we began to call all the cab companies in Sydney.

'Was the taxi yellow, Di?'

'Maybe. I'm not sure. I have no idea.'

It seemed hopeless. After about five hours of racking our brains and calling everyone we could think of, Thom jumped to his feet.

'That's it, no more. St. Jude will find the bag and deliver it to us.'

Harry and I stared at him like he was crazy – he had said it with such conviction.

'Who in hell is St. Jude?' Harry asked blankly.

'The patron saint of the impossible,' replied my unstoppable Thom.

'Well, that won't help me much, I'm Jewish,' Harry smirked. 'Tell me what this Jude has ever done for you. How do you know, it may be just coincidence or chance?'

I'd heard the story Thom now told our new acquaintance. Once he had been in a bad accident and an ambulance attendant had told him about St. Jude.

'Pray to St. Jude to help you through but be careful, he always demands something in return,' the attendant had told him.

Since that time Thom described many incidents in his life where he felt Jude had interceded and he stood firmly by his belief that the saint would help us again in this instance. Hours passed and still we had heard no news about our valuables. It was getting late. We had already called the airlines and moved our flight to the same time next day. I began to have doubts that St. Jude had heard Thom's prayer this time.

Harry insisted that we stay the night with him and we would sort it out tomorrow. As we breakfasted with him the next morning he joked Thom, 'If this St. Jude is going to come through, he better do it quick.'

We sweated it out as the morning passed. We had to be at the airport at three. At two o' clock the phone rang. It was one of the taxi companies. They had found the driver and the bag. Harry was dumbfounded.

'We'd like to give you something for all your kindness,' Thom said as we prepared to leave.

At first Harry would not take a thing but Thom and I insisted.

Finally he said, 'Give me a dollar to remember St. Jude.'

Thom wrote 'Saint Jude' on the dollar note and passed it over.

About six years later as we were again in Sydney, we passed by Harry's store at the airport but he was not there. His son greeted us, telling us that he ran the store now – his dad had recently passed away. We were sad to hear it but had to laugh when his son told us that Harry had gambled on the horses in the name of St. Jude every weekend and never won anything.

It seems Harry had related the story of St. Jude and the missing bag many times to whoever would listen but when he passed away was still waiting for a miracle to work for him.

'Dad gave me the "St. Jude dollar",' the son related, 'and I noticed one day it looked a bit different to the usual dollar bill. I took it to be evaluated and it turns out to be a Silver Certificate Dollar. It's very rare in the US, worth quite a bit of money. I keep it in a safe deposit box.'

Thom and I often had a chuckle about that and wonder what Harry had to say to St. Jude when they met in heaven ... What a dirty trick.

We were back in Nashville and I got a call from Buddy Killen at Tree Music late one afternoon. He sounded very excited.

'I think I have a great song for you, Diana!'

Buddy just did not say things like that lightly so I was thrilled.

'It's perfect for you.' His excitement was infectious.

'I'll be in first thing tomorrow,' I replied.

But between that conversation and the next morning I lost that perfect song as another producer swooped in and commandeered it. The song was 'D.I.V.O.R.C.E.' and the girl to sing it was Tammy Wynette. I was brokenhearted but that was how fast songs came and went and it was to happen to me again and again. Tammy went on to win Female Vocalist of the Year at the 1968 Country Music Association Awards and a Country Gold Award for that song.

We had recorded my version of 'I Fall to Pieces', the Patsy Cline classic, and it did very well. We were on dicey territory as Patsy had not been gone for very long but the fans had accepted my version. I was absolutely thrilled to be nominated along with four others, including Tammy, for Best Country Vocal Performance Female by the National Academy of Recording Arts and Sciences for a 1969 Grammy Award. I attended the ceremony at Nashville in 1970 along with Buddy and Thom. In those days, the Country Music section of the Grammys was held in Nashville as a separate event. With Thom gripping my hand tightly and a smile plastered on my face, I lost to Tammy Wynette and another of her classic hits, 'Stand By Your Man'.

There's no doubt Tammy had a very aggressive producer but she had an incredible, unbeatable voice and she deserved every bit of her success. She seemed to be a very shy, sweet girl, maybe a bit shocked at how far she had gone.

Buddy thought a change would be good and put me together with a hot new producer, Danny Davis of the Nashville Brass. Danny was a great musician and I liked him a lot. We did fairly well together but I still had not found that big hit song that Nashville grinds on. I tried to write my own but my confidence was not there.

I recorded 'Here Comes My Baby' penned by Dottie West and she came to the studio to hear me put it down. She was very sweet and loved the track. I had always liked her throaty sound and boy, could she write. She was well-loved by the fans but was killed tragically on her way to the Opry one night much later.

We had been traveling hard now for about three years with Hank as well as doing our own gigs. I had worked with and alongside many stars. Country was changing, getting more upscale. The Buddy Lee Agency put together a package of five acts to pitch to Las Vegas. The show consisted of The Four Guys, Archie Campbell, me, and the headliner was Ferlin Husky. We would be the first country show to appear on the famous strip in Las Vegas. Until then all country had played downtown and in the lounges, never in a main room on the strip. Buddy landed a booking – we were to open at the Landmark Hotel.

I remember opening night very well because I was scared to death. Don't ask me why, but I walked onstage shaking in my shoes. I had always dreamed of working in Vegas and now I just froze up, delivering a wooden, stilted performance unlike any I have ever delivered before or since. Everyone else in the line up slayed 'em – The Four Guys singing a stunning version of 'Mariah', Ferlin and Archie did their thing. I was the only one who got a bad review.

Once you fall to the bottom it's easy to decide never to go back there. You just don't want to go down that road ever again. I was mad at myself for that performance, mad as hell, and I discovered that I could use that anger to hit a home run next time. That experience was my trigger for developing a mental game plan I called 'Level of Performance' and it was the most important lesson I learned in that industry. I would never perform below a certain level no matter what was happening in or around me. There was to be no coasting.

The next night I came back from the depths to a standing ovation. The show sold out for the run as audiences ate it up. We were booked back at the Landmark and played it each time with a different lineup of stars. Country music – and I too – had arrived mainstream on the Strip.

ELEVEN

Life Upon The Wicked Stage

Thom came home one day with news – the acreage on top of the hill behind us had come up for sale.

'Let's go look,' he said, grabbing me by the hand.

We drove to the top of the hill and stood overlooking the valley and the rolling Tennessee hills. It was simply beautiful. In my imagination my house of dreams was already taking shape – a real family home, a place of our own with plenty of room for the boys to run and explore and fresh air all around, just like I had grown up with back home in Warburton. We purchased the fifteen acres, celebrated with champagne and the serious brainstorming began.

Thom, my Mr. Resourceful, decided to do most of it himself with the help of one local guy, Charlie, as foreman. As the house plans went ahead it all got a lot bigger than we needed but our dreams were coming true. Charlie hired a crew of men recommended by local builders to dig the foundation. I remember it was hot and as the crew swung their pickaxes in that hard clay they sang a song – an *oop ... oof* kind of cadence. I loved to hear them singing my house into being.

When the bottom half of the house was finished we moved in. I was so happy and thanked God for my good fortune. We bought the boys horses, and I had my little chicken coop and beloved ducks. In the summer evenings the air was full of lightning bugs and we would sit out watching the moon rise over the fields. I learned that our property was once the site of a tobacco plantation and old slave quarters, and I loved to roam the fields discovering all manner of plants and animals. We had resident deer that would pose on the lawn in the morning if our German Shepherd dogs were still sleeping.

I loved to be home, gardening every spare minute I could. But spare minutes were few and far between as we continued to travel hard. One year we were only in the house in Tennessee for twenty days. The rest of the time we were on the road.

Johnny Cash was one of the greats of the business and in 1969 I was delighted to appear on television as a guest on *The Johnny Cash Show* in Nashville, which ran to nearly sixty episodes and was very successful for him. Johnny was a big, tall man with an animal charm. I wouldn't say he was a great musician with a guitar but he moved his body like he was consumed with an inner restlessness. His driving beat and the strongly masculine tone of his distinctive voice added to his sexy onstage presence.

There was a good lineup on that episode including Tom T. Hall, the Carter Family, the Statler Brothers and my old friend Pat Boone. My solo was 'Hold on to What You Got' and then Johnny and I did a duet. I panicked when the booker first told me the title of the duet – it was a song I did not know at all. It was the first day I'd met John formally although we had passed on the road before. I asked him if we really had to do the song in question.

'What song do you want to do, Diana?' he asked straight away.

I suggested 'The Last Thing on My Mind' and he called the girl over.

'We are going to do a different song. Tell the band.'

And that was that. He was a joy to work both with and for, and I was very happy in his company. The people who traveled with him all seemed to love him. His eyes were black, gentle and very kind and rested on you curiously as if seeking your approval.

No matter how much experience you have behind you, or how many personal successes, sometimes it still hits you that you are living your dream and you can hardly believe your good fortune. *Working with the legendary Johnny Cash? Singing duets with him?* That's the kind of miracle that was definitely 'the last thing on my mind' when I started out.

Later on John and I worked across the street from each other in Vegas and Thom and I spent great times with him and his lovely wife, June. They were such good people and I admired his devotion to her. There are many Cash stories in the business but the last time we saw him, he and June were telling Thom and I about the time they were robbed at their house in the Caribbean.

'Robbers burst right in the front door,' John explained, passing the rest of the story over to June.

'I laid on the floor,' she said, 'pretending to have a heart attack, you know. But while I was down there I slipped this ring I'm wearing under the furniture.' She grinned slyly as she flashed some serious bling at us. 'Then I went right into the dying act. They were so scared they ran away!' John and June laughed and laughed about that. Good for her, I thought.

Seasons passed and I was so tired I didn't know what town I was in half the time. At some stage earlier we had decided to place the boys in military school to try to solve the eternal babysitting dilemma. We had wrangled the problem from every angle but thought it was the best solution under the circumstances. The day they entered the Castle Heights School in Lebanon, Tennessee, we had to leave straight away in the bus to make a gig. I went to my room in the back of the bus and cried for about five hundred miles, hating that they would be in a boarding school. I remembered that particular loneliness oh so well.

'At least they'll be together,' Thom consoled me. I hung on to that but I always wanted them near me and longed for summertime and school holidays.

It was an appearance at a one-night stint with Roy Clark that set me wondering. I was watching Roy onstage as he worked – what a great star. He had a wicked wit, exuded great warmth and was a fine musician as well. I turned to Thom.

'You know this is a terrific show, I'd love to work more with this guy.'

I didn't think much more of it but as it happened that particular show had not escaped the interest of Roy's management team. They were looking to put together a big package with Roy headlining. At the next annual convention in Nashville we met Jim Halsey, Roy's manager.

Jim was headquartered in Tulsa, Oklahoma, and had a group of entertainers that did well enough, but he was looking to go mainstream and saw the great potential for country music. We all hit it off and after he and Thom went through the usual backroom haggling I was signed to his agency and became Roy Clark's support act. Jim Halsey put us on the road immediately to work out the kinks and then signed us to the Frontier Hotel in Las Vegas. The Frontier! This was a big deal. I'd played the Landmark but the Frontier was right in the middle of the Strip and rated as a top main room. A lot was riding on this booking, not just for me and Roy but for country music itself.

This was the moment where I began this story: waiting in the wings on opening night at the Frontier; the moment when I was part of Nashville's conquest of the Strip; the moment I knew my second chance at this music business was about to launch me mainstream again. The audience was packed and buzzing with speculation. Could country music, even in its reinvented form with pop overlays and a Big Band feel, really satisfy these hardened critics? We had a full band conducted by Al Alvarez, a seasoned conductor, and for the first time, in Roy's words, there were 'no bales of hay on the stage'. Thom stood beside me in the wings. My call came. I released his hand.

'Take your time,' he whispered.

As I walked out into the lights, I closed my eyes and concentrated on my game plan. *Just put yourself in one of those other gigs you've worked to get here, Diana.* I breathed. A vision came into my mind of our first trip south to Nashville in our battered camper van and that evening when I first saw the lights of Vegas sparkling in the desert darkness. It was my time to shine here now.

I picked up the hand mike and opened up. In all my years of performing I had never gotten over the butterflies. I came to regard them as a good thing. Enough butterflies in your stomach and you can fly. As I slid into my opening number the audience came with me immediately and at the end gave me a standing ovation. It was an awesome night. Roy followed and just knocked 'em dead.

The news went out – we were hot! The Frontier main room was packed with Country fans and they were enthusiastic and fervent. After the first few nights I realized with a jolt of joy that it had begun to be fun! The long cold sweat of acceptance was over and now it was just good music and people. For the first time I could really relax and just do what I loved – sing to an audience.

That room had a great feel and Roy was a joy to be with because his standard of performance was high and never slipped. He came from humble beginnings but never flashed his wealth or circumstance and was always the gentleman towards me. The troupe had great times together on and off the stage and the audiences couldn't get enough. The show was a monster hit and Jim Halsey was thrilled. We would play the Frontier many, many times after that.

I was one of the lucky ones who didn't get the 'Vegas Throat'. It is a condition that many singers get there because of the desert dryness. My throat loved it there and stood by me well even after two shows a night for long runs.

After our Las Vegas debut, Roy and I became hot country commodities and hit the road bigger than ever. And not only the roads – Roy owned his own plane and we would sometimes fly to the gigs with him and his pilot. We traveled the length and breadth of the country, winter and summer, in extended tours.

Some time earlier Thom and I had slimmed down our own entourage. After seven years of touring we sold our faithful bus to a rock and roll band and now I personally traveled with only two musicians of my own – a lead man and a drummer. They traveled in a van courtesy of 'Open Road Campers' in exchange for some promo work. My drummer was Jimmy Kelley. He was very 'country', raised in Dog Creek, Tennessee, and had a very bubbly personality. I liked his strong, simple beats, solid as a rock. Jack Watkins was my lead man, accomplished and very reliable. He'd traveled with me before. I felt lost if Jack and Jimmy weren't there behind me as they really knew me and my stuff.

Success moved us back into the mainstream music business and along with the rewards came exposure to many pressures and trials. Thom and I had been married now for nearly ten years and were often questioned quite bluntly about our long-term relationship. Some ladies even took it as a personal challenge to break us up and blatantly threw themselves at Thom. I was worked on too, I think even more so than Thom.

It seemed the more successful we got, the more some people wanted to move in and take us apart. I have often wondered why. Maybe to bolster up their own egos. If someone thinks you're making it big, then a bit of control over you means they get to share your limelight. From time to time I heard the whispers – *Diana's got it all* – and I think I *was* luckier than some. I had my career, husband, children, a happy home – lots of entertainers don't have that. The lifestyle makes it tough to achieve. Temptation was strong around both Thom and I but, thank God, it did not succeed.

We were trying to make our marriage work and bring up the boys against the backdrop of a tough industry that brought all kinds of distractions knocking on the door. Inevitably the strain at times took its toll on us and our marriage, and we had our rough times – some of our spats were legendary.

One awful night we ended up arguing at the tops of our voices out along the highway in front of the house. Thom has the fast fiery temper of the Irish and tends to flare up loudly and quickly. He also cools down faster. Stir me up enough and I'll yell ... and keep yelling. So, as the voices got louder and louder, someone called the police. A patrolman arrived on the scene to find me still going at it, hammer and tongs, so naturally I was the object of his unwelcome attention. I pointed furiously at Thom.

'Arrest *him*! Why don't you arrest *him*?' I demanded.

'Ma'am, I'm not here to arrest him. I'm arresting *you*. *You're* the one disturbing the peace.'

For the record, I did not end up in jail. He took us back to the house, lecturing all the way – an embarrassing incident to say the least.

The best plan we ever came up with was to try to be truthful about our grievances, to put them on the table as they occurred and talk them out. We both suffered from these sessions and plenty of tears flowed but in the end I think it made us stronger as we realized that both of us were pretty normal under the circumstances. Sometimes the grass looked greener to me but I never strayed far and was always true to my dearest friend and lover.

Thom has helped me and persevered with me through all life's terrors and trials, always holding my hand or by just giving me a straight talking to. He always seemed to have enough love for both of us, to see us through the times when we were really down and the whole world seemed to be against us. He would look at me and say, 'Well, this is a really shitty situation.' I'd see the set of his chin and know that *that* would be the moment when things would start to change and we would begin to rise up again. I trust him completely.

Back in Nashville, Tree Music and Buddy Killen were very proud of us and how far we had come. When I decided to become a US citizen, Buddy was the one who stood up for me as sponsor. I felt that as my life was mostly in the US now, I owed my allegiance to it. The citizenship ceremony was made special by the words spoken by the presiding federal judge. He said he had been an immigrant also, that America was a nation of immigrants, and that we were welcome.

I know I will never be anything but Australian-born, but the US has treated me very well. I heard of some negative feedback from the Australian press later, along the lines of: 'Diana Trask had bailed out and become an American'. But to put it simply, I feel that Australia is my mother and America is my father. Which one do I love better? I have a heart for both countries and always will. I have lived for the most part in America but my ashes will rest in Australia where I was born.

The Roy Clark Show was booked to do the annual Whitehouse Correspondents Dinner for President Ford. We had been working hard and I was so tired when we arrived at the hotel that I fell asleep in the lobby as we waited for rooms to be ready. This lasted all of a few minutes when I was firmly shaken awake by a member of the hotel staff.

'No sleeping in the lobby,' I was admonished gruffly.

I dragged myself upright, longing for a sleep before it was time to prepare for the show. Finally Thom and I were in the elevator heading up to our room ... the bellhop was paid off ... shoes were kicked aside ... I was collapsing on the bed ... and the phone was ringing. Thom answered it and gave me a rueful look.

'Cocktail party at six, downstairs,' he relayed to me.

I groaned and put my head under the pillow.

Cocktail parties, especially before a gig, were really hard for me to do. It was like having to get revved up and ready twice. They are all part of the deal, though, especially at a function like that, so I dutifully got dressed, repaired my makeup and hair, and was downstairs by six as ordered, ready to smile and chat. We were ushered into a foyer milling with a crowd of Washington types. Roy was standing with a group and I headed on over towards him. An aide was lying in wait ready to ambush me.

'Oh, Miss Trask, would you please have your photo taken with ... ?' I didn't hear the rest.

I looked at the guy beside me. He seemed to be wearing what looked like a Navy outfit.

'Well, I don't usually have my picture taken with sailors,' I quipped in my usual style of blurting without thinking. Roy spluttered and looked like he might swallow his drink glass and all.

'Well, as a rule that's usually a good idea,' the guy returned without missing a beat. The aide rushed in.

'Ahem, Diana, I'd like you to meet Admiral Zumwalt, the Chief of Naval Operations of the United States.'

Roy disappeared behind his sleeve and now it was my turn to gulp. My thoughts went straight back to my faux pas on the way to Vice President Johnson's ranch in Texas and the blood rose to my face. This was so déjà vu I could not believe it! How many other members of the Whitehouse hierarchy was I doomed to insult? Me and my big mouth once again. The picture was taken and the admiral was quickly hustled out of my company, my only comfort being the hint of a definite twinkle in his eye as he took his leave of me.

We performed for a rather unruly audience that night but I did get to meet President Ford and his lovely First Lady, Betty. I watched the president while I was onstage. He quietly puffed his pipe and seemed to enjoy the performance. There was something so gentle yet strong about the man.

The Roy Clark Show was back in Vegas. It was nearly curtain time on opening night and Jimmy, our drummer, was not onstage. As I've mentioned, curtain time was all but immoveable – it goes up if you are there or not. We made a frantic phone call for Thom to get over to Jimmy's room and find him. When Thom arrived Jimmy opened the door a crack.

'What are you doing, man?' exclaimed Thom. 'We're on in ten minutes!'

Jimmy wailed something incomprehensible.

Thom pushed at the door. 'Everyone is onstage! You need to get dressed. Come *on*, Jimmy!' he insisted.

More sounds of woe. Jimmy released the door and Thom went in.

'Look at my hair!' cried our poor drummer.

Normally Jimmy sported an Afro but right now his hair was plastered down tight to his head in a greasy mass.

'The more I wash it, the worse it gets,' he moaned.

Thom didn't know whether to laugh or cry but time was ticking – save the laughs for later.

'What are you washing your hair with?' he asked.

Jimmy passed him the tube of 'shampoo'. Now, Jimmy was a great drummer but reading was not his strong suit and he often judged things by colors. Sure enough, he thought he was washing his hair with the shampoo he always used. After all, the tube was the same color. Thom looked at it. *Preparation H*. Beautiful. They worked on his hair and Jimmy made it to the stage just in time, looking like a drowned dog.

Jimmy was the source of many a laugh and country tragedy. Another time when we were appearing at the Sands Hotel in Vegas he cornered me.

'Diana, my family's in the audience, all the way from Dog Creek. Do you think you could get them back to Roy's dressing room to meet him?'

I knew that Roy was cool about meeting folks but I just did not take it for granted to load people in on him.

'I'll ask,' I said.

'Roy, Jimmy's family is here but I have to warn you, they are very country. Can I bring them round?'

'Sure, no sweat,' Roy returned easily.

After the show I took Jimmy's mother and uncle backstage. Uncle immediately clamped onto Roy and loudly offered to let him use *any* car on his used car lot if *ever* he was in Dog Creek, Mr. Clark, y'hear? *Ever.* Mother proudly displayed the two hundred dollars she had pinned to her bra, safe from those muggers that were everywhere in the big city. I did not know how Roy would take these folk, but I caught the naughty twinkle as he turned to me.

'I thought you said these folks was country!' he protested, grinning wickedly as Mother and Uncle beamed at him.

Our show was breaking all records in Vegas. Some nights we even packed the audience onto the sides of the stage.

'Just like back at the ole Opry,' I joked to Thom as we saw the extra chairs being brought on stage.

One night at the Sands who should turn up to see the show but my former manager, Mort Farber. He came backstage and we had one of those awkward conversations that can happen between people who are anxious not to mention the reason why their association ended. We skirted around the past and talked about how things were going. He had a passing word to Mr. Cain, the booker, before he left.

'You know, I had this girl first.'

Over time, as a troupe and as individuals, our sound was improving. I was still doing bookings on my own and the hardest thing ever was to leave the Vegas setting and work in a small club or room with a poor sound set up, no singers, no band and no atmosphere. It was extremely difficult to adjust but it had to be done because every audience member deserves your best, no matter where they go to see you.

During this time in the early seventies I appeared on many star-studded television shows and at awards nights. Personalities like Johnny Carson and Merv Griffin – a really fantastic guy – were hot on the scene and I was a guest many times on their shows. *Nashville on the Road, Pop! Goes the Country* and *The Midnight Special* hosted by Marty Robbins were others. I met a myriad of stars and superstars on shows like these where sometimes I was a presenter, sometimes a guest. I also played a guest role in the situation comedy *Love, American Style*, which had a huge international following.

On several occasions in those years I ran into the two young Australian singers who had followed me over to the States and achieved unbelievable success – Helen Reddy and Olivia Newton-John. It would generally be at an awards show or get together with lots of other celebrities where real conversation was difficult, but I was so proud of those girls and told them so. Not only were they great singers, but they represented Australia so beautifully. I would stand in the wings and watch them work, feeling a thrill of kinship and pride.

I was asked the same question a hundred times: 'What's in the water in Australia that so many great singers come from there?'

I had no answer for that one, but I would smile inwardly and take a small bow as both girls had told me independently that they had studied my work and followed my footsteps to some degree as they strived to find their own stardom.

Helen has such a strong, distinctive voice and had a fantastic career. No other song represents the seventies for women so well as her hit 'I am Woman'. She always seemed a very decisive person and one who would not easily be shaken. I have been in contact with Helen in recent times and she recalled being in the audience when I opened for the *Sammy Davis Jr. Show* in Australia at the start of my career. She even sought out Jack White, my first singing coach in Melbourne, because I had been trained by him and remembers buying a copy of my first CBS single, *Long Ago Last Summer*.

Olivia confided she had watched every episode of *The Di Trask Show* in Melbourne after she had done her homework.

'I used to watch you on television when I was a kid and just learning,' she enthused.

It was funny to hear her say that, remembering my own days glued to the set watching all the performers I could. Olivia was always one of my favorites with her sweet lyrical voice and she too has had a wonderful career. I met up with her another time when I was visiting Panda Lisner, my old friend from Melbourne television days. Panda was now living in Las Vegas and on the day I dropped by, Olivia was there also. We spent a happy day sitting around the pool talking and I found her to be good company and a very likeable person.

It was an honor to be a role model for others coming after. It was good to see that the people around both those girls seemed to love them dearly and that they had followed their destiny with a great deal of integrity. That is something I have always admired.

My own integrity was something I cherished right from the start. The casting couch is fully operational in all avenues of entertainment – I found that out very early on back at the start of my career in Melbourne. Producers could be cut-throat and unscrupulous but I can state with pride that I would never lie down on my back for a job, ever. I saw that the girls who tried to get ahead that way had to live with their conscience and remorse later and to my mind they never got anywhere in spite of it.

An opportunity arose for a quick holiday so Thom and I decided to grab the kids and go to Central America. We flew into Belize with all our camping gear as the idea was to hire a truck and drive round to see the countryside. We rented a four-wheel-drive jeep and took off along a fair road that quickly turned into a dirt track with huge potholes. Colorful buses loaded to the gills with people, animals and luggage bumped along beside us as we left the city surrounds.

We found a beautiful campsite alongside a river and set up. It was New Year's Eve and during the evening a local man entered our camp offering us the traditional New Year's food of meat wrapped in banana leaves. We accepted and had some conversation with him. He spoke beautiful English and told us his name was Mr. Ford. That always stuck in my memory as a slightly bizarre moment.

We shopped at local food markets or open-air vendors and this was the first time I saw a woman eating out of a garbage can. Poverty was all around but instead of being mean or rude the people were wonderful to us. It was an eye-opener for us all. I remember visiting Mexico some years before, when Shawn was just a baby. It was when we were living in San Diego and we'd taken my Australian friend Jack Ayling, the television writer, on a visit there. A rake-thin Mexican woman in rags had held out her baby to me. She wanted me to take it, to save it from poverty and starvation. I wanted to, of course, but Thom said it was impossible; we wouldn't even get it across the border. We gave her some money and felt helpless. Thom and I sponsored a child from Haiti for some years and I'll never forget the thanks we received from him for the gift of a goat. A goat! How different are our frames of reference in this world.

We took the boys for a ride across the river in a dugout canoe to visit the Aztec ruins nearby. They rose out of the surrounding jungle in a spectacular wall of stone steps leading to a high altar, aged and worn from centuries of weather. We wondered about the lives that had been lived there and the sacrifices that had taken place on that high altar. At night, trucks ground past our campsite loaded with men toting rifles and guns. We were close to the Guatemalan border.

'They are fighting the revolution,' was the whisper.

A couple of days later we flew out to the surrounding islands and reef. This proved to be a hair-raising ride as I think the pilot got lost.

'Shouldn't we be heading north?' Thom questioned the pilot after he and I had exchanged raised eyebrows.

'Oh, yes,' he muttered and steered the plane on a different heading.

We landed dangerously in a vile crosswind, the plane almost flipping over. I held on to the kids like a limpet, knuckles white and already thinking about leaving. Our courage – or foolhardiness – was rewarded though, as the water and the reef were very beautiful, and once safely on the ground we enjoyed our week enormously in swimming and exploring.

As we had to go straight to Vegas to open, we arrived back at the hotel looking pretty rough, right down to the blackened cooking pots hanging off our backpacks. Who was looking country now? As I got out of the cab, the doorman of the Frontier Hotel walked towards me hesitantly.

'Diana, is that really you?' he asked in disbelief.

The Roy Clark Show had toured solidly for about two years when one night I sat up tiredly in bed. I was in a 'taking stock' mood.

'Why are we working so hard? What's it for? I feel like I've been on this stage all my life,' I moaned miserably to Thom. 'We have to have a goal, some kind of a payoff.'

Thom thought about it and, as usual, came up with the answer.

'Why don't we work towards that boat we've always wanted? We could try for some relaxation time with the kids before they grow up and are gone.'

Our new family goal was born. Thom immersed himself in sailing books and every sailing magazine he could lay his hands on. He took a correspondence course in basic navigation and picked it up quickly, as he does with most things. Thom is very clever with math and has always been a fixer and an inventor. In fact he invented a potato planter as a kid on his uncle's farm. He sold the patent to Massey Ferguson and for all I know they still use it.

I listened and absorbed all I could about navigation too and the day came when we thought we were ready. Practical experience was next. We were strolling along the marina in San Diego one day and saw a sign: 'Sailing lessons'. *That's for us,* says Thom. We enquired and found out the instructor was a little old lady with a small dinghy sailboat. *Why not?* says Thom. *A boat's a boat.* So we signed up for an hour's lesson. She was a good teacher and I can still hear her voice as she taught us the basics of wind and water and craft.

'Push the tiller towards the sail that billows out,' she instructed.

I liked the tiller – although that was the only one we ever used – and I loved the motion of the water. We had one lesson – ONE! – and Thom reckoned we had the basics sorted. *Time to buy the boat,* says Thom. I think I have mentioned he is unstoppable ... ?

We found her in Fort Lauderdale, Florida. She was an island boat, twenty-seven feet with a wide beam and sloop rig. We bought her and named her *Bypass*. This name had its origins in a terrible night we had lived through on the road with the bus some years before. It had been a terrifying experience as we were riding through New Mexico and the diesel engine suddenly ran away with us. The engine emergency stop button did not work and we were pounding along completely out of control, going faster and faster. We came to a steep hill and as we slowed up the incline, Thom struggled and got the thing out of gear. We coasted to a stop with the engine still racing away, winding up in a screaming din.

'Everyone off the bus!' Thom yelled.

I hustled the kids out and the band members tumbled down after us onto the roadside. The engine had to be stopped somehow. We crouched down in the culvert watching Thom cautiously open the engine compartment in the back, a pillow he had grabbed from the bus in his hand. He threw the pillow into the engine intake. It was immediately sucked up but the engine kept going, screaming higher and higher.

'Thom!' I screamed, almost as loud, as next he manhandled a piece of wood across the intake and shoved it in.

Suddenly the noise stopped. Clouds of steam filled the highway and I could make out Thom walking shakily back towards us, his pants burned through. Much later when we had all calmed down, I asked him what he had done to stop the engine.

'I bypassed it,' he said. 'If ever we buy that boat you are always talking about let's call her *Bypass* and we'll know we will always get home.'

I hugged him. And *Bypass* it was.

On a sunny day in Fort Lauderdale, Florida, we took our two excited boys and proudly steered *Bypass* down the New River towards the inlet and the open ocean. We were equipped with a loud horn to signal for the bascule bridges along the way to open up. We were doing fine until we came to the railroad bridge. It came down sharply behind us as we passed and at the same time the 17th Street Bridge in front of us came down before we could get through. We were caught between and had to wait until the road cleared and the bridge ahead could be raised. No problem.

We'll just keep puttering in the middle, we thought.

Just then our engine locked in reverse. Thom had revved it up as he was backing down away from the 17th Street Bridge. The basin we were in was flanked on one side by the Hatteras Boat Works where million-dollar yachts were lined up on the shore waiting for new owners. On the other side was *The Jungle Queen*, a tour boat loaded up with tourists. There we were going round the center in circles, locked in reverse.

A sailboat is very hard to handle when in reverse, as Thom was finding out. First we would scrape by the boat yard, then the bridge, then race by the gaping tourists. The boys were giving their father a hard time as only boys can. I was scarlet to the roots of my hair and Thom was getting frantic and more Irish by the second.

'Throw down the bloody anchor!' Thom yelled to me.

The boys and I raced forward and loosed the anchor. Over she went ... and kept right on going. Too late we saw that it wasn't attached to anything and we watched open-mouthed as the line fed over the side into the river, never to be seen again.

'Oh, shit.'

Thom grappled the helm and we continued our perilous traverse, circling in the middle of the river. After an eternity of embarrassment, the bridge at last opened in front of us. We went through backwards, ignominiously banging our radio antenna on the underside of the bridge. Thom aimed her for the side of the canal and we came to rest alongside a big old wooden boat whose crew appeared from nowhere and manhandled *Bypass* to a halt. Probably drawn by our screams of distress and Thom's colorful language, people were by now lining the dockside, staring at the commotion as our rescuers tied us up alongside.

'Can't take you anywhere without an audience,' joked Thom, rapidly recovering his sense of humor now we were all safe and sound.

The crew of the old boat was sort of hippie-ish but they seemed to know a lot more than us about the ways of seafaring. One fellow told us to always have a broom handle ready to kick the gear lever out of reverse if it stuck. How often in life is there a simple answer to things if only you knew what it was! So the broom had a double purpose from then on.

Having caught our breaths and discovered a second anchor stowed away below, we continued on our way out to the ocean. Nothing was going to stop Thom from sailing this boat out to sea. We passed through the waterway and were doing okay until we came upon a sign that had both a red and a green side to it. *Oh, dear.* We knew that you kept the red to your right and the green to your left on returning from the sea but what about a sign that had both? As we were arguing the point (loudly, I might add) the bow slammed into the mud and we were firmly stuck. *Now what?*

Thom remembered reading that in this sort of situation we should go forward and hoist the sails. *Aye aye, Captain!* We ran up the sails and the gods were with us as we sailed off the sticky mud and into the correct canal. Getting closer to the heads, the traffic was busier and we nervously entered the channel. Then we were out in the open ocean at last! It was wonderful – a beautiful day and smooth seas. We puttered south, keeping close to the shore and dropped anchor (attached this time!) so we could go for a swim. The water was cool and clear and the kids and I played around happily.

'Look at all the boats,' said Paddy a little while later, pointing up the coast.

A line of boats was running hell for leather down on the wind towards us.

'What are they running from?' Thom worried.

We both looked up to the west and there it was – an all-encompassing mass of cloud shaped like an anvil, rising like the Black Death from behind the buildings on the shore.

'Oh, my God! Get the kids! Pull up the anchor!'

We raced to beat the cloud, hauling up the sail and starting to run. Within minutes the squall was upon us and she hit us like a wailing banshee. Now we needed to get the sail down as the edge of the wind raced at us at about fifty knots.

As Thom manned the helm, I moved forward and reached up to get a hold of the sail and haul it in. The boat spun in a slow whirlpool movement and I hung out over the water, grasping the sail and holding on by my toes, staring down into the whirlpool. The boat suddenly righted and the sail banged down.

'Get back here!' Thom hollered. Boy, that man knew how to bark orders.

I crawled back to the cockpit on my hands and knees as Thom told me to take the kids below. I peered up from the cabin as it started to rain, warm at first then freezing cold, pelting Thom in his bathing suit. His teeth chattered as goose bumps appeared all over him and I threw him a towel.

'Where are we going?' I yelled.

A heavy, steamy mist covered us now and we could not see a foot in front of us.

'West!' Thom yelled back, navigator's pride at stake. 'The coast is out there some bloody where!'

After a time the downpour passed as it does in the tropics and the fog lifted. We found we were close to the shore and breathed a sigh of relief as we turned towards home and the marina. I noticed several other boats falling in behind us.

'They're crazy if they are following us,' I laughed at Thom, my spirits rising again.

We limped tiredly back up the river and as we reached our slip we saw that a great big yacht had taken half of our space, leaving us barely an inch to squeeze into. After all we'd been through? I don't think so! Thom gritted his teeth and popped that boat in like a pro. I'd seen that look in his eye before when he meant business. As he stepped ashore an old timer on the dock greeted him.

'Tough day out there, son?'

'You could say that,' Thom replied offhandedly.

'Everyone safe and sound? Then you had a good day,' the old salt replied.

So that was our first day of sailing and it's a wonder we ever went back for more. I often joke that sailing is ninety percent boredom and ten percent terror. We got our taste of the terror that day but it was the start of a great love affair with sailing for both Thom and I. We were hooked on the adventure and the open air.

Bypass had a very slim companionway and if you were not watching your step in a seaway you could bang your arms down hard as you steadied yourself. I was always doing this and my arms became peppered with bruises. As we were opening in Vegas for another date, I had to do something to cover them up as I knew that when the lights hit them they would be very obvious in my sleeveless dresses.

After the rehearsal in the showroom, I walked across the street to a swanky store to find something to cover up the marks.

'I need a good body makeup,' I said to the woman at the counter. She regarded me coolly.

'What are you trying to cover up?' she asked. I showed her my bruises.

'Oh.'

Now that's one little word that says so much, isn't it? She produced a pancake-type cover up, eyeing me suspiciously all the time. I knew she was dying to hear some kind of terrible story.

'Well, you see, there is this tight companionway ... ' I tried to explain. There was no way that lady believed me.

But that wasn't the end of it. After the show I was questioned on the side by the hotel management and others about the bruises. I tried to explain but everything I said sounded worse and worse. Thom was questioned as to whether he had an anger management problem. No one would believe that I simply fell down the blasted hatch!

I tried to watch myself after that but every now and then I would have unexplained bruises and heads would nod knowingly. What they did not know was that Thom and I had an agreement from day one that if he ever lifted his hand to me it would be an automatic divorce. I believe that when a man starts hitting a woman the love affair and marriage is over anyway. He would always tease me about that but I still firmly believe in that idea.

Back at our house in Tennessee we were now putting in the top floors and I had a bigger garden where I grew the world's best tomatoes. Thom built me a wonderful room on the top floor – my studio – that looked out over the rolling fields and trees. Our schedule had eased and I had taken time to advance my hobby of painting and to pursue the countless other projects I had stored up.

I have always loved art and craft projects and took a course in oil painting during my off time, applying all the techniques I had learned long ago in art at school and trying my hand at acrylics and other media. I also had a sewing corner and made a lot of gifts and decorations for our home. It was a beautiful place for writing songs too and I would get lost in there for hours when the ideas were flowing.

When I think back to that time of persistent loneliness and searching I had experienced on first coming to the States, I realize how much it sprang from a deep-seated need for home and family around me. When I was eighteen I ran from these things, determined to go it alone and show them all. But I paid a bitter price. I may have been making it with my singing but I had nothing to go home to when the song was over.

Mort, Roz, Mitch and all the others who ran my life back then had homes and lives at the end of the day. The bookers, the promoters, even the audience members – I saw them all as going home to their loved ones after the show while all I had was an empty room. Then Thom came along and the landscape of both our lives changed. Wherever Thom and the boys were, and especially here in my beautiful house in Tennessee with my garden, my hobbies, my life – that was home and it meant my song was richer and more complete. Thom also helped me resolve my feelings towards my mom. Our relationship had mellowed and I was always glad to see her, but hurtful memories remained.

'Stop looking at her as your mother and see her as a human being,' he encouraged me. 'Her marriage wasn't easy – look what she lived with. She's just a person who made some mistakes.'

He was right. When I took off the 'daughter' spectacles and let myself really look at her as she was, my heart melted and I ceased blaming her for what was past.

Being a very hands-on person, I tried to help Thom and the workmen finish building the house. They did most of the work along with Charlie, but I learned to drywall and finally got pretty good at it.

My 'Waterloo' was window framing. I had been driving five-penny nails to set the window frames and my arm was tiring. I was hanging on to a ladder as well as wielding the hammer and making slow progress.

'Maybe if I hang right out the window and drive from outside it will be better,' I thought. After two minutes of this I was exhausted. I thought some more.

'Maybe if I just put my arm outside the window and drive the nail towards me that will work.'

On the second go the hammer slipped straight off the nail head and right into my mouth.

I clapped my hands over my mouth, pulsating with pain and imagining the worst. I staggered off to find Thom.

'How bad is it?' I asked him. I dared not look in the mirror as we were again opening in Vegas in two days. He took a look.

'Oh, my God! Get the ice!' he exclaimed, running for the refrigerator.

My mouth was swelling up like a bee sting and a huge purple mark discolored my lips. We treated it non-stop for the next two days and the swelling went down in time but I had to do a good job on makeup to try to cover the bruise. Oh, yes ... we got the looks ... Poor Thom.

Times were changing. The country music business had grown and was earning top place in magazines, radio and television, as well as filling the swanky venues. Our show was number one on the Strip, running neck-and-neck with Wayne Newton. Fans were changing too as the more sophisticated folks were cottoning on to the slicker presentation and identifying with the stories of Tom T. Hall and Dolly Parton. Many country stars who had been in the Vegas lounges or only appearing at the fairs suddenly had top spots on the Strip.

Wider audiences were learning what we already knew: that country music spoke to us from the heart about real-life experiences from day one to old age. The appeal was massive and getting bigger.

TWELVE

Dream

When you were a kid did you ever dream about being famous? Did you see yourself surrounded by adoring fans, perhaps modestly accepting an award? Or maybe sauntering from your limousine through the glare of flash bulbs? I had those dreams. When I was five I informed my mother that I would be a famous singer one day ... dreams.

We were back in Australia once more to work and visit the family. My brother's kids, Lisa, Mel, Samantha and Luke, were growing up fast and they loved their Uncle Thom.

'I'm your favorite American uncle,' he would tease them.

'You are our only American uncle!' they would chorus loudly.

Back at the old house in Warburton on that visit I remembered one of my childhood dreams. There I was driving up the main street in a great big fancy car, complete with leopard-skin interior. I would stop in front of the post office right in the center of town, slide out of the limo in heels and furs, and languidly walk past gaping crowds to post a letter:

'Oh, my gosh ... look ... it's Diana Trask!'

'Diana Trask? You're kidding! Wow!' ...

I grinned to myself. What would happen if I lived it out? Would they 'ooh' and 'ahh?' Maybe I should do it ...

I decided to give it the works. I dressed myself carefully with a full makeup – something I *never* did in Warburton. There was no leopard-skin interior in my car but it was pretty nice all the same. I started out

214

and drove slowly up the main street. I pulled up at a lucky parking spot right in front of the post office and got out, letter in hand. A local bus driver barreled out of Martyr's bus booking depot and skidded to a stop in front of me.

'Oh g'day, Di, how's your mom, I hear she's been crook?' he piped good-naturedly and hurried away again intent on his own business.

Oh, well ... You're always just a local in your own hometown.

Back in the States, Jim Halsey decided to play me in Vegas with other headliners. The first was Danny Thomas and we were to play the Sands.

'Welcome to my world,' the legend said as he greeted me warmly at our first rehearsal. Danny was a great entertainer and storyteller and together we made a very saleable package. He was also the first person to give me equal status on the main billboards outside the casino and I was thrilled. We opened to a packed house and rave reviews.

I learned a lot from Danny's professionalism and hung on his advice, especially in honing my audience skills.

'Don't keep saying "Ladies and Gentlemen" all the time,' was his recommendation. I still adhere to his other word of advice – 'Diana, take care of your pipes' – by continuing a daily vocal practice.

I know many entertainers who are incredible readers of people and watch the audience like hawks the whole time they are onstage, sometimes editing their shows to make a greater impact. Sometimes there were weird people in the audience and if you had the confidence you could turn them to good account – in the nicest possible way of course!

So one night at the Sands there was this guy right up front, sitting like he was made of stone – no reactions, no movement whatsoever. People sometimes think that sitting in an audience is a spectator sport but it is a two-way street. I don't know if this guy was drunk, stoned, bored or just catatonic but the situation really tickled me, and by and by I started losing it. Pretty soon the audience and the band caught on and we were all laughing. I knelt down in front of this guy and sang right to him ... absolutely nothing. Before long we were all hysterical.

Danny was in the wings waiting to go on, minus his pants as usual. He had a thing about creased pants and would only put them on a few seconds before coming onstage. The audience was starting to howl at this guy in the front when suddenly on comes Danny in his underwear looking round with a 'What's happening?' face. Now the place went wild and I just had to finish and get out of there … I was helpless.

I've mentioned the hard-and-fast rule about curtain time. Well, there's an exception to every rule. A visiting guest from one of the Arab countries arrived in the showroom late one evening, sweeping in with a bevy of blonde beauties and until they were ushered in and seated, the curtain stayed firmly down. Apparently the gentleman had been upstairs betting at a private table and had lost one million dollars that weekend alone. This was the seventies when a million was still a lot of cash and a good enough reason for management to hold the show while his run of disastrous luck continued.

Backstage, Danny was a terrific person and entertained us all night with stories of his early days on the road as a comic. We were always welcome in his dressing room and he seemed to lift his act during our runs together and performed brilliantly. Audiences were literally rolling in the aisles and it seemed we were made for each other. It was then I found out he too had a dedication to St. Jude.

He told the story that when he was an unknown comic on the road he prayed to St. Jude, the patron saint of hopeless causes, for just enough money to feed and take care of his family. In return he promised he would build a shrine to the saint. Danny prospered to become an entertainment superstar and one of the wealthiest men on earth when I knew him and in return he did build that shrine in the form of the St. Jude's Cancer Research Hospital for children in Memphis. Donations and gifts from wealthy patrons and friends supported the hospital which provides free care to children whose families cannot afford to pay. Later I worked with Danny a little bit at his annual concert to help raise money for the hospital. I know firsthand from my own family the help he has given to people and I, along with thousands of others, thank him and bless his soul.

I was a guest in his home that sits atop a hill in Beverley Hills and met his wife, Rosie, and family. The home was stunning and full of priceless artifacts but somehow still managed to be welcoming. Danny really did live in an amazing world. Rosie was a trip and their family is a credit to them. Although they have both passed on, Danny's memory is beloved by all those he touched and his work is being carried on by his three children, Marlo, Tony and Terre. I bet he is smiling down on us all now and telling stories up there.

Thom and I rented a house on the golf course for one of our stays in Vegas with Danny and I was trying so hard to write a song that had been in my head. I find that in songwriting you have to find the catch word, something that reflects a current trend or awareness in the public, like the word 'body' which became a key word in many songs in the seventies. Well, a word kept coming to me – 'feeling'. I turned that word every way I could trying to get to the hook. I was driving to work one night and switched on the radio and there it was, the hit song 'Feelings' made famous by Morris Albert. Well, at least I knew to trust my own feelings.

A funny story, but true – Thom had a saying which he used to tease me with every now and again: 'If I said you had a beautiful body would you hold it against me?' I think he may have picked it up from an old Groucho Marx movie. Well, I mentioned it in backstage conversation once to a bunch of people and noticed the eyes of one guy absolutely light up. He was a songwriter and guess what? Several years later a song of that title was on the charts and a hit for the Bellamy Brothers.

Many superstars were in the audience during our Vegas days. Lucille Ball came backstage and was adorable. I was nervous when I heard she was in the house until I heard that distinctive laugh, a kind of gut laugh, in response to one of my lines and then I relaxed. She was a great audience. One night Glen Campbell sat right at the footlights, boots up on the stage rail. Glen was a tall, good-looking guy with a strong face and a shock of unruly hair over his forehead. After the show he came backstage to talk to Roy and not long after we had a call from the agency. Glen wanted me to tour with him in England and Scotland and it was all booked to go ahead.

I found the English audiences a bit reserved at first. The tour was sold out, so the interest was there, but it took longer to get them warmed up. There is a moment in every performance called the 'break point', the point where the audience comes over to you and is with you from then on. Lots of things contribute to getting to the break point faster – costumes, lights, set, venue – they can all have an effect on audience mood and reaction. Eventually the English audiences would come to our side and some went wild, mobbing the cars at the stage exit.

Glen had a lovely voice, clear and true as a bell. He was a great 'picker' on the guitar and his warm-ups backstage were lengthy as he got those sure hands ready. He seemed to have unresolved personal demons that showed in his expression at times and a 'little boy lost' look would steal over his face. I also saw those eyes fill up with impish glee onstage.

We played some legendary venues in England like Drury Lane and Festival Hall. Thom handled my lighting and sound men and did a masterful job there. It was a strange feeling to stand on those old stages, many of which were tilted forward, giving you the sensation of falling over into the orchestra pit. On one occasion I didn't stand far enough back for my bows and the big old dusty curtain came down on top of me, leaving me lost in its depths. The curtain was lightning fast and as I glared over at the stage hand operating it I spied a slight smile playing round his lips. I wondered if the fact that I had mentioned that I was of Welsh extraction and we were just over the border in England had anything to do with it?

Geoff Kruger, the promoter, arranged for Thom and I to have a beautiful Daimler to ride around in with a liveried driver who turned out to be a card. He took us off the trail many a time to eat at old castles and fine restaurants we would never have discovered by ourselves.

In Scotland I remember a rather special lunch. I had told Thom I was taking Stewart Dingley, our road manager, and the chauffeur out to lunch while Thom went to a meeting. We went along to a neat little place and as we entered I noticed a whole Scottish salmon about five feet long displayed on a table at the entrance to the dining room. That should have told me something but we went in and let our trusty driver order for us. He was in good form that day. He ordered the finest fare with beautiful wines and cleansing sorbets between courses. When the bill came I swallowed hard and had to ask Stewart for funds to pay in full. Thank God he had enough money to get us out of there as I had stupidly left my credit cards back at the hotel. It was embarrassing but it was a fabulous meal.

'How was lunch?' Thom asked.

'Not bad,' I replied carelessly.

He thought I had just taken the guys for hamburgers. I did not disillusion him until awhile later.

The highlight of that tour was in Edinburgh when Glen marched onstage, kilt swinging, as he played 'The Campbells are Coming' on the bagpipes. The crowd went wild, thundering and stomping. Glen is a fine bagpiper and I would tease him as he warmed up, squeezing the blasted thing like it was a wheezing old woman.

'Shaddup,' I'd holler rudely and he'd grin back good-naturedly and squeeze a bit harder.

I loved Scotland particularly as my darling Scottish grandmother had told me so much about the country her parents had come from. She was such a doughty woman, determined and resilient. If she made up her mind about something, it happened. I felt a bit closer to her and all those strong Scottish ancestors behind her when I was in their country. My interest in herbs was originally sparked by my grandmother's knowledge and that's a connection I treasure now she is gone.

As our tour of the UK came to a close, we played some nights in London and one night Glen just wandered on while I was onstage and we sang a duet. It was wonderful. I loved it and so did the audience – our voices melded so well. I loved to sing duets with the other stars I worked with and wish I could have done it more often – recording too – but those opportunities were rare. Geoff Kruger took wonderful care of us and also arranged for me to sing with the BBC Symphony Orchestra for a radio show, a true thrill for me. The tour closed too fast as I had enjoyed the British Isles immensely. We had not made it to Ireland, though, and as we flew out over the green fields I vowed to return and see the Emerald Isle.

Being so close to Europe, Thom and I took time to fly over to Spain for a week before returning to Nashville. It was a splendid holiday as we sunned ourselves and soaked up the Andalusian scents and sights. We toured the countryside, strolled the ports, and visited the old churches. We sampled the great tastes of Spain, feasting on scampi and other treats in little out-of-the-way places on the docks. It was wonderful.

On the flight back to the US, we heard that a hurricane was brewing and it looked like it would hit Florida. Our boat was there and would need to be moved and lashed down more securely. So Thom and I parted in New York, he to fly on to Florida to see to the boat and I to Topeka, Kansas, for a one-nighter before flying home to Nashville. I was very tired and fell sound asleep on the way to Kansas. I roused a little during the brief stopover in Chicago and was vaguely aware of a passenger slipping into the seat in front of me but I didn't pay much attention and soon slid back into my dreams.

As we landed in Kansas and I gathered myself up to go on to Topeka, I opened my purse and realized I had been robbed. The thief had taken every bit of cash I had apart from two cents (I think, a planned insult) plus all my credit cards. I had pushed my purse under the seat in front of me as the stewardesses all tell you to, had fallen asleep, and now I was stuck. I made my way to the airline office but they really did not want to know and regarded me and my problem with indifference.

What was I to do? Thom would be stranded too as all our cards were the same numbers (not now for sure). I had the name of the booker in Topeka – the first thing was to make contact with him, then figure out the rest. I returned to the desk and asked if I could please make a phone call. The airline official looked doubtful...

'Oh, come on!' I exclaimed. 'Even criminals get one phone call!'

Eventually I was allowed to use the phone. I rang the booker and asked him to pick me up at the airport and, God bless him, he came straight away and took me to the hotel where I phoned Thom and broke the bad news. It was coming up to the weekend and he had little cash either.

'I'll call the bank in Tennessee tomorrow morning and work it out,' he said. 'What the hell is that noise?'

I was wondering the same thing. A siren had started to wail close by. I heard the sound of doors slamming and people moving outside in the hallway. A man's voice sounded.

'Everybody down into the cellar – there's a tornado coming!'

'You hurricane, me tornado,' I told Thom and I beat it downstairs with all the other folks. The tornado passed very close to the town and caused a heap of damage but the show went on later that night anyway. As I boarded the plane for Nashville I sat back and wondered what else could happen in forty-eight hours?

Apparently the thief tried to use my card to buy a first-class ticket to New York but by then the card numbers were posted as stolen and the clerk alerted police. I heard that a cops-and-robbers chase ensued through the airport in Chicago during which the guy got away but my card was picked up. If he had looked a little harder in my purse in the first place, he'd have found a check I had in there for seventeen thousand dollars – part of the tour payment – plus all the identification he'd have ever needed to cash it.

We attended the Catholic church at Lebanon, Nashville, when we were not on tour. The boys' military school was not far from there and they took part in the church activities even when we were away. While we'd been gone in the UK, Patrick had decided to make a trifle for the inter-Church supper. This was a regular get-together of people from some of the local churches and they were mostly teetotalers. He called me and told me what he wanted to make and I directed him to the recipe book.

'How much brandy do I put in?' he asked.

'Just a little, Paddy. It's in the recipe,' I answered.

Well, Patrick did not think that was enough and poured nearly a whole bottle in. Later I heard the remarks.

'The best dessert we've ever had at the Church supper!' the churchgoers enthused. 'Especially the sauce!'

I wondered what they would say if they'd known about the addition. Patrick is a really good chef today, and every now and then I remind him of his 'Church' recipe.

My dad was a heavy drinker but I never remember seeing him drunk and falling down, only a bit silly. I was always worried about alcohol getting a hold of me as it was ever-present and plentiful in Vegas. I found that it was so easy to fall into a habit of ordering a drink between shows and also to 'come down' after a show and relax.

One afternoon the hotel officials were celebrating with Penny Tweedy, the breeder of the horse Secretariat who had won the Kentucky Derby. Roy Clark and I were invited to the party and we started in at about five o' clock, beginning with champagne which always slips down easily. Our first show was at eight. I was fine for that one but the party kicked on all night and, stupidly, we went back to it after the eight o'clock show. There was too much alcohol and not enough food. We did another show at midnight and just made it through, then back to the party which had spilled into the dressing rooms and everywhere backstage. I am not a good drinker and the mixed drinks finished me off. By now I had completely lost my place. Even my false eyelashes had somehow come adrift, one disappearing for all time. *This is a mistake. I need to get out of here.*

I staggered back to my dressing room to find Thom sound asleep on the couch so I decided to go back to our room upstairs. I was trying to walk along the hallway from the backstage area and found myself slamming into the wall on one side and reeling back, taking a few steps, and slamming into the wall on the other side. I was lost and feeling totally out of control. I had never been so drunk. Eventually I reached our suite and had to get a maid to let me in as I could not find the key. I fell onto the bed in a stupor.

'Di ... Diana ... wake up, Di!'

I surfaced very unwillingly, head pulsing and stomach in revolt.

It was late next morning and Thom was rousing me. I opened my eyes and just that slight movement was enough to tip my stomach over the edge. I clawed my way off the bed and rushed to the bathroom where I threw up violently. I was shaking all over and felt so ill and terrible. I continued to throw up every hour for what seemed like forever. Thom sent for milkshakes and toast and by five o'clock that evening I had improved slightly but all I wanted to do was curl up in bed with my eyes shut until the nightmare was over. Unfortunately there was an eight o' clock show to get ready for. Maybe Thom could tell the booker, Mr. Cain, that I was sick?

The phone rang. It was Mr. Cain. Roy Clark was in hospital with alcohol poisoning. Wayne Newton had consented to fill in for the first half and then go on to do his own show. I was to close for him. *Wayne Newton? Close for Wayne Newton? Are you kidding???* I grabbed Thom. Oh no, this was impossible! I was too ill! I could not tell Mr. Cain that I should be in hospital right next to Roy.

Somehow I got dressed and got myself down to the showroom. Wayne was on and killing them as usual but I could barely stand up. He walked off to huge applause, gave me a big smile and I was on. I told the stage hand to place a stand-up mike center stage. I needed to hold on to something. Everyone assumed that I was terrified to follow Wayne and had stage fright that night. Frankly, I preferred they think that than know the truth, but as the room turned over in front of me I vowed that my drinking habits would change forever. After that I arranged with every bartender in the hotel to send me only club soda and lime. There was no way that would happen to me again.

We returned to Sydney to work the clubs and were handled there by Bob Finikiotis, a young tax man and manager who did a marvelous job for us. We had flown from Los Angeles and because of the time difference had to go straight into rehearsals. Just before show time an old problem reappeared – it was the time of my menses and I was flooding. I grabbed a towel and wrapped it tightly around myself and went on. I nearly passed out during the show but pushed through it as I had for years. As I stepped off the stage, weak and trembling, Thom rushed up and grabbed me.

'Straight to bed and rest, baby,' he said.

I knew something was wrong and made a mental note to visit the doctor on my return home; meantime, I would just shake it off. We completed the tour, caught up briefly with my family and then it was back to the States to be with the boys. I did schedule a doctor's appointment when I got back. My friend Polly took me to see a great doctor in Dallas and he very gently examined me and told me his findings.

'I think you have endometriosis,' Diana. 'It's quite severe. You'll need surgery soon.'

A hysterectomy was the only cure for endometriosis back then. Looking back, my troubles had been apparent in my teenage years and should have been picked up and attended to then. I was sad as in the back of my mind was the thought that maybe we would have another child. Thom and I had talked about a daughter. We had even named her Christine. Thom was anxious and I wasn't ready to deal with it so I decided to downplay the whole thing for the time being.

'What did the doctor say?' he asked me.

'I just need to take care of myself,' I reassured him. I would put it on the back burner as long as I could.

THIRTEEN

Oh, Boy!

Patrick developed a bad case of asthma and we decided to move them both to a school in Florida where the atmosphere seemed to suit him better. The boys were getting older and, thank God, better able to take care of themselves. The obligatory letter once a week to the parents always read: 'Dear Mom and Dad, I am fine. How are you?' signed Patrick or Shawn Ewen (just in case we forgot their last name). The separation wore on us emotionally and I longed for the day to see them home all the time. Their beloved Aunt Dutchie, Thom's sister, had recently moved to Tennessee and offered to watch over them when they were old enough to live at home without us. It was a much better option but in the meantime they were still too young.

We traded our original *Bypass* for another boat, a Gulf Star 36 motor Sailor. We kept her in Florida close to the boys and spent every off moment there with them. The Bahaman chain of islands off the coast was our playground in the summers and the boys became expert sailors and divers.

In the next few years we continued to play Vegas with Roy Clark and traveled the world, following our baggage.

'Isn't it a fast-moving world?' one of my companions quipped. 'Just think, breakfast Rome, lunch Hawaii, baggage Hong Kong ... '

I appeared at the Wembley Stadium in England for the annual *Country Music Show* along with many other stars like my friends Charlie

Pride and Dottie West. London became one of my favorite cities in the world and I spent every minute I could scouring the wonderful stores there and taking in the history. Thom and I viewed the fabulous Crown Jewels and I was particularly interested in how beautiful these stones were, even though the craftsmen at the time would not have had the kind of cutting tools available to modern jewelers. Later in life Thom and I worked for a time in the jewelry business in the Virgin Islands and I found myself comparing the machine-cut gems I was handling with the beauty of those ancient Crown Jewels.

We also visited the British Museum, where we saw the display of mummies. I was most uncomfortable with the sight – people had laid out their dear ones thinking they would rest for eternity and here we were viewing the disfigured remains for two dollars. I tiptoed away vowing that I would be cremated.

Our hotel looked out over beautiful parkland and up to the manicured grounds of Buckingham Palace, and I thought I spied the Queen one day sitting on her horse with guards at attention. More to Thom's taste was the view from our hotel to the nearby Playboy Bunny Club where several nudes sunned themselves every day.

Once at another hotel in London we stepped out to eat as soon as we arrived and foolishly left our IDs and money in the room. When we returned everything had been stolen. Is this starting to sound familiar? It was the weekend and it took some time to get hold of anyone to sort it out. We had planned a trip down to Merriott in Somerset, the home of my father's relatives, to look around and visit the churches there and it was only thanks to the good people of the American Express office that we had cash for the trip. Over the years as we returned to London for various television and country shows, we were aware that security was intensifying at all the hotels as the IRA and terrorists were on the loose.

The Vietnam conflict was still raging and I appeared for the US and Canadian military in Germany, France, Italy, Puerto Rico, Guam and the US. Guam was hot and humid, and the first night when I walked onstage and began my opener, nothing came out. I pushed again – nothing. I was completely hoarse. The band had kept going and I turned and signaled to my lead man to take my place as I left the stage to a few hoots from the guys in the audience. There was nothing else I could do.

As it happened, the top official in the audience that night was the father of a member of the Doors rock group, and he arranged for me to be whisked to the military hospital to be checked out. I was told that my voice had completely closed down in the humidity and probably would not come back till I was out of the area. I began swabbing my throat and staying in the air conditioning again and managed two more husky performances, thankfully fulfilling my contract but it was close. High humidity has always caused me a problem but it is a really scary feeling to push for a note that has always been there and have absolutely nothing come out.

I liked working for the boys on those tours, although as an audience they could be a bit unpredictable. In Puerto Rico we did shows for the NCOs as well as the regular troops. For the latter I was assigned a couple of SEALs – the Navy's elite force – whose job it was to accompany me everywhere while I was on the base as the boys tended to be rowdy. I didn't mind one little bit. These two well-built, immaculately uniformed, good-looking guys would walk with me – one fore and one aft – and I had no doubt I was in good hands. One night during the show a couple of boys stood up and made a grab for me. Well, my two guards had them restrained and out of there in no time. They were fantastic.

Thom is never one to let circumstances get the better of him. When he has his mind set on something, you may as well just give in straight away to save time. He is wired to win. A perfect example would be The Battle of the Baggage...

We were booked to tour Europe for the military with a group of my country musicians. Our troubles began in New York when we checked in with a huge pile of extra baggage and instruments, igniting a giant conflagration between Thom and the airlines as to the fee. Thom was an expert negotiator and had previously arranged the entire Wembley tour package – about fifteen entertainers, instruments and baggage – to fly with no extra fees. The man was a pro. I was apt to wait in the wings for these scenes to calm down as they were generally noisy and heated and wore me out. Thom worked his magic again for the European military tour and finally everyone was aboard and we flew to England.

All was fine until we had to board again in Heathrow for the next leg. The whole scene was repeated between Thom and a very dapper, if exasperated, airport official, for the benefit of Heathrow's passing parade. The rest of us stood aside, watching and waiting for the inevitable capitulation. Beaten down by Thom's unique brand of verbal warfare, the airport official eventually threw up his hands and loaded us up at no extra fee, shaking his head like it was all a bad dream. We patted Thom on the back and dubbed him the '50,000-Watt Mouth'.

The baggage problem continued whenever we flew. In Italy the argument worked its way out onto the pavement and even the taxi drivers became involved, screaming furiously in Italian. I suppose we were messing up the flow of traffic for the drivers. I would sip a cappuccino in a corner somewhere and wait. Thom's strategy was to have all the baggage loaded and when they began to charge him the exorbitant fees, he would tell them to take all the baggage off the plane (or the taxi), thereby delaying the whole process for everyone. He was involved in some world-shaking arguments and it did not pay to get in the middle of them. We were on the last leg home and had to go back via Heathrow. The same dapper gentleman saw us coming.

'Just let this group through … I remember … special dispensation.' He smiled through gritted teeth and boarded us, no doubt hoping never to see us hillbillies ever again.

We had some funny experiences in Germany on that trip. We had firmly apprised the musicians of the laws regarding contraband and they understood well but nevertheless we were searched in several countries. Mickey, our guitar player, was very funny about having anyone search him and would jump nervously and cry out as if he was being assaulted. He was a big guy and it was funny to hear him carry on.

'Watch out, I think you're gonna get goosed, Mickey,' Thom would tease. That was his word for a grab for the buttocks.

When we reached Germany, a stern official took the shrinking

Mickey behind a curtain to pat him down. Various screams and a lot of curtain flapping occurred, followed by the emergence of a very upset, red-faced German inspector, embarrassed by the commotion. Mickey was not one to submit quietly.

Thom and I were walking through the Hofbahnhof – the main railway station – in Kaiserslautern one day when a young marine with a baby bottle in his hand stopped us. A woman with a child in her arms waited a little way off. In extremely slow English the marine appealed to Thom.

'Can you ... please ... get ... milk ... for ... the baby?'

Thom took the bottle and walked over to the kiosk, giving it to the woman inside.

'Milch, bitte,' he ordered in his best German. I waited patiently for the outcome of this little joke while the woman washed the bottle and filled it with milk and handed it back to Thom who presented it to the marine.

'Danke,' the soldier said gratefully, holding out the money.

'Hey, that's okay, Mac,' Thom flipped back at him.

The soldier stared at the now-grinning Thom, realized he was a fellow American and began tapping his forehead at his own simplicity, howling with laughter.

'Country! Aw, shay-it! I am country, country, country!'

'Come along, Herr Ewen,' I murmured and we walked away as the soldier was bent in two, laughing helplessly at how he'd been taken in.

Apart from a few basics, we did not speak the language and this made ordering meals a bit hazardous. Once we pointed to what looked good on the menu whilst an unhelpful waiter looked on. No wonder – we had ordered beer and hot potato salad for breakfast. The food in general was wonderful, however, and I especially liked the cheesecakes and Austrian cuisine, although my hips did not.

Keeping my weight in order was a constant struggle and I tried every diet known to man, finally using a low-carb diet and Canadian Air Force exercises to keep at working weight. For people who travel a lot, just the water changes alone can be so destructive to the body. I even tried two years on a vegetarian diet but became too weak on that regime to continue. I think you must definitely know what you are doing to be a full vegetarian or you can cause yourself a problem. As I have gotten wiser, I strive for health first and try to choose a nutritionally-packed diet to preserve my body and keep well.

Once on our way to Australia we stopped over in Hong Kong to sightsee. As we were landing I noticed to my dismay that our health cards were expired – we were supposed to be up to date with a series of shots before entering the country.

'What'll we do?' I said to Thom, anxiously pointing at the cards.

'Give me mine,' he said.

My husband then proceeded to take a dime and trace it out, make a phony stamp marked 'US Virgin Islands', and sign it 'Doctor Higgins'.

'My God! They're going to put you in jail! I'm not doing that!' I grabbed my own card and put it in my purse self-righteously. 'I'll just tell them when I land.'

Upon landing we produced our documents. Thom was ahead of me. The officials seemed to be a very unsmiling bunch, or perhaps that was my nerves jumping. Any minute now I was expecting Thom to be arrested and thrown in jail. Of course, Thom's documents were all stamped straight away (I am sure they had never even seen a US Virgin Island health stamp) but I was grabbed by two security guards and hauled off yelling to destination unknown. Two small white-robed officials held me down and proceeded to inject me with every shot known to Disease Control while I kept up a loud running commentary of protest.

'Ouch! Don't leave marks on my arms ... ouch! I am an entertainer!'

They of course saw nothing, knew nothing, and kept shooting me up. Thom appeared at last at the doorway to get me. Seeing the amusement in his face was the last straw. I raised my arm and pointed an accusatory finger at Thom, shamelessly ready to give him up.

'There he is! Get him! Do you know what he did? He took a dime and ...!' The official cut me off.

'His papers in order,' he pointed out in broken English.

I was in tears and to cap it all off they took my passport as well, ordering me to report back on leaving the country to show my scars and prove the inoculations had indeed taken. I was mortified. I suffered a terrible fever that night, my arms swelling up like balloons and remaining sore for days after. Thom looked after me in a very dedicated way but I knew he was laughing the whole time. Poking my tongue out at the official upon retrieving my passport went a small way to relieving my feelings. Thom was horrified.

'You can't do that!'

'I just did,' I retorted, marching off to the plane. Thom was no respecter of official documents. I can't tell you how many times he has forged a signature to save time – it's terrible.

In Japan I worked for Jim Raines a couple of times, which was quite an experience. He was an Australian businessman living in Japan then and every year he organized an entertainment event in Tokyo. He and his wife Betty became lifelong friends and were great hosts. In fact, I think Betty wins the award for the best hostess I have ever known. I also discovered that Betty was in the audience screaming for me when I toured with Sammy Davis, Jr. in Australia way back before I first went to the States. We worked mainly for the expatriates in Japan, Australians included, but sometimes appeared in Japanese clubs. The Japanese audiences were very different and I was acutely aware of the language barrier. I worked several times for solely Japanese audiences and was concerned that with the differences in customs I may inadvertently offend in some way. I voiced this to a woman of stature at a cocktail party one night. She informed me coldly not to worry, that I was only 'barbarian entertainment' and anything barbarians did was not taken seriously. I was feeling very embarrassed with all this egg on my face when Thom, ex-marine and veteran of World War Two and Korea, stepped in. Taking my arm, he coolly spoke up.

'Barbarians? Maybe. But don't forget, WE are the Conquerors.'

The words hung in the air as the woman turned a sickly shade then, drawing herself to her full height, she turned tail and left the room. Thom does not back down to miserable attacks like that.

'Wow,' I mouthed to him and we raised our glasses to each other. I bet that little darling hasn't forgotten Thom, barbarian or not.

I did not let that experience kill Japan for me, though, and thoroughly enjoyed our sightseeing, even though I was always nearly beheading myself on the doorways of the trains. Being five-foot-nine, I was a very tall woman in Japan. We visited the huge Buddha of Kamakura and went inside. In the half-light I spied a piece of paper on the floor. *Oh no, fancy throwing trash down in here!* I picked it up to dispose of it outside and found it was the equivalent of a five dollar bill in Japanese money. I thanked the Buddha very much.

It was the mid-1970s. Seasons changed, the boys were growing, and each year seemed to go by faster than the one before. The Halsey Agency wasn't happy with us for taking our long summer vacations but I did not really care too much. We had to give some time to the boys before they were gone forever – 'Family first' was my motto. The agency complained that I was worth a lot to them now and if I got hurt they would lose money on their investment. Maybe, it was suggested, I should take out a big insurance policy on the voice alone? I laughed it off. Whatever happened, happened as far as I was concerned, and I did not feel I owed anyone for the way I chose to live my life.

Meanwhile, *Bypass II* was a very comfortable boat and in summertime we had a load of fun with her. We'd take off across the Gulf Stream loaded to the gunwales with provisions and sometimes friends and their kids and discover the beautiful island paradise and spectacular waters of the Bahamas. Food and fresh water in the islands are not always readily available so I learned to plan and ration carefully and we all perfected the saltwater bath and rinse with laundry softener to get the salt off. The water was so clear that sometimes I would be diving under the boat and lose track of how far down I was. You could easily see to a depth of at least eighty feet. I was in total bliss until the day I encountered my first big shark face to face.

It was late in the afternoon and Thom and I had been squabbling about directions all day. He was the navigator and I was the non-believer.

It just doesn't feel right was my line, at which point the kids would mysteriously disappear and Thom would spout irritating explanations capped off by a simple statement that he had studied navigation and I had not. It was very hot and tempers often flared in the tropics, so this evening I broke my own rule about not going into the water near sundown.

I came down the swim ladder and dove into the beautifully clear water. My head eased immediately and all was much better with the world. The bottom was soft, white sand studded with coral and the anchor looked securely set. I swam slowly back up to the surface and was clearing my mask when a small piece of my snorkel jiggled off and dropped to the bottom. *Darn it* ... I took a deep breath and duck dived down about twenty feet to retrieve it.

Back on the surface I reattached the piece, cleared my mask again, and looked back down at where I had just been. Directly underneath me was a very large, black hammerhead shark, angrily swishing his tail from side to side. I had been warned that late summer is the mating season for the hammerheads and as we were just up on the Bahama Bank near very deep water, this was an especially dangerous situation. I had obviously disturbed his territory and he was showing his displeasure.

I felt totally frozen except for thudding heart and racing thoughts. I could focus on one thing only – could I make it to the dinghy before the shark could swim up and get me? I weighed up my chances. *Y ... y ... yes...*

'Shark!' I yelled and in an instant was swimming for dear life to the back of the boat where our dinghy floated. I'm sure I just planed across the water. The worst possible thing you can do is make noise and splash but I forgot my whole Australian heritage and knowledge of sharks and just swam like a mad thing. I reached the dinghy, clawed my way over the side and dropped to the boards. I peered over the side – he was still there, about seven feet long. I was too afraid to even put my hand in the water to haul the dinghy up close to *Bypass II* and get out. Meantime, Thom had run onto the deck and saw me cowering in the dinghy.

'What's the matter?' he yelled.

'Shark! There's a shark!' I blathered.

Thom hauled the dinghy alongside. 'Get in,' he said and dragged me aboard.

I was shaking like a leaf. He poured me a stiff toddy and after a while I calmed down and told the story.

'I knew you shouldn't have gone in swimming, Di,' he said with a grin when I'd finished.

'Why?' I asked with suspicion. *Dumb question, don't encourage him.*

'Oh, you know,' he said in a pretty good imitation of my voice, '*it just didn't feel right.*'

Thank you, Thom … Since then I have seen many sharks and learned they are really quite beautiful creatures with a very important part to play in the health of our oceans, having their own place in the scheme of things. They are something to be aware of and alert around but I was never so terrified as that day.

When we weren't on the boat in the summer we were on the road with Roy Clark for the round of state fairs. I worked out that one year Roy and I had actually put our bodies in front of one million people as we traveled throughout the West and Central states of the US. The stadiums were packed and the show was greeted well everywhere. But the work and the traveling were hard and I was beginning to feel the strain more than ever. One memorable week I flew across the US from coast to coast three times working television and different venues every night.

One overnight stay in New York near the airport brought us another adventure. They did seem to follow us around. I woke during the night to hear the sound of a child crying in the next room. It went on and on, a thin, pathetic wailing, and I could also hear what sounded like a beating noise. Well, I couldn't sleep and I couldn't rest, thinking what might be happening to some poor child on the other side of the wall.

'Thom!' I nudged him awake. 'Listen! You've got to go in there.'

'Don't be crazy! This is New York!'

I pushed him out of bed. 'Get up, go in!' I insisted. You've got to do something!'

He was out of bed, pulling on his pants. 'You're gonna get me killed.'

He opened our door cautiously and looked out, me peering over his shoulder. He knocked cautiously and tried the handle of the next door room. The door opened but it was heavy...

'Something's funny,' he said. The wailing noise was louder. 'The door won't open properly.'

He shoved at it and finally got inside to find a guy hanging by the neck from the hook on the back of the door. He was blue in the face and crying like a child. Nobody else was in the room. Thom got him down while I called the police. It turned out he was beaten and robbed by two prostitutes who left him strung up like that to die.

My recording career had taken a few turns along the way. Buddy Killen had owned Dial, the first country label I recorded with back in 1968; within a year Dial sold out to the Dot label in Nashville. Dot was a major label of that era, whose stable comprised such noted artists as Pat Boone and Billy Vaughn as well as country artists: Roy Clark, Hank Thompson, Don Williams, Donna Fargo, Barbara Mandrell, The Oak Ridge Boys and Ray Price. Now Dot had merged with another label, ABC.

In charge of ABC-Dot was Jim Foglesong, who had been handling my recording career from some time. I remember the day I went to the studio to meet Jim...

'But I know you!'

'Hello again, Diana,' he said with a smile. Jim turned out to be one of the original male singers on *Sing Along*. We had a good chat about old times and caught up with the news about different people we'd worked with in New York. I was very happy to be working with him. Jim was a great gentleman, easy to work with and I felt he had my interests at heart. He carefully managed all my sessions, listening to every aspect of the recording and our first albums did well with songs like 'Everything I Own', 'Country Bumpkin' and 'Jesse'. The late Guy Mitchell was once sweet enough to say, 'Nobody on this earth sings 'Jesse' better than Diana Trask.'

Recording itself was more of a promotional activity than a money-making venture. I knew very few people who actually made much from their records, unless they happened to be songwriters as well. Recordings got you airplay, which got you exposure and hopefully more gigs.

Earlier I had worked with Norro Wilson at ABC-Dot was an accomplished writer and we had a string of hits that did well in the Country Billboard Charts in the late sixties/early seventies – 'Say When', 'It's a Man's World', 'He Took Me for a Ride', 'Lean It All on Me', 'When I Get My Hands on You' – some of which I had a hand in writing. I loved the writing side of things and wished I'd had more faith in my abilities and pursued it properly. Song writing is a powerful gift – to be able to capture a feeling or an experience in a way that cuts right through to the heart of a stranger listening to the radio, that's incredible. To hear your words coming out of another singer's mouth is exciting and humbling.

The more I learned the greater my admiration for the skills of other writers; for instance, Charlie Chaplin wrote 'Smile', one of the best songs ever written. I recently found out I shared that opinion with the best live performer I have ever seen, the late Michael Jackson. Chaplin wrote it for his day, as many writers have, capturing the feel of their times in an unsurpassed way and thereby penning the classics we all know. I learned about the 'hook' – the thing that makes the song stick. We were always searching for the hook.

Jim Foglesong and I had once cut a song by Red Lane called 'Till I Get It Right' that we both thought was great. We were immediately covered by Tammy Wynette who took it right up the charts, so that was that. I was furious – I seemed to come up against Tammy all the time and emerge the loser. That's partly why I wanted to write my own songs – at least I would maintain control of them. But Jim took it all in his stride. He calmed me down and we just resumed our search. One day he called about another song.

'It's called 'Oh Boy' by Tony Romeo. I think you'll like it. Come by and listen.'

I did like it and we included it in our next session which was scheduled for the day after we closed in Vegas. We cut a bunch of songs and squeezed 'Oh Boy' in at the last minute. We both thought it was strong. We all knew that I needed a big song to take me to the next level in the business. I had prayed to St. Jude for a crossover smash, a big hit in both Country and Pop charts. As we listened to the final mix, Jim and I believed that we had done it with 'Oh Boy'.

We were set to release and I went on the road, leaving things with Jim. He called me a few weeks later and I could tell right away he had bad news. ABC-Dot was changing hands yet again and our song was caught in the changeover. Promotion of 'Oh Boy' would not happen. Jim and I were shattered. 'Oh Boy' went on to do well in the country charts with no help at all, but nowhere near as well as it could have. It should have been a monster hit and that thought lingers as one of my biggest professional disappointments.

A few weeks passed and I was on the road when Jim called me.

'Diana? Guess what? 'Oh Boy' has gone crossover in Australia – it's number one!'

I was delighted – we had a hit in my home country and Thom and I celebrated. It may not have been exactly what I was aiming for, but you can always count on St. Jude for a twist. You see, my promise to St. Jude had been this: I will do something in the name of the saint whose feast day falls on the day I am told when and where I have a hit. We checked the calendar. It was Lazarus, the patron saint of lepers, and so The Lazarus Appeal was born and my home country Australia was where I would fulfill my promise.

We contacted Bob Finikiotis, our financial manager in Australia, about the project, and Bob took hold of the thing like it was his own and started running with it. He immediately looked into arranging press conferences and interviews and lining up promoters for some fund-raising concerts. Meantime, I began to study leprosy.

My very first contact with leprosy was back in Texas in the 1960s when I met Dr. Denton Cooley, the famous heart specialist. He had been reading a journal on the disease as I walked in and he mentioned in passing that most doctors in the US would probably not even recognize a leprosy lesion as the disease was not often seen in the US. My later investigations showed that the disease was endemic to the region of Louisiana. I read that the disease had been renamed Hansen's disease to combat the stigma associated with the word 'leper'.

I contacted Carville, the main research hospital for Hansen's disease in Louisiana, and learned that great leaps and bounds in knowledge had been made through studying the humble armadillo, the only animal apart from humans known to be susceptible to leprosy. In developed countries most patients were easily treated as outpatients with the new multidrug antibiotic therapy. There was even a dancer in New York who had the disease and by taking these drugs lived life, fulfilling her dreams onstage. I also learned that there are many types of the disease and that the bacillus debilitates the nervous system and is not particularly contagious unless there is exposure to an infected person over a long period of time.

The disease settles in the cooler regions of the body and causes nerve damage to the extremities, such as the fingers, toes and nose. The resultant numbness then leads to minor infected wounds being unnoticed until damage is permanent, leading to the horrific facial deformities and loss of fingers and toes in an untreated sufferer.

I learned of an island in the Hawaiian chain, Molokai, that had an old leper colony, but there were not many folks left there. Patients were separated and all rights were removed, in fact they had fewer rights than a criminally insane psychopath in many countries. But the most shocking thing I came across was that the Aboriginal people of Australia were still suffering from both the stigma and the disease.

There is a band around the world covering most of the hot climates near the equator, and these are endemic regions for the disease. The northern part of Australia is included, New Guinea also. Leprosy first came to Australia with the Chinese migration to the goldfields in the mid-nineteenth century and spread quickly to the Aborigines who were ignorant of its threat. Combined with other health problems caused by the arrival of Europeans and fearful of the forced segregation of leprosy sufferers, they tended to hide their illness and took to the bush. Most of the world's population is naturally immune; our ancestors were infected perhaps and handed down their immunities.

I learned the Queen of England was patron of a society that tried to help these folks and that other entertainers such as Tallulah Bankhead and the 'Fonz' – Henry Winkler – had also given of themselves to help this cause over the years. The more I read, the more fascinated I became and I felt a personal drive to do what I could.

A treatment hospital was the first idea but of course I discarded that pretty quickly after learning that sufferers could be better helped by early detection, access to affordable multidrug therapy and proper outpatient services. There was less of a stigma attached that way. So our next idea was that of raising consciousness through the Australian newspapers and television about the disease and its treatment. If I could use my name to bring the subject into the light and help reduce the stigma attached to the disease, this would lessen the pain of sufferers.

In Australia we held press conferences in Melbourne and Sydney, which were well supported by television, newspapers, church and medical interest groups, and then came a round of interviews on the subject. This is when the letters began. These were heartbreaking testimonies of discrimination, suffering and separation. People are still terrified to a biblical proportion of this disease as ignorance on the subject reigns around the world. We comforted those we could. Practical help was our next aim and Bob Finikiotis worked hard to set up some fund-raising concerts, the proceeds of which were dedicated to assist in ongoing education and patient support.

At one of the concerts we stood greeting folks at the door when Thom and I saw a couple of old friends from the country. We were a bit shocked to see them – the tickets were deliberately pricey.

'Oh, no worries,' they reassured us. 'Happy to help. Besides, we had a paid trip.'

'How's that?' I asked.

'Our mate in the back of the car, he paid for the trip,' they said, grinning.

I was puzzling over this one, then the light dawned. The 'mate' in the car was a customer, you might say – our friends were undertakers! I hope their 'mate' enjoyed the short rest stop on the way to where he was going.

Many Australians we talked to initially found it hard to believe that such an old disease was still in their midst but we got a lot of good support for our endeavor and we, in turn, gave it all we had. There is still much to be done however. The Leprosy Mission continues to carry out this valuable work of research, education and help for sufferers worldwide. I heard stories of doctors who had crawled through the bush in New Guinea to find sufferers and try to teach them how to take medicine. These truly courageous and magnificent people really cared and showed me pictures of patients they had found with needless disfigurements of distorted feet and ruined noses. I was humbled beyond belief at the work they undertook.

I felt our help was small in comparison but every candle we light pushes back the darkness a little more.

FOURTEEN

Country Roads

Back in the States I was delighted to be booked to be part of a show starring the legendary Bob Hope. It was a charity event at the Hollywood Bowl. Bob Hope was an entertainment king and I thoroughly enjoyed our duet together – 'De-lovely'. Bob had scripted the way it was to go. I was to sing everything except the word 'It's'. That would be his word plus all the shtick that went along with the delivery. In front of the audience he handed me my script which went on and on like a Hebrew scroll. Then, to the audience's delight, he held up his – a tiny scrap of paper.

He was so charming and we got along very well. I introduced him to Thom backstage. This did not stop him from inviting me to his dressing room after the show ... Mr. Hope was famous as a ladies' man. Well, I did go to his dressing room after the show – but I took Thom with me! The look on Bob's face was a picture. He was taken aback but remained charming to us both and every year we would receive a Christmas card from him and his wife. He wrote me a letter once when I was appearing in Vegas with Phil Harris, mainly to warn me that Phil's breath had been known to melt scenery. I still have that letter.

Sometime later Danny Thomas called and asked me as a favor to take a booking with Milton Berle. I was not hot on the idea as we walked such entirely different entertainment roads but said I would do it for him. Milton was very old world and what I imagined old burlesque was like years ago. In his own way he was quite courtly but I thought him very nervous all the time. We did a duet together – the same one I had done with Bob Hope and, I noted with surprise, with the same comic arrangement. I did not say anything about whose material was whose, just went ahead with the deal. Apparently through the years Milton had been accused of stealing other folk's material and vice versa – a long running ragging went on between the old stars.

The early lesson I learned way back at GTV9 television in Melbourne about the art of upstaging stood me in good stead when it came to working with Milton Berle. It wasn't long before I found out that he was a past master too; in fact, he had quite a reputation for taking over the stage. In no time I found myself maneuvered to the point where I had my back to the audience. One night I had had enough and every time *he* stepped back *I* took a step back. We ended flat up against the band.

Milton's mouth started to work in a very agitated manner and he whispered furiously, 'What the hell is the matter with you?'

The audience was snickering and I heard a particularly loud, appreciative noise from Liza Minnelli who was in the audience that night. I just gave him a look and he never did the step back thing again although you could see him fighting it. Milton was a sweetie everywhere except onstage, where he got *very* tense.

Pain from chronic endometriosis was now my constant companion. I was back on the road in the States fulfilling some commitments and could no longer keep the pain at bay. It was affecting my life on both personal and business levels as I was feeling ill and snappy, sometimes spending days in bed. My old habit of 'pushing through' wasn't working so well, and on some gigs I found that taking some brandy was the only thing that helped with the pain and got me onstage. After a particularly bad night where even the brandy didn't help, I came to my senses and

BOB HOPE

July 24, 1975

Ms. Diana Trask
Rte. 2
Mt. Juliet, Tennessee 37122

Dear Diana:

The audience sure did approve of you
Sunday night and rightly so because
you are quite a gal.

The show made a lot of money and so
you can take a deep bow for your
participation.

Hope you have great success in Las Vegas.
I'm sure you will if you can stay out
of the way of Phil Harris' breadth.
He melts scenery, you know.

Regards,

BOB

BH:jg

10346 Moorpark Street
No. Hollywood, California 91602

decided enough was enough. I would have to have surgery. Thom was irate with me for not disclosing the extent of the trouble.

I was admitted to Donelson Hospital not far from home in Tennessee and surgery was performed with great success. The doctor said it was a severe case and that he was glad I had finally made up my mind to do something about it. The hospital was full up, though, and as a result I ended up in the maternity ward. On discharge, administration staff seemed to be on tiptoe around me and I suddenly realized they must all think that, as I was not carrying a baby out, I must have lost one. We had to reassure everyone as we left.

Mom and Dad were planning on a visit to help us out when I came home from hospital but around that time Mom slipped and broke her leg, so we were both on the sick list. My recuperation was slow – it seemed to take me a long time to come back to speed so I used the time to concentrate on writing songs. I spent long hours in my peaceful studio upstairs, the beautiful view of fields and trees as much a part of my cure as any medicine.

In 1979 we took another trip to Australia to tour the Sydney clubs. I tried to get back to Australia every couple of years, particularly as Dad's health was beginning to fail markedly. In the lead up, Thom was unusually preoccupied ... even a bit jittery ... and he seemed to be on the phone *all* the time. What was he up to? I was soon to find out. I was taking my bow at the end of a show at the Castle Hill Returned Services League Club when through the curtain behind me emerged a film crew and a face I seemed to recognize. The audience was going mad. *Is he here to present me with flowers? Then, why the film crew? Is it an award for something?* No, it was Australian television personality Roger Climpson, announcing: 'Diana Trask, This is Your Life'.

I was absolutely stunned. I had no idea at all. Thom said he had never lied so much in the whole of his married life as he set it all up, contacted family and friends and worked out the details. My mom was there, my brother Pete and his wife Marcia, friends from school days – Nola O'Loughlin and Barbara James – even Sr. Lucy and Sr. Concepta from the Presentation Convent; Jack Ayling, the good friend who first encouraged me back to Australia to perform at home; pre-recorded messages from Mitch Miller and Joe Martin (the guy who had scribbled 'Hire Diana Trask' all over the dining room walls at Channel 7 way back when I first went to Sydney); Di Baker (formerly Sindrey) and Brian Syron were there; my two gorgeous boys, Shawn and Patrick. And then my dear father, who I thought was too unwell to travel, arrived in a wheelchair. What a night.

A few months later it was very early spring in the States and I was working in Hot Springs, Arkansas, for my regular gig with Jack Baumgartner, a really wonderful man. He owned a club near the famous spa and race track, and I would always work his best season. I worked for him whenever he asked me to, even though at that time of the year I would always go down with hay fever. In Hot Springs there grows a red cherry tree that is beautiful in bloom, but its pollen, combined with the smoke in the club, tore me up every time and I spent almost the whole gig locked inside in the air conditioning.

I had struggled through most of the two-week booking when one night Thom took me up to our room.

'Sit down,' he said quietly and I knew something bad was coming.

'There is no way to soften this blow,' he said. 'Your father had passed away.'

It was like a punch in the chest. I had worried about Dad last time I saw him. For some years he had suffered strange episodes where he would pass out, and he was frail and ill for the taping of the *This is Your Life* special. That night, sitting in his wheelchair, he told the world that he worshipped the ground I walked on. *Oh, Dad*...

I'd had a funny feeling as the taxi bore him away back to Sydney airport that I would not see him alive again. Strangely enough, as we were preparing to go to Hot Springs, I'd heard Dad's voice in my head saying very clearly, 'Diana!'

'My God, Dad sent me a message,' I cried out to Thom now.

I'd disregarded it at the time, putting it down to his fear of dying communicating itself to me across the miles. As Dad's health deteriorated he would grab at us many times and say, 'Well, just in case I don't have a chance to say goodbye, I'm saying it now.'

'Dad,' I'd say, 'you're only going to die once and you'll do a real good job of it, so relax and go with the flow. We will all love you now and forever.'

He still worried that he would not be able to say goodbye. As it happened he was right. I learned that at the time of his death he was in a nursing hospital where Mom placed him occasionally when he got too much for her to handle. He just dropped to the floor and was gone. Whenever Dad came to see me perform he would always ask to hear 'Danny Boy'. I would sing it for him and watch as his face lit up, his lips moving silently to the words as I sang. The day I learned he died I swore I would never sing that song again and I never have. I just could not.

Mr. Baumgartner released me from the remainder of my contract and I flew directly to Melbourne to be there with Mom for the funeral. Thom had to stay behind for a commitment with the boys, so it was a long, long journey on my own, with plenty of tears. I got into conversation with a man seated near me – he was on his way to Perth for the funeral of his brother and we shared our stories a little.

During the journey I wrote a letter to my dad. I wanted to replace that old one of mine about the kitten, the letter he had cherished for years and which was pickpocketed along with his wallet on my wedding day. He had been so distressed at the time by its loss. I would make up for that loss now, and into that letter I put all my love for the daddy I had adored. I placed it carefully in his pocket on the morning of the funeral, my last gift to him.

Family and friends were around but Mom was very alone, and after the funeral was over I took her for a trip up the east coast to Port Stevens in New South Wales. We walked the wide, white beaches and she began to relax a little. Funny how the ocean can tap into every emotion of the human heart, from joy to desolation. I was on the beach alone one day when a sobbing spell of mourning for Dad swept over me. I looked out at the lonely waste of water and up to the empty sky and cried out our age-old response to death: *Why?*

I cannot explain what happened next very well. All I can say is that an enormous voice filled the sky, a voice that was masculine, intimate and gentle.

'Nature will take its course,' I heard it say.

I was amazed but some of the grieving stopped and I knew Dad was in a safe place and at peace. Although I have sensed his presence occasionally, I never really worried about him after that day. I wrenched myself away from my grieving mother to fulfill contractual obligations back in the US. Life has a way of gathering you up and carrying you along, whether you feel ready or not.

I had heard of a team of prolific songwriters in Nashville – Jerry Foster and Bill Rice – and I decided to go downtown with my compositions and bang on their door. They agreed to listen to my work and also let me sit in with their writers and get a feel for how they worked. One night I was driving my car home from the store and the words just came ... *I have lifted up the corners of my heart*. I burned rubber home, tore upstairs and finished the song that night. First thing in the morning I took it into town to Bill Rice.

'Oh yeah, oh yeah,' he said. 'This is good, Diana. I like this.'

I had a good feeling about that song. Bill suggested one change to the title lyric – from 'I Contemplate Your Lovin'' to 'I Think About Your Lovin'' and we put it down right away in his tiny studio. Ritchie Alves added a few chords on guitar and rhythm was supplied courtesy of a drum stick on a telephone book. So many songs were put down in a day there that it was out of the question to have a full session with lots of musicians around. I drove home excited but knew nothing would happen right away.

The record label ABC-Dot had dropped me from their books some time before – who knows why, an artist is the smallest cog in the machine of these companies – so I currently had no recording contract. 'Oh Boy' hadn't been big in the States and the next song Jim Foglesong and I put down also got lost in the company transition that was taking place. Perhaps the new owners of ABC-Dot saw the label taking a new direction. Thom and I had tried a record producer on the West Coast but things didn't work out there either. Whatever the reasons, I was out in the cold, otherwise I would have recorded my new song myself. As it was, Foster and Rice put it out there in the marketplace and I had to wait.

I had an overseas commitment to fulfill but as soon as we got back I checked in with Foster and Rice. Bill greeted me with a big smile.

'We got your song cut, Diana,' he said. 'Guess who?'

'Who? Who?'

'The Osmond Brothers and it's going up the charts like fire!'

I could not believe it – I was so excited. I almost had an accident in the car the first time I heard the Osmonds singing my song on the radio. Those boys did a fantastic job, singing it just as I had heard it in my head. 'I Think About Your Lovin'' went 17 on the Country charts in 1982 and I was absolutely thrilled. The only sour note was that the producer of the record was named in Billboard as the writer of the song and I received no credit.

'Don't let it get to ya,' advised one of the other writers at Foster and Rice. 'There's no glory in songwriting.'

I didn't agree with him. To me it was an incredible thrill and I wanted to take it further so I was very disappointed when shortly after that Foster and Rice sold out to a huge international publishing company and once more that part of my life was left to drift.

Dad had been gone about a year and I felt the need to get back to Australia. I wanted to see Mom and make sure she was okay, but for my own sake I wanted to soak up the sights and smells of home. I'd toured the length and breadth of the US many times over but my Australian tours had been mainly confined to the club scenes in Melbourne, Sydney and Brisbane, the capital cities along the east coast. There was so much more to Australia – just as there was in the States once I got out to the country and found the real people – and I wanted to get in touch with it again.

Thom wrestled the details with Australian agents, promoters and bookers, I phoned Mom and told her we were on our way, and off we went on an extended three-month tour of my homeland. If you have been to Australia you will know that even three whole months is not enough time to do more than scratch the surface. It is a *big* place.

Our tour began in Victoria, my home state, commencing in the Gippsland region, the scene of our honeymoon adventures. Our venues were whatever held the most people in town – R.S.L. (Returned Services League) Clubs, Town Halls and so on. We travelled with our own sound, lights and crew and used various opening acts booked through a Sydney agent, none other than Tom Spencer, that drummer from so long ago whose fate line the psychic said was twisted with mine.

One memorable night in Gippsland I had slipped into my 'audience participation' bit, a part of the show where I called guys up from the crowd to sing backup with me onstage to a number like 'It's Such a Pretty World Today'. I would teach them their part and to dance a little and it generally got lots of laughs. Often I ended up being the butt of the jokes as I had no idea who I had called up or was talking to.

This particular night I dragged up a big guy with a kind of laid-back attitude and a wide smile. He was so good-natured I decided to get on his case and make him take off his shirt and dance. The response from the crowd was over the top – they were howling. As the act was going so well, I became more demanding of the guy and when I discovered a hole in his undershirt I sent him up without remorse. The audience was hooting and rolling when I finally asked him what he did for a living. He replied gently that he was the local cop ... No wonder they loved it! I think he became very famous that night.

One time on a military base I got a guy up to do the same kind of routine and the boys in the audience nearly went mad. They were in hysterics and the more I teased this fella, the louder they roared. It turned out he was in charge of appropriations for the entire Air Force and was there to be wined and dined by the local brass. I was stringing him along saying that I thought he looked kind of shifty – *don't you think he looks kinda shifty, boys? I'd be careful of this guy if I were you ...* They howled and he took it well, knowing I was as much a butt of the situation as he was.

Speaking of butts, it took an Aussie guy on this tour to get even for all those guys I'd taken the mickey out of for so long. He literally grabbed a hold of mine in a 'show of support' for my act and I thought at the time, well, all's fair in love and war – after all, I'd grabbed hold of everyone else's and teased the heck out of them for long enough.

From Gippsland we moved across the south of Victoria and into the northwestern wine-growing area. White eucalyptus trees held up their ghostly branches like a guard of honor as we passed along the country roads. Here we were being handled by Dennis Smith, a fine promoter who had grown up not far from me in Marysville, Victoria. He produced many successful shows with Barry Humphries – or 'Dame Edna' as he is otherwise known. We visited the wineries and I took pictures of everything with the brand new camera Thom had bought me for my birthday.

As we were in sheep country and it was shearing time, I thought it would be fun to see it in action. In the next small town we stopped by the local New Zealand Dalgety Loan office – an old established firm of woolbrokers operating throughout Australia and New Zealand – and asked if there was a sheep farm nearby that was shearing. The officer responded as if I was a family member dropping by.

'Oh yeah, I'll just phone 'em up and let 'em know you're coming, Di.'

He gave us long instructions, especially about closing gates – it's the same in every farm state in the world I think – and we took off. After about half an hour we found the property and, carefully closing the gates as we went, we ended up at a farm house completely built out of native blue stone. Set back amongst the tall trees and outbuildings it was very beautiful. We were greeted and escorted to the sheds where sheep milled around in the pens waiting to be shorn.

A sheep was taken from the catching pen and led up to the shearing board by the shearer, a brawny Aussie guy. The shearer then tucked it expertly between his knees and went over its whole body with electric shears in a smooth flowing movement. The fleece curled away from the animal in a long creamy wave, revealing the beautiful clean wool beneath the grey, dusty outer surface. The shed smelled strongly of lanolin and the floor seemed to be greased with it. The sheep behaved in a very docile manner and seemed to accept this turn of events with a resolute air.

Expert shearers get the whole fleece off in one single piece in a matter of three minutes or less. It's then picked up by a shed hand or 'roustabout' and tossed onto the wool table, rather like a fisherman throwing a shrimp net. The fleece settles perfectly on the tabletop and the dags (soiled pieces of wool) are removed and saved for other purposes other than that of the finer clean fleece. The fine fleece is then classed and baled ready for shipment. It's a well-orchestrated operation from top to bottom. The most joyous thing to see is the sheep when it is shorn and released. He leaps around like a young colt, seemingly so happy to lose that hot, old coat.

It was a lovely interlude. The family was very gracious and warm, giving us a great lunch before we had to run and prepare for the evening's show, which was playing in the district not far away. We invited them to come and see the show that night as our thanks for their hospitality.

We took a break before moving on to New South Wales where Bob Finikiotis was to meet us and conduct us around. We played a few Sydney venues and then took off into the back country. Now the venues were really makeshift, with chairs added on and rooms bulging at the seams. People showed up out of the back country in jeeps and trucks, hot and dusty from their overland trip. At three o' clock coats and cardigans were draped over the first rows of seats to save places for the night's performance. The crowds were unbelievable – so receptive and loving. This is what I had wanted to do for years, perform for my own people, to do my very best for them and to thank them for their support throughout the years.

The year before I had recorded an album in Australia for Hammard records and Sino Guzzardi entitled *One Day At A Time,* which was getting heavy play and sold very well. We included many of those tracks in the tour. People invited us into their homes to eat after the shows, providing large suppers for us and the whole crew. The clubs also did their best for us and we were reminded constantly of the tremendous Aussie good nature and hospitality.

Funny types do turn up everywhere, though. My mom traveled with us for part of the time and she and I stopped for lunch at one of the R.S.L. clubs along the road. As a matter of course, you are served your salad first in the US and then the entrée. This is not the custom in Australia. Mom and I had ordered a steak and were chattering away absentmindedly, when out of the corner of my eye I noticed that the lady serving us was wearing the usual black outfit with, unexpectedly, pink fluffy slippers. I took this in my stride as she placed the salad on the table and returned to the kitchen. I served myself and began to eat. The woman came out again and I was aware that the fluffy slippers were swooping closer and closer to the table where I was still forking up salad and chattering away to Mom. Finally the woman flourished to a stop beside me.

'You're gonna eat the whole bloody lot before your meat gets here, aren't ya?' she accused.

I stopped eating, my fork dangling lettuce in midair. Mom stared, amazed and then we caught each other's eye and tried hard not to laugh as the slippers turned around and retreated to the kitchen.

'Good God, it's the manners police,' Mom whispered to me.

Most times Thom and I drove separately from the crew and would stop along the way to go for walks along the country roads and fill our lungs with the beautiful fresh air. I found this helped to counteract the smoky atmospheres I sometimes had to sing in. The countryside was all big sky and soft fields smudged with purple shadows. Noisy flocks of budgerigars and cockatoos wheeled overhead, jostling for position along the branches of the trees and swooping above us as we travelled the single lane roads.

One day we were pushing it for time and running low on gas. The country towns were sparse and spread far apart, so it was with a sigh of relief that we saw a little country gas station appear up ahead. We pulled up to find the door shut up tight and a sign on the window. We looked at each other in dismay. Thom got out and read it. *Closed. Gone to see the Diana Trask show.* Oh heck ... We pushed on with fingers crossed, limping over the line with about a thimble-ful of gas left in the tank.

The coast road up towards Queensland was next, passing the magnificent Sapphire Coast on the way. At one spot we stopped for lunch and found kangaroos that frequented the beach, begging for food. This seems cute but is not such a good thing, as they get mad when the food runs out. You'd better be ready to beat it back to the car when that happens as they have long claws and will scratch. Better not to feed them at all and leave wild animals to be wild, I think. Now it was turning tropical and getting hotter. The venues were sometimes outside and sometimes very rough, but the audiences were anything but rough.

We took a left turn, switched to a plane, and flew on towards the center – the red heart of Australia in the Northern Territory. How spectacular it is. From the town of Alice Springs, sometimes just called 'the Alice', we took a small plane out to The Rock – Uluru. Uluru rises out of the surrounding flat country like a sacred temple reaching to heaven, its color fluctuating from deep red to purple and black as the sun shifts and the light alters. It is massive, solitary, unexpected.

In those days access to The Rock was more or less unrestricted, even though for the local Anangu tribe this was a sacred place and on their traditional land. Now the area is more carefully and respectfully managed and visitors are encouraged to view and appreciate but not to climb. Back then only one small motel serviced the tourist industry and from there we hired a guide and climbed the giant monolith. My knees were never the same. It was okay going up – more just a matter of keeping on breathing! But coming down was a real test on the bones and joints. The views were breathtaking in every direction as we looked out over this spiritual center of the Anangu's world.

Our guide explained that this group of people believes Uluru and nearby rock domes called Kata Tjuta were formed by their ancestral spirits during the creation time and that they, as direct descendants, are responsible for caring for the area. Uluru features giant circle shapes on the rock which he said were akin to a woman's breast, the center of life and support for the whole tribe. Cave paintings indicated the water holes found at the base of The Rock. It doesn't rain much in that arid area, but when it does, the rain streams down the side of Uluru into catchment pools which have sustained human and animal life for thousands of years.

Standing five feet high in the scrub were rows and rows of 'magnetic' termite mounds. They looked like headstones in a cemetery, all perfectly aligned to face north-south. This presents their thinnest face to the sun and is thought to help protect the termites from the extremes of summer heat. Clouds of red dust smudged the horizon of the perfectly flat plain as 'road trains' passed in the far distance. These trucks have extra trailers hitched behind, making long 'trains' that carry goods to the most remote parts of this huge country. Their exhausts sat high above the front cabins because of the extremely fine dust.

Everybody needs a conversation starter and I found mine in Alice Springs – I discovered I am allergic to camel urine! I always have a lot of fun whenever doctors ask me if I have any allergies.

'Bull ants and camel urine,' is my jaunty reply.

Eyebrows are raised and they can't resist.

'*How* do you know you are allergic to camel urine?'

'Well ... ' I say, and I tell them this story:

In the Alice there was a place where you could have camel rides. Bob Finikiotis knew all about it and suggested we might like to have a go.

'I don't know ... ' I demurred.

'The fastest camels in Australia,' Bob assured us.

'Come on, Di,' coaxed Thom. 'This one looks like Mort Farber. Take him for a ride. He took you for one.'

I laughed, pulled a face, and gave it a go. I thought it very uncomfortable – fast, yes, but uncomfortable. So I left the others to it and wandered over to see a pair of camels in a separate enclosure. The female was acting very coquettishly, making play with her thick long lashes and large eyes. I was fascinated to see the bull spitting out a bright pink sac from his mouth and inhaling it back in with a loud sucking sound. He pranced around the female, no doubt showing off his muscles. I figured this was mating behavior.

I stood at the fence fascinated by this parade of camel testosterone. Just then the herder ran up and let all the other camels run into the adjacent paddock. One young camel came close up behind me to the fence at which time the big male displaying in front of me began to urinate and flick it on the intruder with his tail. I was in the way and got a load of it in my eyes and all over me. Immediately my eyes began to swell shut and my skin started to mottle. I stumbled over to find Thom.

'My God, what happened to you?' Thom asked anxiously.

'That camel! It ... it ... it peed on me!' I wailed.

'No one is going to believe this one,' he groaned.

Bob was aghast at the turn of events and together they hustled me back to the motel where I spent the next two days in the bathtub trying to get my eyes open.

The Todd River 'flows' through Alice Springs but is, for most of the time, a dry river bed except for occasional flooding. This is a very isolated area and the towns folk of the Alice are hardy stock indeed. Wry Aussie humor is never so clearly demonstrated as in their annual boat racing event – the Henley-on-Todd Regatta – held in a completely dry river! All the 'yachts' are made of cardboard or light timber and have no bottoms so that the competitors can pick their craft up and race hell for leather down the sandy river bed. Should rain fall unexpectedly and flash flooding occur, the regatta has to be cancelled! Teams enter from the around the world and raise money for charity as well as giving everyone lots of fun on the day.

I noticed that local Aborigines were camped along the riverbed and lived in groups in rough shelters. I was told that sometimes they all come up out of the riverbed as if on a silent signal and, sure enough, the river flash floods out of nowhere. No one knows how they can anticipate this, but I'm aware from my contact with these gentle people that they possess many survival techniques and talents that are unknown to us, including a deep knowledge of bush medicine. A doctor once told me that they are the only race that can control blood flow to their extremities.

I have always been very interested in thought transference and mental telepathy – I have had a few personal experiences of it in my life where family is concerned – and I'm sure Aboriginal people share this ability. The Alice has no doubt changed since we were there but in those days the local women gathered in the parks with their babies, sitting quietly in circles – they seemed to talk to each other without sound. I wonder. I own several paintings done by these extremely talented artists that depict their Dreamtime legends. These legends sing that they come from beyond the stars. I think it may be true.

I heard a lovely story from Brian Syron – himself partly Aboriginal – that a group was camped near the Australian space tracking station during the first space travel round the world and they built a large fire that kept going for days. They gathered in large numbers and danced around the fire, chanting and singing the sparks up to the space craft as a sign of goodwill, just as Perth turned on her lights for the space voyagers. I don't know if the story is true, but I do remember hearing that the astronauts reported strange flecks of light passing their windows as they orbited that region. I know for sure that these people love country music and are a fabulous group to perform for.

In the Alice we sampled water buffalo steak – unbelievably tough – and listened to the locals tell yarns. A yarn is a story that really gets you in but you can never be quite sure how much of it is true. They pride themselves on spinning a good yarn in the Territory and if you are too gullible you will hear the joking taunt, 'Come in, Spinner.'

Hamilton Downs is a cattle station not far from the Alice and we were honored to be invited to stay as guests. The station sprawls across thousands of acres – the home paddock alone is three square miles. Stock counts can only be estimated as no person could possibly ride the whole station to count them. The sons, big men when I met them, would take three months to do a roundup. I remembered the stories my dad told me of when, as a young man, he had a job riding the fence line in the outback, checking and repairing as he went. He would ride for up to three weeks at a time, carrying his food and a swag and sleeping each night 'at the Star Hotel', as he called it – on the ground under the great Australian sky.

The lady of the station was Dawn Pryor and she told us something of her early years there with two small babies. She said when she first arrived as a young bride, the sand blew for seven years straight and when the babies came she had to drape the bassinet with wet netting to catch the sand, changing it often so as not to suffocate them. The children received their education via the Alice Springs School of the Air – a two-way radio school that was set up in 1951 to cater for children living on remote 'outback' stations. The Royal Flying Doctor Service, another wonderful outback service, was their sole source of medical help in emergencies. Both these dedicated services have been essential to linking remote families in with the rest of the country.

Dawn's husband, Bill, took us out in the truck to see the big red kangaroos that abound on the property. I sat up in the back of the truck so as to get a good view. The paddocks stretched to the horizon, the dirt deep and dark red in color, scrubby trees and bushes casting sparse shade. The 'roos gather in the shade during the heat of the day, getting more active at dawn and dusk when they move around to feed. As we approached the mob, the males stood up like six-foot-tall statues, regarded us quietly for some moments and then took off, flying across the ground and thumping their thick tails as they ran. The females threw their little joeys from their pouches into the scrub for protection and led us away from them into the trees. We were speeding over the rough terrain at about sixty, keeping pace with the flying 'roos. Suddenly the truck hit a deep rut and now it was my turn to fly – onto the floor where I landed hard on my butt. This time I had a bruise that did not show but it was a beauty.

Dawn had a beautiful aviary of native birds near the house – firetail finches, budgerigars, an old cockatoo that danced and talked and called you 'darling' but would cheerfully take your finger off if you were silly enough to offer it. Huge galvanized iron water tanks stood around the house, a reminder that water is precious here. One night we had a wonderful alfresco dinner of lamb roasted on the barbecue – there is no taste in the world like lamb barbecued in the open.

Aboriginal helpers were invaluable at the stations and I occasionally caught sight of them in the background. They were extremely shy and hard to get to talk to. I had heard that the 'Jackies', the local stockmen, could find water in a desert and had great skill with animals and in riding horses, and their instincts for tracking are well documented. My grandfather George had been up in the Northern Territory as a young man looking for gold and had lived with the people in their humpies. He told many tales of their understanding of how to survive in the arid lands of the interior.

I was sorry to leave Alice Springs as the climate there suited me well – my body loves dry, clear air – but the tour was moving on and our next stop was Mt. Isa in Queensland, the site of one of the largest copper mines in the world. We had a tour down the mine and the miners scared me half to death in the elevator by dropping it really fast on the long dark trip down to the lower levels – 'Just a joke, love ... '

At the bottom we saw long tunnels stretching away on all sides, lined with copper and worked by oversized equipment that seemed to be in operation all day and night. A miner nearby sat in a huge digger, 'mucking out', or working on a wall of dirt and hooked up to an oxygen supply. I remembered playing Harrah's at Lake Tahoe and the oxygen bottle in the wings. This was much worse! I prayed that no one in my family would ever have to do such a job as I found it extremely claustrophobic down below and I'm sure the dangers are real even with modern technology. I gained a new respect for the miners of the world.

The tour moved over to the Queensland coast, also known as the Gold Coast, which is very popular with tourists and holiday makers because of its many magnificent beaches. Thom used to get up early every morning and stand on the balcony of our hotel looking out over the strand. I'm not, as you know, an early riser myself; nevertheless, one morning I pushed out of bed and walked out to see what Thom was finding so special about the view that early in the morning. There, bicycling along the road beneath us, was a young beauty with the tiniest of string bikinis. Oh, yeah, the sheilas look good from up there ...

We ventured as far up as Cairns in Far North Queensland and were now in the real tropical heat. The vegetation was lush and green and the beaches pristine. Ironically you can't swim in this enticing water during 'stinger' jellyfish season but all the motels had pools and the people are laid-back as is often the case in tropical zones. In some places I would walk out of the motel in the morning to find my car covered in flowers that folks had placed there in the night. Our Aussie musicians were a hardy lot, covering many thousands of miles with us through all terrains and weathers and I was grateful for their wonderful work as they really got into the spirit of the tour.

A funny experience along the way showed the deep humor we found amongst the true-blue Aussies out in the bush. Thom and I arrived at a small rural airport – just an airstrip in a paddock and a tiny building where you checked in. We had driven a rental car and were to deposit it at the airport before taking a short hop by plane to the next town. When we arrived we were the only people in the place except for one man behind the airport desk.

'Good morning,' he greeted us cheerily and issued our tickets.

'Where do we check in the car?' asked Thom, looking around.

'The car rental desk is right over there,' he replied helpfully, pointing to a small desk on the other side of the room.

Thom dutifully walked the few steps to the other counter. No-one was in attendance. The man finished what he was doing behind the desk, whipped off his coat and changed into a blazer that spelled out the name of the car rental company. He moved over behind the other counter and smiled largely.

'Good morning,' he greeted Thom as if he had never seen him before. 'May I help you?'

Thom, the joker of all times, had at last met his match. He meekly handed over the car agreement and paid the bill.

'Thank you, sir, have a nice trip.' The man took off the blazer and donned a dustcoat.

'Good morning, sir. May I check your luggage?' he asked.

Thom was completely gone by now. 'I don't believe this guy,' he whispered. 'I hope he doesn't fly the plane.'

A few minutes later the small airplane taxied in whilst the human chameleon changed yet again back into the original uniform and stood by the exit door.

'Good morning, sir, ma'am, may I take your tickets?' he inquired as we boarded. What a character.

One of my favorite towns was Grafton in New South Wales. The town is small and sometimes the planes would have to circle the local landing strip while the kangaroos were cleared off it. Grafton is famous for its spectacular jacaranda trees and the townsfolk host the Jacaranda Festival each year. Huge trees planted many years ago line the main thoroughfares and form beautiful arcades of purple flowers in the summertime.

The club we played there was great and I especially remember a ladies-only audience that was incredible. They were all members of the local ladies' lawn bowls club and the afternoon show was packed out with ladies, not all of them too young in body anymore but very young in heart and ready for a good time. In the troupe was a young Indian bass player – a very sexy, personable guy with a good stage presence. I saw the ladies' eyes light up at the sight of him so decided to build it up a bit. We sang a duet together and I moved in close and fixed him with my eyes. The ladies were clapping and whistling and the wine was flowing. My bass man played along, gyrated his hips and strutted his stuff as we turned up the heat. Pretty soon the Grafton ladies were up on the tables, screaming and tearing off their twinsets. They were even on the stage with us in their efforts to get at him, their menfolk glued to the doors trying to see inside at the cause of the commotion. What a fun afternoon we all had. My bass man only did the one tour with me – maybe one was enough.

It was in Grafton that I started to write songs again and penned my first version of 'Christmas in Australia' inspired by those beautiful purple jacarandas that herald the arrival of summer here. I finished the song later with a co-writer, Tim Connor, and it was recorded beautifully by the Irish Drovers.

I remember one night on that tour experiencing for the first time what I call 'a stream of golden light.' It's when standing onstage during a performance you sense an electric current of golden light over your head, tiny balls of light in a wide stream. All you have to do is hook on and the whole thing plays by itself. You have the sensation of standing in the wings and looking at yourself, and no matter what you do you cannot make a mistake.

I have heard of other entertainers experiencing something similar. I believe Shirley MacLaine calls it 'dancing in the light.' It is not a spooky thing, rather a very joyous experience. The audience is all part of the experience and as I looked out at their faces that night I saw joy. I'm intrigued that after all those years of performing in world-class venues in Vegas and beyond that it was back in Australia on a country town tour that I received this gift.

We finished the tour back in Sydney and returned quite a few more times to play in Australia but never in such an extensive way. I will always treasure the experience of meeting firsthand all those wonderful people and making those memories. There were so many hotels and restaurants and RSL clubs and lawn bowls clubs that bent over backwards to make our tour a special event. I felt like Australia opened her arms and held me to her breast, cradling me like a favorite child.

FIFTEEN

Smile

Shawn received admittance to the prestigious Kings Point Merchant Marine Academy in New York and a couple of years later Patrick joined the army and went overseas. We were empty nesters already. We spent a lot more time resting and relaxing on the boat, banging around all the little nooks and crannies of Florida.

Shawn came home on college break to stay with us on *Bypass II*. One night we were cocktailing with some dear friends, The Guys, aboard their boat which was moored close by our slip. I had spent all afternoon preparing a large pot of fabulous soup and left it on the stove ready for our return. Coming back on board *Bypass II* through the companionway, I saw to my horror two enormous water rats on the stove helping themselves to my soup! They heard us and bolted, one through the exit and the other into the cupboard behind the dining table. Out went my lovely pot of soup – with much weeping and grinding of teeth – and the search began for that blasted rat but we could not find hide nor hair.

The rat was well and truly aboard and so began its nightly raids as it banged around and foraged in the pantry. It tore up a whole roll of aluminum foil, ate two bites out of each piece of fruit I had in the fruit sling, and got into the flour and pasta – everything. There was no way we could put poison down on a boat as it might crawl into some inaccessible place and die, causing a mighty stink. We tried different traps – catch and release and every other kind – nothing. I was beside myself at night as I could hear it above my head, tearing with its claws at the fiberglass and thumping around in the engine room. Thom sat straight up in bed one night swearing that the rat had run right over him. Shawn built a wall of socks around his bunk at night.

'He'll have to pass the 'agony of de feet' to get to me!' he laughed.

But he wasn't laughing when he misplaced two hundred dollars his father gave him for his return to college. He looked everywhere on board and couldn't find it. And I wasn't laughing when he left for school and Thom had to go to a convention – I was alone with the rat. I pleaded with Thom's good friend Woody, the Marina owner:

'Woody, you've got to help me. I can't sleep with this thing around!' Woody pulled out the big guns.

'This is the trap you need,' he said, producing the monster with a flourish. 'Bait it with bacon and put it down in the engine room in a corner – and don't touch it whatever you do!'

I carefully baited the trap with a big piece of bacon and left it tucked up in an alcove in the engine room. For three more nights I listened as the rat banged around below. Then on the fourth night I heard the sound I'd been waiting for – the snap of the trap mechanism and a long hiss. *Maybe*, I thought hopefully and went to sleep at last. The next morning I was preparing to go down and deal with whatever was in there when a guy turned up to mount an antenna on our mast. I'd forgotten he was coming. *Perfect – he can see what's down there!* As he entered the engine room I heard the exclamations.

'Oh, my! We have a big rat here!'

Yes!

He appeared on deck holding out the trap, complete with the remains of our unwanted lodger – a very large and very pregnant female. We disposed of her and that was that, to my great relief. The postscript to this story happened about three months later. Thom was inspecting the steering fulcrum which was located under a seat and only needed checking every now and then. I heard an exclamation and then a holler.

'Good God, come and look at this!'

I charged over to see. There was the rat's nest composed of about a boxful of tissues, two pairs of my undies and a neatly folded wad of bills – two hundred dollars to be exact. From then on our intruder was known as the 'Two Hundred Dollar Rat'.

I was reading in my bunk on the boat just a short time later, when I had a strange grasping feeling in my chest, followed by a fluttering sensation. I knew I was not having a heart attack as there was no pain and yet that's what it felt like. Thom was worried and checked me out. My breathing and all other signs were normal and after a time the feeling passed. Three days later I got word that my mom was in hospital after suffering a heart attack. She was very ill and not expected to live. I flew home immediately to be at her side, Thom following a few days later.

I stayed at the house in Brighton and visited her every day in the hospital. She would hold my hand and we talked through our life together, laughing about the way we had always butted heads. Family visited but only in short spurts as the doctor had restricted her visits.

'What is the prognosis?' I asked him.

'We could operate but I don't know if she could take it,' he replied.

'How long?' I asked.

'It could be months, it could be hours,' was his response.

It was an odd step out of time, sitting in the hospital room day after day, measuring the hours by quiet conversations and squeezes of the hand rather than by miles travelled and performances given. Mom told me she was dying.

'I can see my parents waiting for me,' she said.

She also imagined she could see Dad. 'He's leaning against that wall over there, smoking his pipe and just waiting.' She smiled, 'He looks about thirty-five.'

I brought her a bunch of violets, her favorite flowers from when she and Dad were courting, and she gently smelled the sweet fragrance.

What makes a marriage? So many things and it's different for all of us. Troubles always come but I know Mom and Dad spent a lot of time in their later years ruminating about their past. I believe they came to a point of settlement and peace in their relationship. As a girl, Mom had been swept off her feet by Dad. She thought him the handsomest man she had ever seen. It was far from perfect but something grew between them which, although not a love affair, became love. They honored their contract to stay together.

A few days later I left for the airport to pick up Thom who was coming in on a morning flight. I meant to take him to the house first to eat but for some unknown reason, a feeling, I piled him back in the car to go see her at the hospital first. He was tired from the flight and I usually visited later in the day but I had that strong feeling. As we stood by her bed we could see that she was very weak.

'The writing's on the wall,' she mumbled to Thom, her words more slurred than they had been.

She was wearing her prettiest nightie as she knew that Thom would be visiting her that day. They were always very close friends and she had stood up for Thom all the way when things were hard for him in Australia in the early days. She seemed to fall asleep so we left for the house to once again get Thom something to eat. We had just finished a sandwich when the phone rang. I knew straight away. I listened to the nurse's formal words of sympathy and put the phone down. I turned around to Thom and opened my mouth but no words came out.

He contacted the rest of the family, got me back into the car and we drove the familiar route to the hospital for the last time. My brother Pete met us there. I stood by her bed and combed her hair.

'Walk towards the light, Mom, walk towards the light.'

One of her dear friends had delivered a striking orchid from her greenhouse earlier in the day and it lay on her pillow beside her now tranquil face. I leaned over her, touching her arm and time seemed to stand still... I was in a vacant place. Out of the mist a small child with a pinafore and long dark sausage curls swept towards me in a swirl of wind and pulled on my skirt. *Can I go now?* she pleaded. I replied without speaking, *No, you must wait a little more time.* The child pulled a face, looked away, and then she was gone.

I stepped back from the bed in shock. 'Oh my God, I saw her!' It was an overpowering experience. At a family reunion a short time later the old photograph album was pulled out and there she was, the little girl I had seen. It was my mother at eight years old with her hair in long sausage curls.

Patrick and Shawn flew in to spend the vacation in Warburton. She had loved all her grandchildren to pieces. We all missed her so much and laid her ashes to rest on the mountain range she had loved. My mother and music – they went hand in hand. *Smile, though your heart is aching…* the song played over in my mind.

Time passed and the sting grew less. I had been on the stage now for twenty-five years. Several years before, Thom and I had planned to give only three more years to the business as it was taking a heavy toll on our family and health and the clock was ticking with me. We both felt the need to get off the treadmill. My contract was due to be renewed with the Halsey agency and I was dragging my feet about signing up for more years.

I got the feeling my career opportunities had plateaued. I'd reached a certain point and had good success to that level but could not clearly see a way to elevate my status in the business any further. I was disenchanted and just plain tired. Music changes all the time and it's a constant battle to reinvent your sound so as to remain fresh and new. Touring was an exhausting, non-stop roundabout.

Thom and I talked it over at length. He felt we could handle a few years on our own and then hopefully retire. He had dreams of his own – to go blue-water sailing. I wanted that to happen for him. And so, not without some regret, we informed Jim Halsey of our decision and in 1983 stepped away after a good long run. Jim was always a true gentleman and had been a great supporter throughout the time his agency represented me. Thom took over booking our fate for the next few years. The upside of that arrangement was that when we wanted down time we took it.

One of our trips was to Portugal and other parts of Europe. The countryside was beautiful there and we relaxed in the land of Vasco da Gama and his brave ships that had discovered the new world. It was so strange to see all the eucalyptus trees in Portugal and I wondered if they had originated in Australia. In the old quarter of Lisbon known as Alfama we wandered the maze of winding narrow streets listening to the earthy voices of the local *fado* singers.

I wore my shoes out in Rome and dearly wanted to call the nuns back at the convent to say: 'You were right! It's all here!' We traveled to Vienna and had a laugh when we saw one of Chopin's apartments perched over a McDonald's. We attended a performance of the Lipizzan Stallions and marveled at their precision. Travelling by train we passed through the Alps and Switzerland and finally ended up in Spain for a while watching the sardine fishermen fight the big surf of the coastal region. We wandered slowly and enjoyed everything.

In May 1984 Shawn finished his term at Kings Point Merchant Marine Academy in New York and was to graduate. We were extremely proud of him and his prowess. He was one of only two candidates from Tennessee to be accepted into Kings Point. He is very brainy (not from me I'm sure) and had excelled in all his classes. To help us celebrate, I invited my brother and his new girlfriend (Pete and Marcia had unfortunately been through a divorce) plus my childhood friend Nola O'Loughlin to the States for the event.

The group gathered in Nashville and we took a trailer and drove up the coast to New York. Patrick drove his motorcycle alongside of us and we made a motorcade, showing the group the sights. We passed through Amish country and Maryland and Virginia. Arriving at the grand old school, we were greeted by Shawn and met with our extended family from Connecticut. The campus is extensive, spread over an old estate that belonged to the Chrysler family before they bequeathed it to the state. It is on the river and has a view straight down to the Chrysler building in New York.

Shawn's girlfriend flew down from Canada and joined us. Patrick donned his uniform for the event and saluted his brother formally upon reunion, a strange moment for us. There was a parting ceremony in the chapel with speeches and beautiful singing then out on the campus all the men threw their hats in the air, yelling and howling in relief. It was all over, they had graduated. It had been a long, hard four-year grind for Shawn and he was ready to party. We led the relatives back to the hotel and the kids attended the military ball and celebrations.

Patrick had to return to Germany, but we took the rest of the group to the Bahamas for a few weeks aboard *Bypass II*. Everyone loved the ocean and beaches and the Aussies frolicked in the water and the sun. My brother caught a big fish on the way across the Gulf Stream. I had trolled for years in the very same place and never caught a thing but first time out he catches the big one. Brothers!

I always had a line over the back trolling when we moved the boat, much to the captain's chagrin. He reckoned the boat could go on the reef when a fish got hooked, as whoever was steering just let go and rushed back to the lines. Fishing was serious business to me, no sport whatsoever. Fish was food and there was no throwing them back unless they were undersize or inedible.

About six months later I was called by my step-son Tommy to help out with the children as Karen, my daughter-in-law, was about to give birth. I was so happy to be there for the big moment. Karen was very heavy with child and in slow labor I think.

'Have you ever heard of a baby that didn't come out?' she moaned, trying to hold the weight of her distended tummy up with her hands. Oh, yeah, I knew that feeling alright.

She was overdue and I got her to put on her sneakers and we went for a walk, Karen moaning all the way. She had the baby that night. It was an amazing honor to be there and to assist at the birth. Karen surprised me and named her new daughter Krissy ... now we finally had our baby Christina. She was gorgeous and this was the first actual birth I had ever seen other than those of my own babies which are hardly fun to watch. Kristina was in my arms a few seconds after birth and I told her I was her Nanna and that she was in Los Angeles and she was okay. I stayed with the family to help, loving taking care of the baby and bathing her and watching the other kids. My lovely Krissy has grown up to be a herbalist like me.

Shawn surprised us when he came home one night by producing a ring from his pocket.

'I'm going to get married,' he announced. He would marry his girl from Canada and the ceremony would be up there where her family was.

Married? Thom and I couldn't believe it. It only seemed like yesterday we were juggling babysitters and now our boy was launching out on his own. The wedding was set for early spring and after much arranging and rearranging, we decided we would travel up across the border in a trailer and truck, gathering together with everyone in a campground near the church. That way we could do a little sightseeing trip afterwards. Best laid plans ...

We had got as far as Kansas City when a green pickup truck pulled out in front of us and promptly stomped on its brakes. There was no way we could stop in time. The pickup truck exited merrily via the off ramp, never looking back, but we were in trouble. The trailer bucked like a pony and Thom tried to do a quick turn to stop it but it toppled over on its side with the truck still attached up in the air. I was screaming in panic as the trailer whumped down on the pavement behind us. Of course it was about five o' clock high-drive time and the city was emptying out. The traffic was held up for miles as we were sprawled completely across the highway.

The police arrived and heard the story. The officer sniffed the air as we walked over to the trailer and looked at me accusingly.

'I smell liquor.'

'It's for the wedding,' I stammered.

He moved close to me and took a little sniff.

'Open up folks. I'll have to see inside,' he ordered.

To see if what I said is true, I added mentally.

A tow truck had appeared and pulled the trailer upright and cleared it to the side of the road. In we went through the bashed in door. I looked around in disbelief. Somehow tomato ketchup and oatmeal had met midair and plastered themselves all over the interior, along with the broken champagne bottles. It smelt like a wine bar.

'You've got yourself a bit of a mess,' the policeman observed.

You said it.

The trailer was a write-off so we packed up what we could and proceeded to Canada in the truck alone. I was so nervous when the wedding finally took place that I broke out in hives and scratched my way through the whole ceremony. It was hard, having to let Shawn go. He was my first baby.

... Smile, and maybe tomorrow ...

The kids went on their honeymoon and we took a ride up into the beautiful Canadian Rockies. We only had the truck to sleep in and camped in a rough fashion wherever we felt like stopping. My itching eased as I calmed down. We found a National Park called Wells Gray and stayed a few days. It was May and still cold but I needed a bath. We had worked out a way to take a camp shower by draping a towel around the tailgate but I thought I would like to wash my hair. I wandered down to the river, shampoo in hand, and scooped up the cold water and lathered up. It was very cold but felt so good. My problem was how to get the soap out of my hair. I scooped up the water ineffectively. *I'll just immerse my head and get a good rinse,* I thought. As I dipped my head in that freezing water I saw stars and almost passed out. I could not believe it was so cold.

The park offered a boat ride up the river to see a huge waterfall that spouted out from the mountain sixty feet in a thundering spray. As the boat moved toward the waterfall the captain noted that the usual viewing point was flooded and he would need to anchor out farther. Thom reached forward to loosen the anchor and I watched in horror as he lost his footing and went over the side into the freezing, swirling mass.

As the water closed over his head I was convinced I would never see him again. I ran to the side of the boat and time hung for long minutes until his head bobbed up alongside. I cried out in relief and made a grab for his clothing. Another couple of guys grabbed his arms, trying to pull him in but the side of the boat was too high.

'Let me go, let me go, I'll go to the back and climb on,' Thom panted.

I didn't want to let him go. He would never come out again! My head had been in that water and I knew how cold it was. Perhaps he wasn't thinking clearly? The other men pulled my hands away and Thom swam to the back of the boat and clambered up, willing hands helping him. He was shivering and blue as we loaded clothes on him and the boat returned to camp. How he had the presence of mind to go to the back of the boat was beyond me. I suppose his experience aboard *Bypass II* just kicked in. I was really shaken and fussed over him the rest of the trip. There always seemed to be an adventure when we went anywhere!

I had an adventure myself in Canada. I met Elvis. Elvis Grizzly. We were walking with a ranger-led group in an area inhabited by grizzly bears and I got myself separated from the group. We were just above a river in a spot frequented by two grizzlies nicknamed Elvis and Priscilla. As I came out from some trees, I saw a huge male below me, just hooking a salmon from the water. He started up the bank, I froze, and he stopped and looked at me. I kept my gaze down. I knew to appear subjugated and not to threaten him in any way with movement or eye contact but my heartbeat took off like a rocket.

Looking but not looking, I was aware of his appraisal of me. Primal. Unnerving. Very, very grumpy. I should have been petrified but all I felt was elation at seeing him up so close. True, part of my mind was estimating just how fast that bear could cover the distance to me and slash at me with his claws or bite me but basically I took the opportunity as a gift. After a few seconds Elvis padded off and up came the ranger at the double with a can of mace. Nature up close can be a little unsettling.

I'm always surprised by the number of people who have no respect for the power of nature, though. Once when working in Cypress Gardens, Florida, a beautiful old Southern plantation with open stages and alfresco entertainment, I witnessed a woman trying to get her four-year-old daughter to pose next to an alligator. I could not believe my eyes. The alligators would come up out of the swamp and rest on the grass and if you kept your distance you were okay because they're pretty docile and not that fast on the ground. I was transfixed by the sight of this woman coaxing her little one to get closer so she could get a better photo!

'Come on, now, honey, get closer to the nice alligator.' A guard came up at the double.

'Ma'am! Ma'am, the alligators are dangerous. Move your daughter away.'

'Oh, aren't they tame? I thought they were tame.' Goodness me.

In September that year I was delighted to be asked to sing at the opening of the 1985 Australian Rules Football Grand Final in Melbourne, Australia. This was a big affair for Melbourne's football community and the city as a whole, and it was a real privilege to be invited, especially as I was the first female artist to ever get this gig. A long-time fan of mine, Helene Davidson, who had become a very good promoter arranged the booking. She was from Horsham in Victoria and was a wonderful organizer. Thom and I flew in for a week or so and had some time to catch up with family and friends before the event. It was a different feeling coming home and not being greeted by either of my parents, though. A lot of changes had happened in the last few years.

I sang 'Waltzing Matilda', the bush ballad by 'Banjo' Paterson that has become a de facto national anthem in Australia. It's a song about a swaggie, or drifter, who stole a sheep for food and, when cornered, drowned himself in a billabong – a small waterhole – rather than be taken by the troopers for his crime. It must have struck a chord in the national consciousness at the time – free spirits who challenge the system have often found a sympathetic ear in Australian society. The song has a soaring refrain and the packed stadium of 100,000 people at the Melbourne Cricket Ground was a sight to behold as the song came to an end. I felt very humbled – quite a long trail for a little girl from up the road in Warburton.

While we were away, our baby son Patrick surprised us with the news that he was engaged and that he and his girl wished to marry before the end of the year. We flew home from Australia to prepare for another marriage in quick succession. The wedding was to be held in Tennessee this time with the reception at our home. I must have been possessed when I agreed to that one, but with some help I catered for the reception myself. The candlelight wedding was held at a little church nearby, with the hundred or so family members and friends coming up the hill to the house after the ceremony. Patrick had asked Thom if he could borrow six pairs of black socks for the groomsmen.

'Come on, Dad, we need the socks,' Pat wheedled. Thom passed them over, knowing he would never see them again. Sure enough he never saw them again.

The kids pulled out in a stretch caddy for their honeymoon and Thom and I looked at each other.

... Smile, through your tears and sorrow ...

In 1987 we had signed on to do a gig in Reno, Nevada, for the opening of a new hotel being run by our good friend Jack Pieper who also ran The Frontier Hotel in Vegas. I'd been hired on the basis of the kind of show I had done there with Roy Clark but that was with a big band in a completely different style of venue. This was a lounge and when I tried to translate the show into that setting it didn't work, mainly because we hadn't hired the right mix of musicians for the feel of a lounge. Quite honestly it was a bit of a trial, as every night I worked basically to the wall with no customers. Jack was disappointed with me, Thom was upset, and I kicked myself for not paying more attention to my work. But we had a lot more trouble coming ...

It was Thom's turn to cause us both worry and anxiety. He was not feeling at all well and, on checking with a doctor, we discovered his blood pressure was through the roof and he was in danger of heart attack or stroke. He immediately started on medication and I watched him like a hawk. Our 'six months' had spun out way past our original expectations when we first got married and Thom always seemed like such an unstoppable person, but now all the fears for his health that surrounded our early years together resurfaced and I was really worried about him.

... Smile ...

Some time later on the boat Thom had a strange fever followed by exhaustion and lethargy. We returned home and he had another bad night. We visited the doctor the next day, who said that Thom had suffered a serious stroke. After further examination, he concluded that Thom needed a carotid artery repair to deal with a major blockage. At that time this was still an iffy operation but we felt we had to go ahead anyway. I was with him right after surgery and he had a zipper-like suture closing the wound in the neck. It was scary to look at and one of the young nurses ran out crying when Thom turned towards her and she saw it. Thom was trying hard to get on top of it but he was not doing well. There had been some damage and it would be a long recuperation.

... Smile, though a tear may be ever so near ...

We stayed close to home for quite a long time as Thom struggled to get his balance and health back. An old pal visited and saw the violent scar on his neck.

'What the hell happened to you?' he exclaimed.

'Oh, some Indian came at me with a knife,' Thom flipped back. (The surgeon was from India).

'Well, where's this guy now?' his friend said heatedly.

'Oh, he's in the hospital in Nashville,' Thom returned.

'Serves that sucker right,' his pal retorted.

It was my turn for the sick list again. I had been experiencing some ongoing nausea since my last Australian tour. It flared up every now and again and made life very uncomfortable. Thom was in conference with a British recording company that wanted to record me when things suddenly got worse and I was admitted to hospital for gall bladder surgery. Once again life was put on hold while I recuperated. Thom was a wonderful nurse during this time.

I picked up again but I was still concerned about Thom's prowess. He was not doing well. He seemed to be fighting wild mood swings and wasn't bouncing back in his usual Irish way. He had always been the life of the party and always made me laugh – but not now. Glimpses of that old Thom humor were few and far between.

I dragged him to the doctor. His advice was blunt.

'Change your lifestyle or the man will be dead.' He recommended retirement and a complete change of pace.

I have to admit, it wasn't an easy decision. I knew I would do it for Thom because more than anything I wanted him well and for us to grow old together, but at the same time I was afraid. What would it mean to relinquish my identity as Diana Trask the singer, the entertainer, the recording artist, the star? Would I miss the applause?

I was known for getting a standing ovation of thunderous applause nearly every night in Vegas. My fans were many and faithful. People told me my stage presence was a powerful experience for them. I had always tried to reach across the footlights and influence people's lives in a good way, singing with truth about family and love always being deeper and stronger than we knew. Did I owe anybody more than what I'd given? Should I go on? What would it be like to be just Diana Trask, housewife? Music and singing had formed my life. What would I do without them? I went to our local church to think and pray – I felt scared and churned up inside. I sat alone and called out from my heart.

God, what am I going to do without my singing?

I heard him answer me.

Well, Diana, you could sing for me.

That pulled me up. Tears started to flow. Yes, I could do that. I could stop being the old Diana, pushing her way through every difficulty and trying to control every situation. I could stop trying to stage manage my life and simply celebrate every day with God and live in his life. I knew that could be enough.

I found Thom in the barn and when he told me with tears in his eyes that he did not think he would ever reach his dream of going blue-water sailing, my answer was unhesitating. We would buy that blue-water boat and go cruising the Caribbean. My dear Thom had given about all there was to give without rest. We both needed time off both spiritually and emotionally. The boys were grown and flown and I had been on the stage for over thirty years. Time for a change.

... You'll see the sun come shining through ... Smile.

SIXTEEN

Sailing

I'd like to say that my moment of revelation in the church put an end to my fears and that I embraced my new life as a first mate with equanimity, but that would be asking too much. We'd had plenty of fun over the years sailing for relaxation but did I want it as a career? No way. My decision was made and I knew it was the right one, but my feelings continued to swing from calm acceptance of my new life to real resentment that I had been uprooted – probably permanently – from the life I knew and loved as an entertainer.

It wasn't only my public persona I was walking away from. I worried about leaving the kids. We wouldn't be easily able to see them or be there for them if they needed us. And what about my beautiful house and garden, my herbs and vegetables? I loved my home and did not want to leave it. My misgivings were very real and at night I would lie awake going over and over the arguments for and against my decision. Everything I'd worked for was at an end. I was giving up the person I thought I was.

I hid my worries as best I could and, with an elated Thom, began our search for the blue-water boat we wanted. Waking and sleeping, our thoughts seemed to be filled with all things nautical. First, we sat down and compiled a list of our specific needs and desires, like automatic steering or spacious heads. We combed books and catalogues, consulted a yacht broker, and Thom went off on boat-hunting trips as far as Maine. In three months we had found her and funnily enough she wasn't far away – sitting just down the dock from *Bypass II* in Bradenton, Florida. The moment we stepped aboard I turned and winked at Thom behind the salesman's back.

'This is it,' I whispered. '*Bypass III!*'

She was forty-seven feet and ketch rigged, set up in such a way that we felt we could easily learn to handle her. She looked spacious and sea-kindly with a commanding cockpit and much bigger rigging than our other boats. Her salon was sumptuous as she had been on duty as a party boat ... a title that stuck with her. We took her out for a test run with Bob, our yacht broker, and she handled well but seemed large and ungainly compared to our other boat. Bob assured us we would grow accustomed to the different feel of her and that she would get us where we were going. I stole a glance at Thom. His eyes were shining, his dream was near. Our decision was made and after a few more hassles with the various banks and brokers involved, she was ours, *Bypass II* was sold, the house closed up and we were ready to set off. I promised Thom I would stay aboard for five years and we shook on it officially.

We had never made an overnight passage or spent an extended time out at sea in our previous boats and the thought was a little daunting to me. I remember passing a tiny vessel one dark night as she banged her way south of Puerto Rico through big seas. I had looked down on her from the deck of a huge, well-lit cruise ship and hoped that would never be me ...

Our plan was to head for Venezuela, making a large circle of the Caribbean Sea. We did our homework, reading up on different routes to the Caribbean, purchasing charts and questioning many sailors who had made the trip. Our next job was to run her round the Florida coast and through the keys and bridges to Fort Myers to provision and ready her for the long trip to the Caribbean. In classic Ewen style – a little like the Griswalds on holiday when I look back on our many adventures with campers, buses, planes and boats – the 'fun' began almost immediately.

We took off through the early morning quiet of the marina and into the Gulf of Mexico, under motor all day as there was little wind and also because we wanted to get a hold of the way the boat moved before trying her under sail. Down south where the water was shallow there were thousands of lobster pots and we planned to move under sail there so as not to foul the prop. As our first day wore on and the sun started heading for the horizon, it dawned on us that we had always sailed these waters in summer – we'd forgotten that in winter time the sun goes down early. That meant we had miscalculated our distances and would not find an anchorage until after dark. As the enormous sun went down in a bright orange fireball, we sipped our wine and smiled at each other. Oh well, let the party begin ...

Darkness fell like a blackout curtain. I hauled out the Florida navigation guide and we searched for a suitable safe entrance into the inter-coastal waterway, as this would be the best way south to lower Florida. At night the whole world looks different, especially off an unfamiliar coast. Thom, I must say, is a fantastic navigator but it was a tense situation. Lights spangled the shoreline but the entrances were shallow, and we had to stand off from the oh-so-tempting shore. Thom chose an entrance further on that was wide and safe but had a long dog leg opening from the south. As we approached, the lights were very confusing and we could not clearly see the way in. I began to pray for a ship to show us the way.

'Please, God, send us a ship,' I prayed out loud, over and over.

After about half an hour of worry, out of the darkness and gathering fog a lightweight container ship appeared with all her lights on and turned into the channel.

'Follow that ship!' I yelled to Thom on the wheel. 'The Lord sent us a ship!' Many strange and inexplicable things happen at sea and this was one. We turned in behind the container ship and felt our way up the channel. The fog was thickening and visibility lessened as we ran up the entrance.

'What's it doing now?' Thom gestured off in the dark towards the container.

We peered together through the night towards the large freighter.

'It looks like it's turning round. Get the glasses and take a look,' he ordered.

I strained my eyes forward and saw the ship was coming right at us. I passed Thom the glasses and took the wheel. 'Do you see what I see?'

Thom saw.

'Bloody hell! Swing her port side, now!' Thom yelled.

I didn't need telling. I scooted over to port as the freighter slid past us much too close for comfort, leaving us bouncing around in her wake. Looking up at her, I saw there was not a soul on deck and I have no idea if they even saw us. Still, I bless that ship for getting us in, even though she nearly ran us down in the process.

We entered the turning basin and cast around for the inter-coastal waterway that would take us south. It would be well marked but the fog was not helping. We had to find a safe spot to anchor for what was left of the night. I was down below in the navigation station glued to the Florida guide and calling up instructions but visibility continued to worsen. I came up top and we hauled out the spotlight, trying to find the big red markers that showed the channel but they were hard to see and we would be right on top of them before we saw them. According to the navigation guide, the water on each side of the markers was only inches deep and we were in danger of running aground at any minute.

My adrenalin was pumping hard – I did not like this situation one bit but Thom seemed calm enough. If anything, he was enjoying himself. One by one we picked out the triangular-shaped markers through the gloom, catching sight of the sandy bottom of the channel close at hand as the spotlight moved over the surface of the water. We were moving forward at a crawl.

'Where's the next one?' was our cry as we slowly picked our way along from marker to marker.

The night was wearing on, we hadn't eaten since noon, and only adrenalin was keeping me going now. How could we get into this much trouble on our first night out? And we weren't even at the blue-water sailing bit of the trip yet – this was only Florida on the way to the dock to get the boat fitted out! On the guide I'd located a spot that indicated a tiny bay where we could stop and make safe. We just had to find it.

'We have to get the anchor down, this fog is getting worse,' called Thom. 'Where's that spot you found?'

I struggled with the guide. 'We have to find the right marker and then turn left ... ' I trailed off, staring at the guide and peering ahead into the gloom. 'I think we might be almost there!'

It was a tiny bay. It was on the left – it would do. Thom crept forward to anchor.

'You sure? This looks really tight,' he said shaking his head doubtfully. 'We have to get out again in the morning.'

'I don't bloody care! Drop the damn thing!' I yelled back bad-temperedly. He dropped the hook in what seemed like the middle and we drew a breath of relief. It was now close to midnight and we were exhausted and starving. I made some beans, we had a glass of wine and dropped into our bunk, dead to the world in minutes.

Thom was first up in the morning and called down through the hatch.

'Diana, get a look at this.'

I came up on the deck and looked out at our anchorage. We were in a strange foggy calm in dead-still water and through the mist I could see we were completely surrounded by houses like a subdivision. We were in the tiniest of bays and Thom was clearly worried. The night had been still and of course the fog was now denser than ever. You could barely see the bow of the boat as it swirled around us.

'There's no swinging room at all,' he said worriedly. 'We have to move out now.'

'Now? In this fog?' I protested.

'Yes, now,' he said sternly. 'If we don't and a wind comes up we'll be on those rocks.'

I peered across to where he was pointing. There were definitely very large rocks across the entrance where we had sidled in blind last night... Oh, boy.

First things first – food. Thom argued but I insisted we eat before anything else was attempted. One of the things I have learned in my life is that fatigue and hunger can be very dangerous things in an emergency, not to mention anything about preserving a relationship. Also, I fretted about Thom's health – this was too worrisome for him. But he seemed consumed with the problem and just focused on getting on top of it. I tried to stay calm.

We threw down coffee and cereal, pulled up the anchor, and edged out of our hidey hole. We were looking for the main channel we'd turned off last night. As we maneuvered, the fog rolled in so thickly we could barely see the length of the boat ahead. We came to our heading and just steered blindly for it. I was on the bow peering forward when a red marker loomed up out of the mist.

'Left! Go left!' I screamed.

Thom rounded smartly and we were back in the main channel. A little further along we found a wide spot alongside another marker, put down the anchor and clung there like little lobsters. We could hear other boats moving along the canal in the fog.

'We'll wait it out awhile,' said Thom, 'but as soon as the fog lifts we move – some fool could hit us here for sure.'

'Yeah, why don't we just hang here and relax,' I said. 'We're supposed to be relaxing, right?'

We laughed and the tension slackened a little. We were still scared but the excitement buoyed us up – we'd made it through! It was mid-morning before the fog lifted and we up anchored and turned south. A local boat showed us the way and once again we saw how wonderful the boating community is at helping each other. We came up with a little song – 'Sea Rescue' ... about Captain Thom and his ever faithful companion, Roselyn (my middle name). *Da da dah dum ta da dah dum.* Over the next few years there would be many opportunities to sing this song as we sailed out of one scrape into another.

The weather was clearing to a sparkling day as we eased down the waterway towards Fort Myers. Thom was at the wheel whistling and I was leaning on the rail with the sun on my back – dramas in the fog were a thing of the past. By afternoon we were safely anchored behind Sanibel

Island for a couple of nights to take a breather. The beaches there are beautiful and we walked and walked, picking up shells and enjoying the winter season in sunny Florida. It was there I first began collecting sea-washed glass – old bottles smashed by surf and rocks and sand-blasted smooth by the sea. We met a great couple at Sanibel Island – a preacher and his wife on vacation who were a lot of fun.

A few days later we were heading into the channel towards the harbor at Fort Myers. As we motored gently along, a cigarette boat sped out towards us, a really cool-looking guy at the helm. He was standing with legs astride, sunglasses on and a cap set at a jaunty angle upon his head. A cigarette boat is your average drug runner or playboy-type boat, being big, sleek and fast – something for the rich and powerful to play with. At that moment a scrap of wind lifted the gentleman's hat clean off and unfortunately took his hair with it. Both flew off down the waterway. The look on the guy's face was a picture as he punched down his boat and jammed it into reverse. He headed back for the dock, barely glancing at us slowpoke sailboaters. Good thing, because Thom and I were bent over with helpless laughter.

Passing through Florida Bay, we did pick up lobster traps around our prop. A thick rope became tightly bound around and we had to get someone to cut through the tight weave to free us. Our good pals The Guys – the friends we had supper with that night the Two Hundred Dollar Rat took up residence on *Bypass II* – joined us down in the keys and we learned what *Bypass III* could do under sail. Ted is a great sailor and, in showing Thom her paces, he tipped her on her side. The only problem with that was his wife Sherry and I down in the salon found us a flood coming in through the portholes. Just one more thing to fix before we took off for the long trip.

I was not keen when she heeled right over; this was now my house after all, and no amount of talk about seamanship could alleviate my discomfort when things started flying round or my little house was on its ear. Thom was great about that and generally tried to keep us on a fairly even keel. The sail plan was different for this boat to our previous vessels, meaning the sails needed to be arranged in a different way to keep her stable. That was an important lesson to get under our belt before we headed out. I could see already that the challenge of mastering the boat was having a positive effect on Thom. He was completely into it and rose to the challenge of trying to work out all the problems as they cropped up.

In the boatyard we completely worked over the bottom of the boat, raising her waterline and working on the thousand-and-one things that needed to be done. I worried about power as we would be spending a lot of time at anchor and off the grid. Sailboats are notoriously under-powered for regular living at anchor and I talked Thom into getting a generator just in case it was too hot and he needed air conditioning. At the time we installed it, it didn't seem to run very loudly but later on it became a real problem.

We were finally ready. Ted and Sherry Guy saw us off and we moved down the coast to West Palm as a jumping-off spot for the Bahamas. When we arrived at West Palm the dock master assigned us a slip on the inside of the marina. It was really hard to get to but we tried for it, not knowing that the tide rips through there at a really fast clip. As we made the turn into our slip, the current was sending us straight into a concrete dock. A power boat could have done it easily but we were unable to turn fast enough with the water moving as quickly as it was. I was yelling and several boaters jumped to our assistance but we hit hard alongside and took a hunk of teak off our toe rail. A booboo on our new boat! I was as mad as fire and had a piece of the dock master who reeled back in surprise.

'What were you thinking putting us into that slip?' I ranted. 'In case you haven't noticed we are not a power boat!'

He was a big beefy guy but my temper was up and I flew at him. Thom grabbed me and hauled me off. I hope he thought twice about putting sailors into that slip again. Probably, though, he just wrote me off as a sailboat nut. There is a healthy edge between owners of sail boats and power boats – 'blow boats' and 'stink pots', they call each other – but I have to say I've never seen any boater deny help to another boater no matter what he's driving.

We left Freeport and passed across the Gulf Stream, a dangerous piece of ocean at any time, and began drifting down through the Bahama chain of islands. It was a dead-calm clear day, the sargasso grass lying on the surface of the ocean in clumps as tiny fish darted through and around. Sargasso grass is an important part of the food chain out here. We had our lines out the back and hooked a school of dorado, but only managed to bring in two as the new boat was higher off the stern than our old one and we ended up losing quite a few over the side. We solved that problem later when I hooked our trolls to the cockpit area and fished from there. I have been known to fight a big fish all the way from the stern right down the companionway and into the salon, throwing towels over it and holding it in a stranglehold. It was a marvelous day and as I scanned the horizon I saw a huge marlin break the water and skim across the surface in four or five joyful leaps.

We had sailed this area many times so were seasoned to this part of the adventure but you never know what the ocean will throw at you so it does not pay to be blasé. *Bypass III* became easier to manage as time went by and we dawdled our way along. We had questioned other sailors mercilessly about what to expect on each leg of the trip but there is never enough knowledge. Sailors swap weather and news about upcoming ports at the watering holes along the way and via the radio. First mates – the wives and partners – were a tight-knit group, swapping good places to eat and buy produce, even making little maps out to pass along to the next group.

In the Berry Island group we found a delightful little cay, completely deserted, and we dropped anchor in a small horseshoe bay. We sat there for a few days, fishing and diving and swimming across to the white sandy beach. One day I noticed native people on the beach setting out chairs and umbrellas. A man emerged from the trees with a number of empty bleach bottles and I watched as he carefully strung them off the beach, making a little partition in the water. I guessed this was meant to be the safe swimming area – but who for?

'Look behind you,' Thom said.

A gigantic cruise ship was anchoring off the little cay and as we watched, passengers were being unloaded into dinghies and ferried to the beach. Musicians appeared and bars were set up as food materialized from nowhere. I dove off the boat and swam in to join the festivities. I had to laugh as the passengers only swam in the little area marked off by the bleach bottles. I had been all over the lagoon diving for lobster and fish. At the end of the day all the people were ferried back to the ship, which then lifted her anchor and departed, leaving us to our tranquil island once again. The only thing that disturbed our quiet was the generator which out here sounded like a 707 landing. By now we were finding we really did not need the thing and were wishing we could dump it somewhere.

We traveled loosely with other sailors who were going in the same direction, meeting up at different ports of call. We met a lot of interesting and lovely people as we moved from place to place, but I was aware in those early months of sailing that I had to carve out a different footing for myself when we were in company. It had been a hard jolt to stop life in the fast lane. I had been 'Diana Trask, the personality' for so many years and in that role I had been the center of things. Now I was just another first mate. In conversations with people my words were not listened to just because Diana Trask said them – I had to earn a place in the conversation.

In another way it was a relief not to be on constant guard with people. There are those who wear you on their sleeve when you are a personality and drop you like a hot potato if you start to slip out of the limelight. I had always found this tiresome and tricky when trying to figure out who was being real and who wasn't.

There's no doubt, though, I felt a huge void at first. I used to sit out on deck at night and stare at the stars, questioning the universe and its purposes. It was beautiful, no doubt about it, but was I really meant to be here on a boat in the middle of the sea doing *nothing*? For a long time I was so impatient with the pace of our new life. My restlessness was always bubbling away below the surface, often finding expression in a madly tapping foot. There were days I swear I couldn't bear to sit on that boat another moment, sidelined, seemingly without purpose and with no outlet for my creative juices. The world I knew – the world of entertainment – was slipping away behind me as fast as the ocean currents slipped past the boat.

I simply missed singing for an audience. I had grown to love the excitement and even the sense of fear when confronting a big crowd and conquering the night. I still had that full head of steam inside me; the drive and desire, the skill and the smarts. Thom's illness, bringing everything to a grinding halt, was a punch to the stomach that left me feeling stranded. I was all dressed up with nowhere to go.

I was also fearful about whether we could really handle this adventure. Sure we had sailing experience – plenty of it – but soon we would be coming to the limit of our previous travels and sailing into much more challenging waters. Were we ready for this?

We met up with a fun young couple in the Exumas chain – Mark and Donna – who were slowly wandering south. Mark was an expert diver, and he and I immediately became a diving team and would go out cruising the reefs for lobster and fish. He was completely unafraid of sharks and often posted me outside a cave as he scouted it out. More than once, startled sharks, disturbed from their resting spots, hurtled by me as Mark explored. I don't know who got the biggest shock, me or them.

Mark was a really incredible diver and the most beautiful thing to watch in the water I have ever seen. He could go down about eighty or ninety feet and spear a fish effortlessly. We both dove without tanks but about thirty feet was my limit and then I would puff.

'It's all in your head,' Mark would say to me.

Yeah, right.

I would float on the surface in the crystal water, distracting the fish and he would dive down behind and spear it. Some fish were so big that it became a gargantuan fight in the deep water with the fish trying to dive back into a hole. He would put a hand either side of the speared fish's head and slowly come to the surface, rising with his catch in a deadly ballet.

Mark and I were swimming (that is, I was attempting to keep up with him) on the ocean side of Cat Island one day when we saw the biggest barracuda – about seven feet long – I have ever seen. He was swimming lazily in the open ocean with a much smaller barracuda in attendance. His huge presence dominated my vision. I knew that the barracuda is the fastest fish in the ocean and that if he wants you, he's got you and that's that. I also remembered that they seldom attack. Still, we were definitely on his turf and Mark signaled me to move away slowly. It was a spooky moment, turning my back on such a large, dangerous fish and I gave a little look back as we swam off. He was just hanging there in the water, watching.

Mark and I hunted rock pools for lobster. Large waves crashed over the pools and one day I got stuck down in one of them. Every time I tried to take air and get myself out, a wave would break over me and I'd be smashed up against the wall of the cave underneath. The water was a bubbling mass and I could not see anything. I tried curling up in a ball then pushing off with my feet, but the force of the waves was too strong. I was there for quite some time until I finally got smart and dove down to the other end of the cave and came up in a different spot where the waves were less fierce. Mark had been keeping a look-out and was waiting for me.

'You okay?' he questioned.

I nodded, dragging in air. I suppose my years in the surf in Australia served me well that day.

We feasted on all the sea offered – even conch, which was new to me and not my favorite as it could easily taste just like fishy leather. Luckily, Donna was an expert conch cook and after it had been through her hands I eventually found a taste for it.

We entered George Town Harbor or 'Chicken Harbor Number One' as the salts called it. This was about as far as most boats from Florida ventured. From here on it was the business of the serious cruisers. This harbor was regarded as a 'hurricane hole' – a place for boats to run for refuge during a hurricane as it had sheltered lagoons in the center. This is where I first heard the words: 'The wind is the enemy, Mon,' – a true saying if I ever heard one.

Hurricane season lasts for about six months, from June to December, and you have to know where to run if you and your boat are to survive. Amongst mangroves is a good choice. Thom would bring the boat in close and we'd tie her down securely with lines running off in many different directions. The mangrove roots would absorb the swell of the ocean and in amongst the growth you were sheltered from the winds.

I was alone on the boat reading one day when an older couple passed in their brand-spanking-new inflatable dinghy. She sat up proudly in the prow as he steered the boat for a beach near where we were anchored. Suddenly there was a loud bang that had me leaping up from my seat. The front of the dinghy had exploded and the lady was sinking into the briny deep, screaming like a banshee for her husband to help her. Her husband seemed to have weighed up his options and was in the back furiously trying to save the motor. I jumped on the radio and sent some guys nearby to help them out. Eventually they were hauled out onto the beach, soaking wet and beside themselves. Frankly, there is no way you can ride in a dinghy and keep dry. We always called ours *Wet Ass One*.

We moved further south. Fewer and fewer boats. Fewer and fewer people. The harbors were smaller and more remote. Ornate little palm shacks dotted the beaches, each with an intricately woven roof in an individual pattern of palm fronds, a sign of the weaver's identity. Most of the islands were flat, ringed by shallow water and reefs and fully exposed to the tides and winds. Delicate coral and huge pounding seas laced the Atlantic side of the islands and we even found pink beaches with sand that inexplicable color.

After lingering along the way we were almost out of the lower Bahama chain and onto the Turks Caicos islands. So far we had mainly been motorsailing, as the wind was always on the nose, and I was wondering if this boat would ever sail at all. We were headed for a flat island for an overnight stop before arrival in the Turks. There had been a light wind all day and it was warm and sunny. Suddenly, the engine stopped cold. We were in deep water and reluctant to jump over the side and see what was up, but in the distance we could make out the flat jut of land that was our destination.

Up went the sails and we tacked for hours towards it, making painfully slow progress in the slight wind. At dusk we at last dropped anchor in pure clear water with a sandy bottom. We hurriedly donned goggles and jumped in. Our prop was a complete ball of plastic drop cloth, bound tightly around in an impossible knot. We took turns hacking at the thing for an hour or two to free ourselves of it and luckily there was no damage to the prop. Talk about pollution! We had been miles away from shipping lanes or other boats or people when we picked up that plastic. What else is floating around out there?

We hung off the end of the island for a while before crossing to the township. There were several boats in the area and it seemed from the radio chatter that we were all getting low on fresh produce. I know we were down to beans, beans or beans on our boat. Thom was making things a lot worse by getting on the radio and reciting all the mouth-watering menus we were supposedly eating on *Bypass III*. They even sounded delicious to me. Years later those menus would crop up in talk amongst us: 'Remember that week we were all eating beans and Thom was doing menus ... '

Not everyone sailing those waters knew what they were doing. I mean, we made mistakes, but at least we made an effort to do our homework and sail safely. This particular night we had cleared the Turks and were headed for Hispaniola. The entrance was tricky so the passage was best done at night, making for an arrival in full light. One other sailboat was visible, travelling at a safe distance about a half mile from us and nothing else was in sight. Suddenly from out of the darkness we saw a blaze of lights coming at us. A very large sports-fishing vessel was bearing down on us, music blaring. We heard the captain hailing us on the radio.

'Hey, sailboat, sailboat – over.'

Thom picked up the receiver. 'This is the *Bypass III* – over.'

'Hey, man, where the hell are we?' came the voice.

Thom looked at me, shaking his head, and gave the guy our location.

'I hear there are sand banks somewhere around here. How far away d'y'reckon they are?' was the next question.

Thom rolled his eyes. 'Look at your chart! They are straight off your bow, about twenty miles ahead.'

'Hey, thanks, man,' he drawled casually and switched off.

'Some people shouldn't be let out,' Thom intoned as the boat took off into the night, music and lights blazing. I couldn't agree more.

We plodded on through the night and sighted Hispaniola through a thick haze early in the morning. The island of Hispaniola comprises the countries of Haiti and The Dominican Republic, sites of the first European colonies of the New World founded by Christopher Columbus in the 1400s. It was the capital of the Dominican province that we were approaching. As we neared I thought I was seeing high clouds, but instead a colossal mountain emerged from the mist. It was strange to see after the flatness of the Bahamas. We navigated the tricky entrance and entered the harbor, which was striking for all the wrong reasons – dirty water and dilapidated docks. We soon dubbed it 'Port-a-Potty' instead of Puerto Plata, its real and far more romantic name.

It was here that we earned our second rat story. We were secured from stern to the docks with rat guards designed to prevent rats coming aboard when we were in harbor, but the tide dropped so far here that at certain times the lines were in the water. The rats here swam like fish. The first night we closed up our hatches except for the mosquito netting and thought we were safe. It was a hot night and I was in the back cabin alone while Thom was stretched out under the big hatch forward. In the middle of the night something woke me up – a presence ... *something is at my feet!* My heart jolted and I sat up in bed, frenziedly groping for the light. There on my bed was a rat.

Well, I screamed loud enough to wake the dead. I was kicking at that thing like a demented woman and running forward, still screaming, to find Thom.

'There's a rat! There's a rat in my bed!' I gibbered, thrashing out at thin air as if there were man-eating rats all over me.

Thom leaped up and we ventured back to the cabin looking for the intruder, me peering over his shoulder and screeching at every shadow. There was a neatly chewed hole in the mosquito netting but no sign of the rat. Needless to say there was not much sleep for me for the rest of the night. I lay awake imagining a scene from the film *Willard* and planning a shopping spree for the biggest damn rat traps in Port-a-Potty. Next day I got into conversation with a French couple in the boat beside us – and wished I hadn't ...

'What about the rats? Do you have a problem too?' I asked innocently.

'Oh, we don't do anything. We just leave everything open on the boat,' was the unconcerned reply.

'But, but don't they come aboard?' I asked incredulously.

'Oh, yes,' the woman replied. 'They come but they only wake us up when they reach the new skin on our feet. You see they blow very gently on your feet and eat the dead skin. You feel nothing until they bite the new skin which has feeling.'

I recoiled in horror from the idea of this novel approach to the French pedicure and marched Thom off to buy the traps. I would *not* share my boat with rats. We lingered a few weeks traveling the island of Hispaniola and visiting with the people. They were truly wonderful folks and we learned something of their lengthy and colorful history peppered with colonists, pirates and slave traders. We decided to see more of the coast and moved on to Santa Barbara de Samana at the east end of the island. The harbor in Samana Bay was beautiful and clean for the most part except when it rained hard and the streams dumped tons of garbage into the waterway. I could not believe the street-cleaning method there. A man would use a palm frond to sweep rubbish up into an old license plate, then the refuse would be tossed into a ramshackle truck and that was it. The dry streambeds were littered beyond belief with trash, hence the pollution in the harbor when it rained.

Traveling around by local bus or hired motorcycle (me on the back) were our best options for exploring the country and each had their advantages over the other. The buses were very crowded but they ran frequently and were pretty reliable. On the other hand, the motorcycle gave us the freedom to come and go when we pleased but gave me a badly aching behind. In one way or another we toured all around the capital which was named, we were told, after Queen Barbara de Braganza, wife of King Ferdinand VI of Spain. We also saw the tomb of Columbus at Santo Domingo and generally took in the beautiful coastal and mountain sights.

We were on the bus to the capital one day when Thom managed to convey in broken Spanish that it was his birthday. In no time faces were breaking out into smiles and the entire busload sang 'Happy Birthday', offering small gifts like chewing gum and band-aids in honor of the occasion. Thom's Spanish was not perfect but his love of people was, and they just adored that he was trying to speak their language. My Spanish was improving in leaps and bounds – I just seemed to have an ear for it. Years ago my good friend Jim Raines had gifted me with a set of his language courses and I had studied them a little, but if you want to make progress total immersion is definitely the way to learn.

We had spent longer than planned in Samana as I came down with Salmonella poisoning, which kept recurring until a sailor friend of ours who was a nurse supervised my recovery. We had made good friends there as well. I fell in love with a lady in the market who teased me and my Spanish when buying vegetables. She was a lovely spirit and we laughed across the language barrier as she would holler 'Here is Enchola!', whereupon everyone would fall down laughing at my murder of the Spanish word for passion fruit.

We had long since decided to get rid of the generator and, after negotiating for a while with a garage owner, Thom swapped it for groceries and we were shed of the noisy beast at last. We later installed solar panels and were very happy with them. We parted ways with Donna and Mark as they had to return to work where they lived further up the island and we prepared for the next big jump to Puerto Rico across the dreaded Mona Passage. We double-checked *Bypass III* was all shipshape and finally we were ready to move on.

The Mona Passage is the slice of ocean between Puerto Rico and The Dominican Republic. It's a long, dangerous passage for a small boat – the entire Atlantic Ocean pours through a slot into the Caribbean Sea at this point. The current is strong and tries to push you onto the Washerwoman Shoals a submerged reef that agitates like a washing machine. A small boat does not have the power to overcome the current and is locked there unless a powerful engine comes along. We researched the passage and listened to all the horror stories around the bars about rogue waves and the like – I was definitely scared.

The morning came to leave. Thom had listened to the advice of other sailors and placed a seasickness patch on his skin near his ear, just in case. I decided not to – I had never been troubled by seasickness. It was 5am as we left the anchorage and headed out to sea. As we passed the point we were greeted by our first whale. She came very close and turned on her side, waving her colossal fin in the air as she flopped back into the water. All morning long the humpback whales accompanied us. One very large one came up on our bow and Thom turned white as she sprayed us with fishy breath and dove right under the boat. The humpbacks spend a few months in these waters giving birth to their young and then return up north.

We were following the curve of the island east. The plan was that when we hit the concrete ship – an old wreck on the coast – we would make a turn out to sea for twenty miles and then run a course for Puerto Rico. Simple enough. But as the afternoon wore on I noticed with concern that Thom was not sailing the boat as usual. He was acting a little strangely but when I questioned him he said he was fine. Dusk was upon us as we reached the concrete wreck that marked our turn.

We made the turn, talking on the radio to another boat that was ahead of us and on the same course. What a blessing a ship's radio is! Hearing another voice coming back at you from the emptiness of the ocean is so reassuring. Looking back from the convenience of these high-tech days, we had no cell phones then and no GPS – those things were not invented as yet. I had bought a Loran back in Turks – a simple precursor to GPS – which picked up our position on the satellite grid and bleeped it back to us and that was as high-tech as it got. Thank God, Thom was a natural navigator.

He was the 'ocean navigator' – the one up top calculating our position from point to point with nothing but a compass, a watch, a bleep from a satellite and the skills of dead-reckoning along a line. He was brilliant at it – we wouldn't have made it otherwise – but as a wife I was always careful to tell him when I 'had a feeling' he was wrong I was the 'close end navigator' – the one who hauled out the maps, charts and guides or hung out over the bow and scanned the coral beds and guided us through harbors and waterways close to shore.

The Mona Passage is unreliable as far as weather is concerned, as sailboats move slowly compared to weather systems. It would be easy to get caught out so I made supper early so as not to be in the galley if it got rough. It was going to get rough alright.

Back on deck, Thom was looking terrible. I got him to eat something but he promptly threw up his meal, and as darkness fell and the weather worsened, his condition also worsened. Squally conditions blew up but luckily we had already shortened sail so our canvas was not dangerous and excessive. I blessed that lesson when we had learned to shorten sail at night. We motor-sailed into the weather and *Bypass III* began bucking and tossing with the squall. Thom was now throwing up violently every few minutes, running to the gunwales and holding on. His glasses went over the side. I could see he was losing it.

'Thom! Thom, come below,' I insisted. 'You've got to rest for a while.'

'I'm alright,' he tried to say but I engaged the automatic steering and dragged him away and made him lie down.

Back to the wheel. Gusts of rain hit hard, stinging my face as I made my way along the deck. The night was dark and full of noise from whipping winds, slapping canvas and straining ropes. The lights of the boat somewhere ahead had disappeared. After a few minutes I went back down to check on Thom, willing him to be better – surely that stupid seasickness patch was supposed to prevent this? But Thom was hallucinating, seeing headless bodies melting down the cabin wall.

What was I to do? I was alone, no help was available. I worried that he would go into convulsions. I remembered my brother-in-law's advice. He was a nurse and had stocked the medicine chest for us. I heard his voice in my head: *When a person is incapacitated or injured keep them quiet and still.* Okay. I reached for the post-operative knock-out pill that he had put in the chest.

'Thom, take the pill. Swallow it down.'

He was so sick he could barely lift his head, but I got the pill down his throat and watched anxiously to make sure he didn't throw it straight back up again. Curious memory – just then a cockroach staggered out from under the stairs looking about as stunned as I was feeling. I had been after the roaches for weeks and this one just turned around and staggered back under the stairs wondering what the hell was going on. No time to sit. *Bypass III* was reeling and lurching as the rain and seas worsened and I had to get back up top. Earlier we had run through the checkpoints and times of our runs and I knew roughly how long it would take to get to each checkpoint. We'd passed the concrete wreck some time ago.

'Puerto Rico – do you think it is time to make the turn?' I yelled to Thom.

'Make the turn, make the turn, check the watch,' Thom managed and then the pills kicked in and he fell back in the bunk. He was out.

I went up on deck and turned the boat onto the course for Puerto Rico, praying I would not end up on Washerwoman Shoal. As we turned, the movement in the boat steadied a bit and the sky miraculously cleared. Stars hung out on a jet-black sky, but the seas were running very high and the water looked dark and uneasy. I left her on automatic steering, re-checked my safety harness, and stood watch in the cockpit. Thom and I had made an agreement – never leave the cockpit at night if you are alone. The night wore on and the weather was slowly clearing. *Bypass* was handling the ocean well and Thom was sleeping comfortably. All seemed well – until I heard it.

We'd been told lots of stories by boaties at gatherings and in the bars about rogue waves running in the center of the Mona Passage. I heard it coming like a hissing cat. The wave was bearing down against the wind, breaking and hissing on the way. I was caught, helpless. There was no way I could turn the boat quickly enough so I just clung there staring windward, waiting for it to appear. It was enormous, cresting on top in white curls of phosphorescence that caught the light of the stars. I held my breath and it hit us. *Bypass* just lifted herself right out over the top of it as it curled under us amidships and hissed away to port into the black night.

I was dancing like a mad thing on the deck. 'Ha, ha! You didn't get me!' and I broke into a wild version of 'Waltzing Matilda' that hopefully would never reach a recording studio. The fear had been real and total. When the wave hit and the boat fell over on her side in the aftermath, I looked overboard and saw a dark black hole in the ocean. The thought whipped through my mind: *I could go over the side and there would be no help, I would never be found,...* I have no doubt I saw death that night – it was a sobering experience.

Shock set in and I started shivering. What else could happen this night? I berated myself: *Diana, why are you in this position? This is crazy to put yourself here. Never do this again.* Thousands of things raced through my mind and as I ranted at the sky, my eyes fell to the horizon and there hung the Southern Cross ... home! Tears fell and I prayed for our safety.

I needed to talk to another human being. Thom was out cold ... the radio! I jumped on it and radioed the boat ahead. Every now and then I'd see his stern light far in the distance and then it was gone. Aboard was a professional captain and he told me the owners were in their cabin deathly sick. His voice was comforting and steady and I thought of telling him about my predicament, that I was sailing the boat alone, but what could he do really? I would just check in with him from time to time for company.

I fingered my safety harness, checking the lock again as I had heard of people not snapping it well and going over the side. I looked up. On the horizon in front of me, a large clear light had appeared. Was it a ship or a liner? I radioed ahead to my sailing buddy.

'Yes, Diana, I see it,' the captain replied. 'I'm not sure what it is yet. Watch yourself. If it closes, take steps to avoid.'

We always moved out of the way of big ships as half the time they just plow ahead not checking for small vessels. I kept my eye on it but it did not move at all, just kept glaring at me. After staring at the light for about fifteen minutes I realized it was Venus, enlarged by its proximity to the horizon and sitting like a beacon over Puerto Rico. I took it as a good omen that we would come safe to harbor. Then I smelled it, the somewhat odd combination of flowers and gasoline. Strange to be at sea and smell flowers. The offshore winds had blown their scent towards me and I knew

I wasn't too far off the coast. I breathed it in and fixed my eyes on Venus. Thom dreamed on.

But the night was not done with us just yet. The weather was changing yet again with a sharp breeze on the nose. My original fears about drifting towards Washerwoman Shoal returned. Morning was not far away as the wind whipped my forward sheets, the lines that steer the jib, and wrapped themselves firmly around the two fresh water jugs we had up forward. This was not good. Now if I had to change course due to weather or some other emergency I could not do so unless I crawled forward and undid the mess of lines.

We had sworn on our lives never to leave the cockpit at night but what if I just had to? I thought about it and figured out that I could crawl on my belly up amidships, hooking onto safe spots on the way. I would be okay, I reasoned to myself, if I just moved slowly and carefully. I had been on deck for thirty hours now and fatigue was kicking in but it had to be done. It was not fun on a tossing deck in the middle of the night and I was on pins and needles all the way as I crawled, untangled and crawled back. As dawn broke I saw the mountains of beautiful Puerto Rico and the jagged coastline to my left. *Thank you, God.*

I went below and shook Thom. He sat up groggily and staggered up to the deck.

'Where are we?' he asked.

'Look and see – mountains,' I answered.

'How long was I out? Do we have coffee?'

Now that I had finished sailing us out of mortal danger, making coffee was a comfortingly ordinary thing to do. As we sipped the brew in the early morning light, one last whale came up alongside and gave us an incredible view of her tail as she plunged and headed out to sea.

'Go below, I can take her,' Thom ordered me down to rest but my adrenalin was still up and try as I might I could not sleep. The night had been too stressful. I ended up back on the deck as the day passed and we wended our way through the reefs and into Boqueron anchorage.

We puttered into the harbor at about 5.30 in the afternoon as other cruisers we knew came up on deck of their boats to greet us.

'How was it?' they yelled as we passed.

My tired, grim expression said it all. Another first mate sped over in her dinghy with curried chicken and vegetables for dinner. We were so tired and hungry and I bless her to this day. It is amazing how kindness and thoughtfulness from another human being can change and restore your life.

I have reflected on that night, the danger we faced and the isolation I felt as I battled the boat and the elements and my own fears. I agreed to go blue-water sailing for Thom's sake, to save his life. And it did. But more than this, our sailing years saved my life in a different way, and I think Thom saw this well before I did. I thought my life was over when I said goodbye to the world I knew but he could see where I could not that this experience would set me up for the rest of my life.

That night spent traversing the Mona Passage brought out all the strength, tenacity, courage, sheer stubbornness and instinct for self-preservation that had seen me through my worst moments in show business. I took the skills I had honed in thirty years of handling audiences, agents, critics, media, other performers and all the others who make up that tough, tough industry, and held on until the dawn. I knew that the fear of the moment would pass and that exultation would be the prize. This is the essence of human resilience – to rise above.

I believe Thom set out on our trip not expecting to return. For him it was his last great adventure but he knew I would need something to carry me through the rest of my life when he was gone. This trip would be a building block for me; a time to slow down and find other strengths, including patience and the confidence to tackle new experiences. Conquering the Mona Passage signaled the beginning of my acceptance of the adventure we were on and what it might bring for me personally. From the confined space of a little boat tossing on the vast ocean, I was beginning to grow.

SEVENTEEN

Livin' The Vida Loca

It was an all-consuming thing, just getting the boat to the next spot and facing all the hazards that came with it. I have reflected many times with other sailing couples that it takes a strong pair to stand the trials of sailing and the challenges it brings to your marriage or relationship. Here's a man you have known for years and suddenly he speaks a completely different language. You were always a partner and a friend and now you are the crew and expected to react to the master immediately. You know he depends on you and in some ways you are more of a full-time partner than you bargained for. When it's just the two of you against the entire planet with all its twists and turns, strange things can happen.

It took a long time for me to realize that it's like a symphony orchestra – there can be only one maestro. For our safety alone this was the rule but sometimes I thought he worried more about the boat than me ... This was a common complaint I heard many times from other first mates in what turned out to be eight years of sailing aboard *Bypass III* in the Caribbean.

In Venezuela, during our last years of sailing, we put together a 'First Mate Club' – a group of ladies who had in common a life at sea and a litany of complaints about their respective Captain Blighs. We enjoyed some legendary luncheons and were asked to leave more than one restaurant as we were a somewhat noisy bunch. One French girl who joined our group would regularly burst into tears as she came through the door: 'When will it get better?' she would sob. We would generally ply her with good Venezuelan liquor and comfort her as best we could.

I've seen many a first mate jump ship and many a captain left wondering why. Some ladies just cannot take it and won't take it, yet there are others who just live for the adventure. Charlie is a famous 'single-hander' we met who sails by herself into foreign ports and all over the oceans. I take my hat off to her and to others like her. Life aboard a sailboat is not for everyone.

At one point I realized that Thom was using automatic steering, GPS radar – his new toy – and all the electronic equipment while I was doing the laundry in a bucket. What is wrong with this picture?! Speaking of laundry, I had seen the native women washing in the streams all through the chain of islands and had shaken my head, thinking how dreadful it would be to have to do that all the time. We had not even reached as far as Venezuela and I was already in the streams with the best of them, dipping and scrubbing in my little washing and rinsing pools. If there was a fresh water stream nearby I was in it doing the washing, usually in my swimsuit, which would then come off as well and go in with the rest. I was merrily engaged in the above one day when I heard Thom thoughtfully honking the horn on *Bypass* to warn me of impending invasion. I turned to find a large group of day picnickers coming into our previously deserted anchorage. I dragged on my wringing wet, soapy suit – not that easy when you're in a hurry – and continued on.

Our sailing stories could have made a book in themselves as we made our way down the island chain to Venezuela. Gerri and Flip were our cruising buddies for a while and we had wonderful times, plenty of laughs and many, many scrapes and adventures. We all liked the joke: 'Do you know the difference between a fairy story and a sea story? Well, one begins with *Once upon a time*, the other starts with *Honest to God, this is no shit.*' One of those 'Honest to God' moments had to be when we were caught in Egmont Cay, Grenada, in tropical storm Arthur with winds of seventy knots going over the deck in the anchorage. *Bypass III* heeled right over on her side with her ports in the water. It was very scary.

We cruised intermittently with many other characters: Hartley and

Barbara on *Northern Magic,* and Bill and Jenny aboard *Marjorie Grace.* Bill's best joke was to hurtle up the anchorage and go twice around our boat, rocking us out of our bunks and yelling at the top of his voice: *Wake up, you big Irish bastard!* Then he'd tear off down the anchorage, laughing all the way. There were families with wise young children sailing too, like Donna and her family from Canada; a Hawaiian guy called Fred and his wife aboard *Holopuni*; a very funny Puerto Rican couple, Mommi and Paul; so many great people. We all stuck together like glue, sharing information and advice from hurricanes and all the other weather problems that beset us, to the best places to shop and the ones to avoid. The radio net was so important to us. When Thom came down with Dengue fever we were hanging off the end of a small island down near Grenada. I was on the radio all the way up to St. Thomas with the girls helping me and telling me what to do.

We had reached Grenada and the Grenadines – such a beautiful chain of islands – where we teamed up with a wonderful Californian couple, Alan and Gretchen, aboard *Scallasa.* They were both expert sailors and we learned a lot from them, plus I found a new diving buddy in Alan and we paired up to dive for lobster and fish. I found the freedom and sensory pleasure of swimming and diving was a great help at those times when my mood was low or restlessness threatened. Gradually I was melting and merging into the life of a blue-water sailor and learning to take life more slowly.

We sailed to the Testigos Islands with Alan and Gretchen – I was very excited as this was territory with a very different feel to that of the Caribbean. The islands came up out of an empty ocean in a dramatic display of steep sand dunes. The population was sparse, mainly shark fishermen and there was a small military outpost. On a clear day you could see the coast of South America way off in the distance, a line of incredibly blue mountains hinting at Venezuela.

We were ashore one night eating with a woman called Toocha, a female shark fisher we had become friendly with, when we got the news that a big blow was coming and we should run to Margarita Island where better shelter could be found. It was a scramble to get back to our boats and pull up anchor. We were especially anxious as previously one of our through hull fittings had failed and Thom had driven a regular bung, like a bung in a bottle, into the hole in our bottom. Would it hold? We didn't know but we had to run. That was another hairy night but we made it in behind the big island by the time the weather hit.

Venezuela was such a contrast to any other place I had ever been; in fact, South America itself was a completely different experience. You had the feeling of being a speck on a vast continent with a huge personality of its own. We had been told that the mainland was dangerous, there were highwaymen and bandits, and that as a woman I should not go out alone. So to be careful I hired a driver to take me to the open air market when I was on my own. This went on for about a week when I realized that I could see plenty of women walking around by themselves. How could it be so dangerous? Next day I walked over to the bus stop and climbed on and went downtown to shop. No problem. Another lesson: never listen to anyone about a place unless you have been there and judged the situation for yourself. From that day on I relaxed completely and enjoyed every bit of our time in Venezuela.

By now I was speaking fairly good Spanish and could order my Lomito and special cheeses and so on. The central market in Cumana was incredible with fresh food of every type on display in the open underneath a large tin roof. I would hire a little boy to trundle a wheelbarrow alongside me. He acted as my 'shopping bag' and I would fill the barrow with my groceries from the market stalls. One day I was in company with an American lady who happened to be very skinny. As we passed a group of farmers leaning against a wall in the market, I heard them talking about her.

'Hey, why don't you eat some good Venezuelan food and fatten yourself up?' they teased, laughing and pointing to her. 'Look, she is skin and bone.'

'What are they saying?' she asked me nervously.

'Oh, just that the Venezuelan food will build you up. It's very good food,' I said hastily and hurried her away. Understanding and speaking

Spanish was not always a good thing as I was constantly being asked to translate for the 'gringos'. After a while I soft-pedaled the fact that I spoke Spanish or else I ended up working at every outing and it became uncomfortable.

We stayed in Venezuela for two years, loving the people and the country and especially the food. We were guests in highbrow mansions and little shacks and the hospitality was always the same. We ate everything and never gained an ounce as it was nearly all low-fat and cooked from scratch. We sailed over to the edge of Colombia and left the boat for a while to go backpacking in the Andes. The countryside and little villages were very beautiful. Lupines and frailejons bloomed along the highway as we chugged in our bus up and over the high mountain pass at Apartaderos.

Sometimes we thumbed our way and once got a lift in a truck up a winding road high in the Andes with a group of Indians who farmed the hillside terraces. They looked oriental and spoke a language I had never heard before. We stood in the back of their truck as it roared up that twisting, climbing road, steadying ourselves as best we could as there were no real handholds. Another hitchhiker was with us – a guy with a terrible hangover – and as we climbed and lurched he kept up a hilarious monologue. We did not understand the words but the face and the groans said it all.

Piccala came to us in Venezuela, too. Piccala was a little stray dog with attitude who ended up as the sweetheart of the boatie world, the star canine of the docks known up and down the Caribbean Sea and, most importantly, part of our family aboard *Bypass III*. We had seen her eating out of garbage cans around the dock at Cumana, a mangy stray with a large weeping hole in her side. We did not know her breed but she was some kind of a little terrier and she quite simply stole my heart. I don't think I have ever bought a dog. Dogs just find me. With some tender loving care Piccala was transformed from a sick, ragged stray on the docks to a charming little ball of fur and personality. Everywhere she went with us after that, people everywhere were always trying to buy 'that American dog'.

At the time we found Piccala, I had been reading one of Amy Tan's books in which she recounts a funny story about her mother. It seems her mom spoke little English and when she came to meet her daughter for lunch one day, the older woman was spitting with disdain. As I recall, it went something like this:

'This man I rent to is a very stupid man,' the mother complained. 'This stupid man yelled at me that I was the worst fookin' landlady he had ever known. So stupid! ... everyone knows that I come from Canton not Fukien!'

Thom loved the story and one day near Christmas when a big fat lady driving a brand new BMW coasted up alongside him in St. Thomas saying that she wanted to buy that dog for her children, he stopped in his tracks.

'What kind of a dog is that anyway?' the fat woman asked.

A light went on in Thom's brain and he gave what would be his standard reply from that moment on.

'It's a registered Cumana Fook-in dog,' he replied, dead pan.

'I knew that was some kind of a Chinese dog,' she huffed.

'Sorry, no sale,' said Thom straight-faced as the woman drove off.

Piccala was the source of many laughs. One day we were in Venezuela and Thom had to take her to the vet. Our only mode of travel was by bus of course so he stood at the bus stop waiting. The bus pulled up and the driver told Thom he could not take the dog on the bus.

'But this is a seeing-eye dog!' Thom protested innocently.

'I thought all seeing-eye dogs were big dogs,' the bus driver replied suspiciously.

Thom hit right back, 'You mean, this isn't a big dog?'

The bus driver sighed and let Thom on the bus. On the return trip, lo and behold, Thom got the same driver. This time the guy just rolled his eyes and muttered.

'Okay, seeing-eye dog. Okay, okay.'

After a time spent dawdling along the north coast of Venezuela we headed towards the east, trailing along the coastline towards Trinidad.

Brightly colored fishing boats were strung out all along the coast as we passed. We travelled night and day, stopping finally at a little anchorage called San Francisco to rest and get ready for the Mouth of the Dragon – the entrance to Trinidad. We arrived early and of course I went over the side to fish and just see what was under the boat. It was not long before I discovered a plentiful supply of very large mussels clinging to underwater branches and rocks – delicious! I filled up three buckets in fifteen minutes. That night a group of us had a feast on the beach after the guys had spent the afternoon scrubbing and cleaning the catch. Howling monkeys serenaded us from the tropical forest that came down from the cliffs and the night was sparkling around the open fire.

Several boats left in the morning and we lingered on, waiting for some other friends to catch up so we could go on together. Thom was ashore later in the day walking Piccala when I heard what seemed to be the rumbling of a huge motor beside us. The vibrations shook the boat and brought me topside to scan the horizon. No boat. That was strange... Thom came back with a tale. We'd been shaken by an earthquake. As he was walking the dog he saw hundreds of crabs suddenly run up out of the water and into the scrub just before the earth began to shake. After the shuddering stopped they all marched back again.

Our friends arrived and we entered the Mouth of the Dragon, an inauspicious name for sure, but we actually enjoyed a smooth passage in and under a very stiff wind we made harbor in Trinidad. It was Carnivale time and we stayed at the marina for the event, the whole island getting into it. At night we went downtown into the heart of it, the packed crowd bordering on dangerous as people milled and jostled in a sweaty frenzy. At one point I was inching along behind Thom when a young and enthusiastic fella jumped on my back, moving sinuously against me to the pounding beat of Carnivale. I crunched forward into Thom for support.

'Thom – a little help here!'

My new acquaintance was dislodged and melted into the crowd, grinning widely. Gee, I usually get dinner first ...

Trinidad was a marvelous island with wide sparkling beaches

and incredibly rich flora and birdlife. One day I took a magical walk through the forest with a naturalist from the university. It seemed that in this tropical wonderland everything had a poisonous or toxic element, depending on how it was prepared or cooked or dried. He pointed to a leaf that had dried and fallen on the ground. Piccala promptly rolled around in it and ate it and became as silly as a wheel. She was not herself until the next day and then I think she had a hangover.

My interest in herbal and natural cures was ever increasing and I questioned anyone who would sit still about the native herbal knowledge. One particular woman in Bequia was raking the garden in front of the post office when I saw her grandchildren race toward her. They were strikingly healthy with shining skins and eyes, in contrast to some of the children I had been seeing. On speaking with the lady she gave me her secret.

'I have no money,' she explained. 'My daughter leave me with these children so I work here at the post office. I feed those children aloe and coconut every day ... just a little. Maybe we are not rich but they are healthy.'

I had to agree and that was not the only time I had heard about miracles attributed to aloe, a succulent plant in abundance in the islands. It seemed the women were the doctors and practiced traditional medicine, largely imported from English and South African folklore.

On one of our sightseeing trips I was unfortunate enough to be in the company of a woman who scoffed loudly at every possible moment about all she saw: 'My God, they live in filth! The poverty is disgusting!'

I took a good long look. Was this real poverty? Yes, the people lived in shacks and sometimes there were walls missing but there were plenty of old folks sitting around in the sun along with physically impaired people. They were all in a family setting, not being force fed or locked away. They seemed to be helping themselves and laughing, not isolated and helpless. They were not obese or stressed out. I looked again at my traveling companion. She was overweight and oppressive and unable to conceive of a way of life other than her own. Just who was living in poverty here?

'Livin' the vida' in the sunshine was a vibrant life and as I had brought my paints along and inspiration was all around, I began to paint in earnest. This brilliant, many-hued tropical paradise would inspire anyone. I learned to underpaint the white glare of the coral beaches and called my works my 'Caribbean period'. They later all sold well in Puerto Rico where I was represented by my friends Miriam and Oochie, who had a gallery there. Painting and songwriting were a lot alike to me. I would work like crazy to finish the project and when it was done I did not care if I saw it or looked at it again. A lot like growing vegetables – when it's ripe, it's ripe.

Painting was also a way of letting off the creative steam that continued to build up inside me. Performing may have been off the agenda but I had to find some way to satisfy my need to express what was inside me and to harness the enormous energy that used to go into my singing career. Immersing myself in painting and in the study of herbs helped to fill the gap.

Across the Mouth of the Snake back towards Venezuela lay the wild regions around the many mouths of the Orinoco River. This river is a major artery and connects back through the Rio Negro to the Amazon River. The mouth of the Orinoco is seventy miles long with absolutely no physical navigation aids. We had spent an evening with a French missionary and I had wheedled from him the Loran numbers of the only navigable entrance in this wilderness apart from the main entrance many miles south.

Thom and I wanted to try to find it but we knew of no sailboats of our size that had attempted it. We tried to gather information about the river and found it was extremely temperamental, rising and falling by seventy feet depending on tropical rainfalls miles away. We had some sailing pals, Jan and Jeff aboard *Clarity*, and they decided to follow us if we made the trip. My old school chum, Nola Loughlin, was visiting with us at that time too and made up the rest of the crew.

After taking as much care as possible with our planning, we decided to make the attempt and set out on the tide to cross the wide expanse of water and locate the pesky entrance with just the Loran to help us with our position.

The Frenchman had told me to watch out for a particular line of trees – 'you will see two dark trees that stand out on their own'.

What does he mean two dark trees? There are mangroves as far as the eye can see! But just on dusk they appeared – at least I hoped they were the ones he meant. We nosed in closer, a wide, shallow entrance revealing itself. Bump! We were scraping the bottom – not good. Thom put *Bypass* along carefully and thankfully she soon surged through into deeper water and we nervously puttered up towards the trees that rose out of the river in a ragged line. A stilt house hovered above the water's edge as we neared and we dropped anchor with fingers crossed – who knows what was on the bottom? Still, so far, so good, and as we all relaxed with a cocktail thousands of scarlet ibis flew in to roost for the night. Where before the trees were green, now they were lit up as for Christmas, each branch glowing with its beautiful burden of living, scarlet decorations. It was worth it just to see that sight.

That trip was an amazing experience. In the days that followed we ventured further up the river, sometimes passing natives in dugout canoes or wildly gesturing people on the banks of the river holding up brightly colored birds or monkeys or vessels for sale. One man came alongside in a dugout with his three wives. He seemed to be of German descent and we spoke briefly. His wives were very young and when they smiled, alas, lacked most of their teeth. One day a fisherman came up to sell us his fish. They looked like catfish but had prehistoric kind of claws down the back and a bright yellow belly. I was not too keen but told the guys: 'If you skin it, I'll cook it'. The fish was delicious but I must say I let the dog have the bright yellow bits. I had done some research earlier at the public library about the fish in that region as I had to sort out what to eat from our fishing lines – what was good and what to avoid. It seemed from my reading that many of the fish in that region looked prehistoric in their features.

Amazing birds and animals dotted the shore as we felt our way up the river but the most amazing thing I ever saw occurred one night when everyone else was asleep. I was restless and hot and went up on deck in the moonlight to view the river. I looked across at *Clarity* – no lights showed. Jan and Jeff were asleep too and the only light was the full moon. On the spur of the moment I decided to take a bucket bath on the deck. The river was moving swiftly out in the center at about six knots and it was full of debris forming fast-moving islands that slipped by silently. I went forward and threw the bucket over, ready to haul up. The water was brown but I figured it was clean enough.

The jungle was alive with noise, the odd howling monkey sounding like a screaming woman. There were no insects so I stripped down and pulled up the bucket. I was just soaping up when I heard a sharp exhalation of breath. I looked over the side and there was a family of pink freshwater dolphins playing around the boat. I called to them as they jumped and danced and performed around *Bypass* for about fifteen minutes. Too soon they had slipped off into a side lagoon and were gone. It was one of the blessed moments of my life.

An unwelcome noise in the steering hailed the end of our trip up the Orinoco. Thom hailed one of the natives who appeared infrequently on the river and I asked him in halting Spanish if there was a spot we could go to jump over the side and see what was up.

'Can you dive and look for us?' I asked him hopefully.

The native slowly shook his head. 'Big yellow snake ... piranha.'

'Ask him what should we do then,' Thom said. 'What about over there by the bank?' I tried again.

'Will you dive for us over there?' I questioned.

Once again the man shook his head. 'Crocodillos.'

'Well, that's that,' said Thom. 'Back we go.'

Back down towards the mouth of the river we went at an easy pace and soon enough were headed back towards St. Thomas and anchored in front of the town with repairs underway. Docking for repairs prior to sailing on may have been the plan but before we knew it our lives had taken another diversion. A fellow cruiser asked Thom for advice and help regarding a business venture in the town and in no time Thom was involved with Colombian Emeralds in St. Thomas and we were back to being weekend sailors. It was no fun being alone during the week while Thom was occupied all day so I ended up going to work for them too as a salesperson.

Colombian Emeralds serviced the cruise ships that visited the islands and sold beautiful emeralds and other gems along with high ticket watches and various other items. We enjoyed our time with the company and they treated us well but it sure was a change for me. I had never sold anything to anyone before – except my voice to an agent or booker – and I was grateful to Pam, another cruiser, for taking a chance on me. I liked the job well enough but found it could be stressful at times amongst the staff. I made good friends though – my favorite was Dawn, a tall, blonde from Minnesota. We got along well and had lots of good laughs as we were by far the oldest two on staff and were competing every day with all the little *chicas* on the sales floor.

Dawn was a very funny girl and my favorite story of hers was when she worked at the nursing home where it was her job to clean all the oldies' false teeth. She figured this was slow work doing it one by one so she would collect them all at once and clean them in one go. The only problem was whose teeth belonged where. Apparently it was bedlam and she would rock with laughter telling the story.

Thom came to me after work one day with a look in his eye that could mean only one thing – something was up.

'Sick of tropical paradise yet?' he asked me.

'Why?'

'How would you like to live in Alaska?'

'Alaska?!'

I was sitting on deck with a cocktail in my hand watching the sunset glow deepen in the sky. Birds were wheeling overhead. The air was balmy and the clear blue water slapped gently against the hull. I had actually become used to this life! *Alaska??*

'The company has a store there. Place called Juno. They want us to work there just for a season.'

'What about the boat?' I asked.

'I think we'll have to sell her.'

That was a tough decision. But the truth was with both of us working and spending less time aboard, she had not been getting the daily care she needed as it was, and Thom hated to see his 'other woman' going to seed. It would be even harder to manage if we were based in Alaska.

In a matter of weeks *Bypass III* was cleaned from top to toe, sold off to another blue-water adventurer, and Thom and I were heading north to Alaska.

EIGHTEEN

On The Road Again

We loved Alaska and although our schedule was tough, we took as many small moments as we could to head out and explore. We would leave early and drive up over the mountain to Whitehorse in the Yukon Territory to do the shopping. You could see everything on the roads – giant puma, wolves, snow birds and of course lots of bears. I thought about my grandfather George who, as a young man and before he met my grandmother, had sworn to seek his fortune in the gold mines of the Yukon. They did meet and he never did make it to the Yukon. Love takes us down many unexpected paths.

Our main problem when we made the decision to come to Alaska – apart from the boat – was what to do with our little dog. It would be a wrench to lose her, but Piccala did not travel well as she was quite old though still perky. I thought of some dear friends of ours, The Guys, dog-lovers from way back.

'I'll ask Sherry,' I told Thom.

Sure enough, Sherry and Ted took her with loving arms and Piccala ended up their darling, living in the air conditioning and sleeping with them in their king-size bed – a long way from the garbage dumps of Venezuela for that little pooch.

We worked the season in Juno for Colombian Emeralds and then ended up changing companies to Little Switzerland, for whom Thom was eventually asked to start up a new store in Skagway. He was enthused and I agreed to try it as long as everybody stayed healthy. We landed in Skagway on a windswept day, driving our camper off the ferry and up an incredibly steep ramp as I white-knuckled it in fear at the incline. The mountains rose ten thousand feet on either side of the fjord and the whole scene was deep in snow.

The people of Skagway are incredible and we loved the town. I especially loved the scent of the air. A fast river rushes through the town and on my time off I would go searching for the huge plate-sized mushrooms that grow in the area and gathering tall bush cranberries, bitter but great in a jam. My love of plants and herbs was still growing and I studied whenever I could, scanning libraries wherever I was for local information.

Alaska has a frontier feeling. The long distances, the open spaces, the rough roads, the wildlife, mountains and glaciers – it was spectacular and reminiscent in some ways of Australia, which is also huge and in many respects 'empty'. The people of Alaska are survivors, resourceful, practical. Some communities live right off the grid – no power, no water laid on. They bake, hunt, make and mend for themselves, coming into town for supplies. One of the girls who made jewelry for the business came from a community like that and we were invited to meet them. That was my introduction to the best thing I have ever tasted – moose ribs. We sat under the stars around leaping fires and worked our way from one end of that moose's rib to the other. It was a like a clip from *The Flintstones*. Our new dog, Clarence (yes, it didn't take long for the next stray to turn up), was beside himself with excitement, trailing this huge bone in his jaws that bumped along as he ran.

It was the mid-1990s. We worked very hard to get the new store up and running and, although mentally Thom was built to handle a challenge, his past history was always at the forefront of my mind and I worried that his health would slip backwards if he was under too much pressure. The grind of the store was constant, every day for long hours. Sometimes I would stop and shake my head in disbelief at the twists and turns my life had taken – *What am I doing here?! I am a singer! Who took my audience?!*

Thom handled the scene a lot better than I – often I felt quite overwhelmed, but as the months passed I could see signs of stress building in him and thought to myself that we would soon have to make another change. Sure enough, after two years Thom's health was declining. When we visited doctors they gave him medicines galore, but at the time I knew no better and didn't question the treatment. His old problems with heart and blood pressure were resurfacing. There was no doctor in Skagway or even a pharmacy for that matter. We had a nurse and a clinic of sorts but I was anxious about what would happen if something really went wrong.

It was during our time in Skagway that I received a return invitation to perform at the Australian Rules Football 1996 Grand Final back home in Melbourne. It was a very welcome invitation – I had loved doing it back in 1985. The same promoter, Helene Davidson, who had got me the gig in '85 again arranged for my appearance and I was thrilled to be asked back. Helene had been a terrific support for me in various concert promotions back in Australia and I loved her and her family.

We flew down for just a week and quickly touched base with family and friends and rehearsed for the opening, the Melbourne skies teeming with rain. I was delighted to meet up with old friends John Farnham, Slim Dusty, Barry Crocker and other headliners, who were all part of the event. I hadn't performed for some years now but I slipped right back into it without batting an eyelid. I wasn't nervous, I wasn't anxious about my voice. I had practiced for about six weeks to get the pipes together and thoroughly enjoyed going home and reveled in singing for an audience again.

The time came and we all marched out into the center of the stadium to do the routine. Everything was going fine until the smoke machine was let loose. We had not practiced with the smoke effects although we had been assured they were very safe. As the smoke was released, a waft of wind pushed it back towards us in a thick stifling fog. I looked back at Barry Crocker who was reeling against the upright, gasping. I was struggling too when at last the wind took the smoke away and we all thankfully sucked in some fresh air. The Grand Final was a special event, however, and I was again honored to be there.

We stayed in Skagway for three summers until the chain changed hands and we felt we could not do well under the new management. Besides, I felt it was time to lay down the law to Thom – retire and get healthy again. This time he agreed. As compensation for selling *Bypass III* we had purchased a large comfortable fifth wheel RV trailer to move around in during our off time as we were always interested in seeing the countryside around. So when our final decision was made not to return to the business, we packed up again and set off down the road on the next adventure.

We were headed for the Baja California Peninsula in western Mexico. I had always wanted to go there since I'd heard Jack Davey, a popular radio personality in Australia in the forties and fifties, talking about the long-distance car trials there. Jack Davey had a lifelong interest in cars and the challenge of entering long-distance trials in difficult terrain. He did an all-around-Australia drive which he compared to the Baja run. Wow, what a trip. That road in the Baja is paved now, of course, but is still extremely narrow and our rig was wide. The Mexican truck drivers are very skilled and handle that nightmare road every day. The trip was hairy in some spots but the beauty of the area was worth it.

We fell in with a group of Canadians and had a heap of fun. A memorable stop was at Todos Santos, where we camped right on the beach along with groups of surfers from all around the world. I loved the Pacific Ocean and the white sand, and although the surf was very rough I found little rock pools to lie in and soak myself. Whales and their babies played close to shore right in front of our camp. They were very numerous in the winter and we'd often see six or seven with their calves right up close where the beach shelved away very steeply into deep water.

One day I was walking with my Canadian friend Elsie when a mother whale and a baby whale came in very near to the shore, maybe forty yards.

'Let's swim out and touch them!' a couple of young girls nearby suggested.

Without thinking I yelled back, 'Yeah, let's go!'

Mistake. There seemed to be a slight break in the big surf as we started out but the undertow was very strong. I was out just a little way when I looked up and saw a giant wave coming at me. I had been a strong swimmer all my life and the size of the waves didn't scare me. I took a deep breath and dove down under. The wave came down on me like a giant press. It was the heaviest I had ever felt and it pushed me to the bottom. Only I couldn't touch the bottom.

'Gee, it's suddenly very deep,' I thought. Of course it was deep, how else could the whales be swimming so close to shore? I hadn't thought this through properly.

I surfaced just in time to exhale a tiny bit before another giant swept over me. Again I dove down, trying to stay a little closer to the surface this time but the breaking wave pushed me down heavily again and I had to fight back to the surface. One small puff out but, again, no time to inhale. By now I was definitely in need of oxygen. Each time I went down it took longer to float up to the surface and I still couldn't feel the bottom. Thank goodness for all those breathing exercises when I was younger. Another wave grabbed me and tumbled me over and I was not sure where I was. All I knew was the water was pushing me down yet again.

'Maybe this is it?' ran through my mind. Then: 'Thom will be so mad at me.'

Thom was constantly complaining when he watched me swim that I was always the farthest swimmer out from the beach and always by myself.

'Well, I better get a breath this time,' I decided, 'or I'm going to pass out.'

I pushed my legs down hard as I began to rise and – a miracle – I touched the bottom. The wave had thrown me towards the shore and I was on the edge of the backward drag of the undertow. I ran as hard as I could up the slope, lungs feeling like watermelons, and threw myself down at the edge, dragging in huge gulps of air. I saw the other girls away to my left, helping each other out. The whales had disappeared.

It was an extremely scary experience and I later found out that

Todos Santos is a class five surf beach – very dangerous. The waves are called pile drivers because of the way they mount up across the ocean and hit the slope then drop their load like a ton of bricks on the shelf. No wonder they felt so heavy. Not two weeks later a fellow camper broke his neck at exactly the same spot. And, yes, Thom *was* mad at me.

We traveled back from Mexico to Maryland to babysit Shawn's house for a few weeks while they were away. During the night Thom woke up struggling to breathe. We tried a few things to make him comfortable but he worsened and I finally called 911. The ambulance whizzed him off, me following in the truck along the unfamiliar streets. During the trip the ambulance suddenly sped up, leaving me sitting at a stoplight unable to follow. I watched the red tail lights turn the corner up ahead and they were gone. *Thom ...*

I started to panic – why did the ambulance speed up? What was happening to Thom? I was in a strange town and had no idea where the hospital was. I had to stop to ask directions and by the time I finally arrived Thom was intubated and critical. I sobbed alone in the waiting room not knowing what to do or who to talk to. The English doctor was kind but not enthusiastic about Thom's chances. They admitted him to intensive care and I was confronted with a host of strange doctors all spouting different opinions. I ended up talking to a nurse who was the most help. She told me to get him to a doctor I trusted for continued care. I prayed to St. Jude.

Thom survived the attack but his heart was fragile and he would have to take things even easier. As soon as the kids returned we set off for Florida, a place Thom loves. We visited my stepson Tommy and his family and parked the rig there while Thom made his recovery. The doctors had installed a defibrillator and pacemaker in his chest and he was doing a lot better. Shawn and Patrick and their families all visited him and slowly, slowly he recovered.

... And a time for every purpose under heaven ... This was our time for drifting. When Thom was well enough to move on we drifted like gypsies, stopping here and there along the gulf shore towards Mexico

Beach. I pursued my art projects using my store of sea-washed glass and worked at odd jobs. It was interesting – nothing really fazed me anymore when it came to tackling a different job or managing a challenge. Thom had been right – our time aboard the boat had freed me up to face pretty much anything.

We coasted down to old Mexico for the winter and spent the summer in Yellowstone Park. The opportunity came up to take jobs as camp hosts in the National Forest in Washington State. *Sure, why not?* There we camped alongside a pristine stream with no water or electricity, using our generator and cooking over an open fire when we could. Surrounded by 700-year-old fir trees and about three miles from the glacier, it was an idyllic spot. The silence at night was profound. Berries of every type and wild flowers and herbs were everywhere and I wild-harvested many, picking blackberries at every chance.

About a year earlier I had finally followed my dream and got back to formal education, enrolling in the School of Natural Healing. I was studying hard and getting good marks. I loved every minute of it and could not believe my straight-'A' performance. My last venture into higher education had been way back when I was a new mom living in Huntingdon Beach, California. I'd found it too hard then to keep it up but I always knew I wanted to pursue studies in health. Now at my current stage in life I was worried I wouldn't retain anything but I was pleased to see the old grey matter was still working well.

My cousin in Australia, Yvonne Trask, is a naturopath and very competent. She lives in Cowes on Phillip Island, south of Melbourne – the place where we witnessed the nightly 'penguin parade' when Paddy and Shawn were tiny – and she became my mentor, encouraging and helping me at every turn. We emailed often as I sought her advice and together we worked through Thom's problems, plus a few of mine. I greatly benefited from her experience. She still is my guru.

Word got around that I was into herbal medicine and campers began to seek me out for help with various troubles. Poison Ivy was a common problem – for me too when I stumbled against the bush and developed the rash. I explained the natural methods of treatment and said it was really a matter of choice which way they wanted to go. Most people readily accepted the holistic option I described, having already spent a lot of money on regular treatments for no result.

One woman sought out my help for her little dog. I had seen the poor little thing outside a few times while the husband tried to make it go potty. Sometimes going to the toilet on command is hard on our animals and I immediately had some ideas. So often, as in humans, I see an extremely unbalanced diet, overloaded with grain products. This is so hard on dogs and can cause Candida.

I told the woman about our dog Clarence. He had a problem with his tummy when we first found him and I suspected gall bladder and other problems. He had been abandoned and was constantly drooling in fear and often throwing up. I devised a fish soup to feed him and he slowly pulled out of it. He rarely drools now and can eat anything put in front of him. The woman made the soup and the little pet relished it, lapping it up like crazy. I saw them later, the bowel problem was gone and the dog was thriving. They were ecstatic – they really loved that little pet.

We took another position in Arizona under the same deal but here we had power and water. This was a beautiful little park in the Coconino National Forest near Sedona. The whole area is surrounded by purple and red painted hills with inspiring bluffs that have been featured many times in all those old John Wayne movies and other Westerns. Indian tribes had lived in the area for centuries, digging out the cliffs for dwellings, and folks come from all over the world to soak up the reputed spiritual vibes of the area. I wild-crafted many plants and dried them, making medicines as I had in Washington State. I thrived in the high desert but Thom did not...

One night he took ill again. He was bleeding badly and I rushed him to hospital where he was quickly admitted to intensive care. He almost bled to death – the blood thinner he was on was killing him. I went round and round with the doctors again but now I was wiser and did not accept what they said without thinking of the consequences and making them explain their points of view and back them up. I had learned at school that the body will strive for good health but we have to nourish it and help it along. We changed the meds and he came home. Shortly after, he had a bad heart attack.

I was at my wits' end. I knew that a lot of meds are very bad for the body but in his case he needed intervention. The question was, which ones and how much? In hospital corridors I saw quite a few other women like me trying to make decisions about an older husband's life. I was constantly being intimidated by medical personnel. One woman told me that if I gave Thom herbs I would put him in the ground. I immediately stopped and Thom almost went into the ground. I sought help from my professors and Thom and I agreed amongst ourselves that we could combine a sensible course of action using herbs, nutrition, vitamins, minerals, hydrotherapy and meds. We just had to find the right balance. We both worked hard on diet and supplements and gradually his outlook steadied. *Breathe, Diana*. We summered quietly in Oregon with the intention of returning to Florida for the winter.

As we prepared to leave Oregon and visit our friends in Eugene, Thom went down again with heart failure and needed to be hospitalized. A fellow Australian who lived in Oregon, Anita Sanders, was there for us and helped us enormously at that time. Anita and I had met by chance a little while before and in conversation had discovered we had both grown up in Warburton – although some years apart – and were the only girls from the town to each marry an American. Angels come in unexpected forms and at the most amazing times. Anita was our angel then, throwing open her home and, along with her husband Steve and family, insisting that we stay there until Thom was able to travel.

I knew I had to get Thom south and stabilized and get the option of continuous care in the future. My problem was that Ole Man Winter was at the door and snow was flying on top of the ranges that marked our route south. We needed to get to the other side of the pass before we were iced in. Shawn solved the problem by steering by from a business trip in San Francisco and very bravely driving the truck over the mountains for me, never having driven a big rig like that before.

Once again Thom rallied but I knew I would have to drive the 3,000-mile trip back to Florida. His spirits were soon on the rise, though, and before long he was teasing me about this and that.

'Are you sure you didn't say, Love, Honor and Ebay?'

This was a crack about my wedding vows when I had deliberately left out 'obey', not thinking I'd be any good at that part. Thom was always bringing that up in company, especially when we were sailing and he was captain.

'Well, you know, she never *did* say she'd obey,' he'd remind whoever was listening.

The boys offered to help with the journey but I decided I could do it. Thom had always trained me to take over in an emergency and I felt I could make it. When we picked up the rig over the pass there had already been a freeze and all the batteries were flat and the whole rig was unusable. I had to haul out the generator and charge everything before we could even leave the parking lot and get set up for the night. Thom was weak and I had to move fast.

I muttered to myself, 'Well, it's a good thing I'm a big strong Australian b**ch – I'm gonna need to be.' Thom overheard me and started laughing.

'What did you just say?'

After a few nights out I got the thing down to a fine art – except for stopping. We would seem to go on forever after I had applied the brakes. I had to learn to think well ahead on that one. Thom was able to help me in tricky parking situations and so we beat it south with the weather trailing behind us like a dark shadow in the rear-view mirror.

I was doing okay until I decided to take a shortcut through a desert turnoff that would cut about thirty miles. The road turned out to be as twisted and as narrow as a snake. As I came up over a hillside turn, I saw to my horror a long house trailer chuffing up the hill, its bulk swung right out into the middle of the road. I couldn't do anything but keep up my forward impetus as there was a steep drop on my right and no road on my left. I think Jesus took the wheel as I aimed for a tiny slice of light I saw between myself and the now wildly swinging trailer. I headed for the space between us and held my breath thinking I would surely hear the crunch as the tail end hit him. We passed, Thom reckoned, with an inch to spare. Afterwards I found a tiny paint scrape on the rear bumper. *That was close*. I pulled off the road and took a breather. Oh, boy ...

Setting up the camper one night in the desert, I bent over to connect the water line. *Pow!* I was hit in the behind by a sharp cactus. What a shot! I turned round and took a knife and sliced the thing back, unceremoniously picking a long barb out of my rear end. As we were leaving, I was having a time with the water connection again and I bent over in a different direction. *Pow!* The blasted thing got me again.

We traced our way through the southern route of the US. I knew that this would probably be our last long trip through these parts and savored the fine fall air and views. The boys all visited with us when we finally made it back to Florida. We celebrated Thanksgiving and it was a marvelous family reunion. We wanted to be close to them now and hunted around for a location that would soothe our souls and serve our needs. Shortly after, Tommy and Karen found us a great place in the southernmost part of Georgia, close to the Florida border, and there we gratefully threw down the anchor after many years of travel and adventure by land and sea.

My studies into natural medicine continued and I graduated with honors as a Master Herbalist – a very proud moment representing lots of hard work and plenty of time wrestling with the computer to complete papers. When your work disappears from under your hand leaving nothing but a blank screen, it's as well to have a son at the other end of the phone to tell you how to bring it back from outer space.

In the last couple of years I've also had the unexpected thrill of returning to the recording studio for the first time in a long time. My old friend Dennis Sindrey is now living not far from us and with his help another dream of mine has recently come true – a CD album of my own original songs. Dennis was one of the first muso friends I made back on that Queensland holiday at the Corroboree Club so many years ago when I was just starting out. How amazing that our lives should come full circle and bring us together again to make music at the other end of life. He was a guest in our house the first summer we were here in Georgia and he gave me a fifteen-minute lecture on practicing every day without fail. It was wonderful to get back into a studio again. My song for Thom, *Little Bit* – the one I wrote just before we first tried our luck in Nashville – is on the album.

In 2007 Thom turned eighty and the family all gathered once more to celebrate. The house was full of our children, grandchildren, in-laws, extended family and friends. During the afternoon I was sitting by Thom on the sofa as people came and went and conversations ebbed and flowed around us, flavored with reminiscences and spiked with laughter. Thom was king of the castle, still the funniest person in the room, the one who had rescued us all at one time or another.

At one point in the buzz of chatter he took my hand and we exchanged a long look and a quiet smile. Through all our years of working, travelling and adventuring, our ups and downs, our successes and failures, what we had here now all around us was the best thing we could ever have shared together in life – our beautiful, wonderful family.

'Honey,' I asked him curiously, 'if there was anything you could change in all your life, what would it be?'

He squeezed my hand and answered without thinking twice, 'I wouldn't change one thing. Not one damn thing.'

***

Post-script: During the latter production of this book, my Thom passed away. Another ending, another beginning ... The journey continues. The climb takes you places you never expected.

NINETEEN

Thanks For The Memory
– Last Words

Many times in my life I have been asked: *What is the secret to your success?* or *How come you two are so happy?* or *You seem to have it all!* Oh, boy! Well, here for the record are some of the hard lessons and truths I have been taught along the way.

1. *You, You, You.*

So many times I have wanted to watch that act or performer who preceded me on stage, and every time I did that, things did not go well. In my early years I watched from the sidelines and learned from everyone but *never* if I had to follow them onstage. I'm not sure what it does to you but somehow you never measure up. The confidence is just not there. Don't compare yourself to others when you have to perform next.

2. *Take It Easy on Yourself.*

My grandmother told me this on the verandah in Warby years ago and it still holds true. Addiction is a terrible thing. I have watched many people go down that road and most of it started as a joke or a dare or just trying to fit in with peers.

I have always feared alcohol addiction because I saw a lot of drunks in my time and always thought they were awful. I think it would be so easy for me to become addicted. I know that once in hospital they were giving me pain meds and I was yelling for more after a few doses.

Drug addiction sneaks up on people. I have never taken drugs but

I know people who started with something they thought they could control and all of a sudden they were locked on with the monkey on their backs. There are a lot of traps out there – sex addiction, food addiction. Just put on the brakes whenever you think you are being pushed or are falling down that road. It's too hard to get back from there.

3. *It's a Beautiful World.*

In convent school we sure had to examine our consciences. It was one of the things we routinely did before confession. It was always boring as a child but I have now learned it is the foundation of a clear mind. Sometimes things surface years later that you have pushed back in your mind. It happened to me when an incident concerning my mother surfaced twenty years after her death. I literally sprang out of bed with the realization: 'Oh, my God! That's why!'

I had an answer to a situation that had made me unhappy and caused me so much grief for years. If I had really sized up the problem at the time or had someone to confide in or just been able to look at things differently, what a change that would have made. The simplest things that are so embarrassing to children or young adults can become a crippling emotional hurt for years. I learned that if you can face up to facts they are not half as bad as you think. Take it out and give it a look under a different light.

We make mistakes, big mistakes. We make fools of ourselves or others do it for us. Give yourself a break, tell yourself you won't make that mistake again, and move on. Find the things that are at the bottom of your unhappiness and just get rid of them by confession to yourself or to others. Tell someone – they don't see your problems the same way you do and generally don't care either. Do some good deeds and things will change for the better.

4. *Say a Little Prayer for Me.*

I am quite sure that Sr. Lucy saved my life. I was at a function in Melbourne once when an agitated young woman fronted up to me.

'I hate you!' she announced dramatically.

I could see she meant it and I stepped back and waited.

'Sr. Lucy made me pray for you every night of my life at school!' She sighed and her voice changed a little, 'You ruined my knees!'

I found out that she had lived at the convent as a boarder and Sr. Lucy had mentioned me lengthily and thoroughly in group prayers every night. Thank you, Sr. Lucy, and all the little girls on their knees who prayed for me at that time. I was alone in New York City – just raw bait for the sharks in very dangerous territory. I really believe those prayers led me out of danger, found me helpers and eventually found me Thom. To those of you who prayed for me, I hope someone prays for you. I know I do.

5. *Looking for Love.*

Don't go *Looking For Love* as the song title says. That is a sure way to never find it. You know, we would all like a tall handsome millionaire who is crazy about us to take us home to mother, but that's generally not how it goes. Love can find you at the most inopportune moments and through the most unlikely people.

Maybe it's the love of a grandmother or a dog or a pal or sister. One never knows where or when. It always pains me to see people who complain that love never finds them. Maybe they couldn't see it if they fell over it. Life and love will never be exactly the way you plan it. You can't control love. When it finds you (and you will know it if you are smiling) just accept the blessing and embrace the fact that love is there for you. Nurture it, and nurture the person that shows you their love. Love requires work. It is a gift that you earn every day.

'Better to have loved and lost then never to have loved at all.' For those who feel love has left – love is still out there, the world is full of it. Take time and think. Mistakes teach us. Next time, hold on. I know in my marriage love came and went a few times. We just worked through it and waited until we found it again. Don't let the sun go down on an argument. Solve the problem or at least air the problem. It's those things you put off that hurt you later. Write that love letter. Love without conditions.

6. *Are You Lonesome Tonight?*

The loneliest I have ever been was as a young woman in the US. It is a dreadful, empty feeling with no happy end in sight. The only way out is through the intervention of others or taking hard steps yourself and reaching out to strangers. Remember, other people are lonely too. Seek help. Look for someone who is smiling. Smile too.

Fatigue is a killer, not only at sea but in relationships too. It's hard to be a young mother or a young father these days. It's hard to be any kind of worker and still have a life. Take those times that you have off and sink it into the needs of your partner or those you love. Whenever you give, somehow it turns around and refreshes you, incredible as it seems. Don't make heavy decisions when you are tired. Don't go to sea if you are tired. Heave to and rest. Look for the triggers that make you sad or tired and recognize that sometimes it can be a physical problem. Look at a change in water or diet or maybe herbal medicine or meditation. Try alternative ways to finding health, peace and happiness. It worked for me.

7. *Happy Birthday, Baby.*

Some folks are too proud to take or don't know how to take with grace. I used to be one of the latter. When a gift or a compliment comes, learn to take that feather in your cap and don't look for the down side. (I still find it hard to take a compliment.) Not every person you meet is out for themselves, so take with grace. Enjoy the gift with the giver. Don't grab from others or discourage them – show them how you appreciate and receive applause with grace.

8. *You Make Me So Very Happy.*

One of the secrets I learned onstage was to look straight over the head of the heckler in the front row. Just proceed like they were not there to demean you and pretend as if they are encouraging you. If nothing else, it sure baffles them. Milton Berle had a great line.

'Oh, I remember you!' he'd holler back at a heckler. 'You heckled me twenty years ago. I never forget a suit!'

So if you think people are laughing at you just come up with a really good line or pretend that they are applauding you instead. It works. Find things or people that make you laugh. It's good medicine.

9. *Inside Out.*

We visited a small orphanage in Mexico to see if there was anything we could do for them. I remembered my Mexican friend Rosario who always said, 'Bring bread,' so I purchased a large bundle of rolls and bread to take along. The nuns were delighted and I asked what else we could bring.

'Live chickens,' was the reply. Definitely something I would not have thought of.

There was a little boy about six standing nearby with a listless expression, kicking the dust at his feet in a bored fashion. I began to play with him, teaching him a game I had played as a child. I found a tennis ball and showed him how to throw it against the brick wall, let it bounce once, then catch it. After a few attempts he caught the ball. This transformation in that child was literally stunning to behold. The eyes were suddenly shining and he was completely engaged. Maybe hope was born that he too was able to achieve. Sometimes we need to see things from the inside out instead of the outside in.

10. *Mama.*

Mama always said, 'You can never change a man.' I believe she is fundamentally one hundred percent right about that one. If you try and he lets you, then he's not the same man you originally knew, so why do it?

11. *You'll Never Know.*

I was on the beach in Oregon running with our new dog Clarence when I spotted a man fishing in the surf. *I wonder what bait he uses up here?* A woman was sitting reading not too far away. *Probably his wife.* I began walking towards her, intending to ask.

She lifted her head with a smile and said hello at the same time I did and as she spoke I noticed her accent.

'You're Australian!' we both said at the same time.

'Where do you come from?' tumbled out next.

'The Upper Yarra Valley,' I said.

'Me too!' she squeaked. 'Where?'

'I'm from Warburton,' I said.

'Me too!' she looked at me incredulously.

'My name is Diana Trask,' I offered.

'Oh, my God!' she yelled, 'I was at your wedding!'

This was Anita Sanders, the angel who helped us when Thom took ill in Oregon. Now what are the odds of meeting a person from a small town like Warburton on the beach in the US, a country of three hundred million plus? It turned out that we had many friends and acquaintances in common. She was a few years younger than I (a fact she always enjoyed mentioning) so we had just missed being in the same groups, although I remembered her mother and others from the family.

We became the absolute best of friends and Thom used to say we needed our jaws greased whenever we met. How unbelievable was that meeting! Just walk with faith and know there is a good plan for you and that you will meet the people you need to meet. You just never know. Prepare to be amazed.

12. *Thanks for the Memory.*

I'm so glad you have taken this journey through my story with me. There are far too many people to acknowledge for their help and guidance both in the US and Australia, but you know who you are and I want you to know how deeply I appreciate your time, help and love throughout my life. I know that I never would have made it without you. Thank you. Peace, good health.

I am, with love to you all,
Diana Roselyn Margaret Veronica Trask Ewen.

In my school uniform waiting for Dad to drive me to the Mercy Convent in Lilydale.

Nightlife at Lee's Nightclub, 1958.

Singing at a New York nightclub.

Chatting with Panda Lisner at my twenty-first birthday party in Melbourne.

Publicity shot from the sixties.

Leaving our Warburton home with Dad on my wedding day.

Our wedding group.
Back row, left to right: My brother Peter, Mom, Thom, myself, Di Sindrey and Dad.
Front row: our flower girls, the Mullumby sisters.

Marching to 'Sound Off' on *The Di Trask Show*, 1964.

Thom and I with comic Joe Martin and his wife.

Surrounded by the stars of Dial Records at Tree Music in Nashville, 1969.

A group of fans join my boys and I alongside our tour bus.

On the road with my band, The VIP's.

Danny Thomas, one of my dearest friends.

With George Burns
in Las Vegas.

Country music headlining at The Landmark Hotel in Las Vegas with Bob
Luman, Archie Campbell, Ferlin Husky and I.

A treasured meeting with President Gerald Ford.

Roy Clark and I were delighted to catch up with my friend
Helen Reddy.

Roy Clark and I with Admiral Zumwalt, a fine sailor.

On tour with Morey Amsterdam from *The Dick Van Dyke Show*.

Sharing a birthday kiss, backstage at The Frontier Hotel, while Roy Clark and Buck Trent look on.

With my good mate, Australian country singer Reg Lindsay.

Onstage with two Australian stars, Rolf Harris and Col Joye, in Knoxville, Tennessee.

Family time with Patrick, Shawn and Thom.

Thom kept the secret till Roger Climpson walked onstage during my stage show and said, 'Diana Trask, This is your life!'

This is Your Life group shot. Our two beautiful boys Patrick and Shawn are behind my mom.

Publicity shot for my back home Australian tour.

Singing at the AFL Grand final in Melbourne, 1985.

Onboard our yacht *Bypass*.